Religion and
Social Problems

Routledge Advances in Sociology

For a full list of titles in this series, please visit www.routledge.com

19. Social Isolation in Modern Society
Roelof Hortulanus, Anja Machielse and Ludwien Meeuwesen

20. Weber and the Persistence of Religion
Social Theory, Capitalism and the Sublime
Joseph W. H. Lough

21. Globalization, Uncertainty and Late Careers in Society
Edited by Hans-Peter Blossfeld, Sandra Buchholz and Dirk Hofäcker

22. Bourdieu's Politics
Problems and Possibilities
Jeremy F. Lane

23. Media Bias in Reporting Social Research?
The Case of Reviewing Ethnic Inequalities in Education
Martyn Hammersley

24. A General Theory of Emotions and Social Life
Warren D. TenHouten

25. Sociology, Religion and Grace
Arpad Szakolczai

26. Youth Cultures
Scenes, Subcultures and Tribes
Edited by Paul Hodkinson and Wolfgang Deicke

27. The Obituary as Collective Memory
Bridget Fowler

28. Tocqueville's Virus
Utopia and Dystopia in Western Social and Political Thought
Mark Featherstone

29. Jewish Eating and Identity Through the Ages
David Kraemer

30. The Institutionalization of Social Welfare
A Study of Medicalizing Management
Mikael Holmqvist

31. The Role of Religion in Modern Societies
Edited by Detlef Pollack and Daniel V. A. Olson

32. Sex Research and Sex Therapy
A Sociology Analysis of Masters and Johnson
Ross Morrow

33. A Crisis of Waste?
Understanding the Rubbish Society
Martin O'Brien

34. Globalization and Transformations of Local Socioeconomic Practices
Edited by Ulrike Schuerkens

35. The Culture of Welfare Markets
The International Recasting of Pension and Care Systems
Ingo Bode

36. Cohabitation, Family and Society
Tiziana Nazio

37. Latin America and Contemporary Modernity
A Sociological Interpretation
José Maurício Domingues

38. Exploring the Networked Worlds of Popular Music
Milieu Cultures
Peter Webb

39. The Cultural Significance of the Child Star
Jane O'Connor

40. European Integration as an Elite Process
The Failure of a Dream?
Max Haller

41. Queer Political Performance and Protest
Benjamin Shepard

42. Cosmopolitan Spaces
Europe, Globalization, Theory
Chris Rumford

43. Contexts of Social Capital
Social Networks in Communities, Markets and Organizations
Edited by Ray-May Hsung, Nan Lin, and Ronald Breiger

44. Feminism, Domesticity and Popular Culture
Edited by Stacy Gillis and Joanne Hollows

45. Changing Relationships
Edited by Malcolm Brynin and John Ermisch

46. Formal and Informal Work
The Hidden Work Regime in Europe
Edited by Birgit Pfau-Effinger, Lluis Flaquer, and Per H. Jensen

47. Interpreting Human Rights
Social Science Perspectives
Edited by Rhiannon Morgan and Bryan S. Turner

48. Club Cultures
Boundaries, Identities and Otherness
Silvia Rief

49. Eastern European Immigrant Families
Mihaela Robila

50. People and Societies
Rom Harré and Designing the Social Sciences
Luk van Langenhove

51. Legislating Creativity
The Intersections of Art and Politics
Dustin Kidd

52. Youth in Contemporary Europe
Edited by Jeremy Leaman and Martha Wörsching

53. Globalization and Transformations of Social Inequality
Edited by Ulrike Schuerkens

54. Twentieth Century Music and the Question of Modernity
Eduardo De La Fuente

55. The American Surfer
Radical Culture and Capitalism
Kristin Lawler

56. Religion and Social Problems
Edited by Titus Hjelm

Religion and Social Problems

Edited by Titus Hjelm

Routledge
Taylor & Francis Group
New York   London

First published 2011
by Routledge
270 Madison Avenue, New York, NY 10016

Simultaneously published in the UK
by Routledge
2 Park Square, Milton Park, Abingdon, Oxon OX14 4RN

Routledge is an imprint of the Taylor & Francis Group, an informa business

Typeset in Sabon by IBT Global.
Printed and bound in the United States of America on acid-free paper by IBT Global.

Library of Congress Cataloging-in-Publication Data

Religion and social problems / edited by Titus Hjelm.
   p. cm. — (Routledge advances in sociology ; 56)
   Includes bibliographical references and index.
  1. Religion and social problems. 2. Church and social problems. 3. Social policy.
4. Religion and state. I. Hjelm, Titus.
  HN31.R453 2011
  201'.76—dc22
  2010024928

ISBN13: 978-0-415-80056-3 (hbk)
ISBN13: 978-0-203-83510-4 (ebk)

Contents

List of Tables   ix
List of Figures   xi
Preface and Acknowledgments   xiii

1   Religion and Social Problems: Three Perspectives   1
    TITUS HJELM

PART I
The Impact of Religion on Social Problems

2   The Indirect Result of Religious Norms and Practices:
    Explaining Islam's Role in Limiting the Spread of HIV/AIDS   15
    AMY ADAMCZYK

3   Islam and Labor Market Integration in Denmark   32
    PETER B. ANDERSEN AND PETER LÜCHAU

PART II
Religion as a Solution to Social Problems

4   Religious Diversity and Social Problems: The Case of Britain   53
    JAMES A. BECKFORD

5   Fighting Against Unemployment: Finnish Parishes as Agents in
    European Social Fund Projects   67
    SANNA LEHTINEN

6   Religion as a Solution to Social Problems: A Christian
    Orthodox Approach to International Humanitarian Issues   82
    LINA MOLOKOTOS-LIEDERMAN

7   Religion and Social Capital Research in South Africa: Mapping
an Agenda in Progress   98
IGNATIUS SWART

8   Campaigning for Justice: Religious and Legal Activism in
Challenging Illegal Immigration as a Social Problem in the U.S.   122
GASTÓN ESPINOSA

9   Missionaries and Social Workers: Visions of Sexuality in
Religious Discourse   142
MARIAN BURCHARDT

PART III
Religion as a Social Problem

10 Perception of Muslims and Islam in Australian Schools:
A National Survey   159
ABE W. ATA

11 Religious Problems in Contemporary Japanese Society:
Two Cases after the Aum Shinrikyo Affair   173
MICHIAKI OKUYAMA

12 George W. Bush and Church-State Partnerships to Administer
Social Service Programs: Cautions and Concerns   186
DEREK H. DAVIS

13 The Cult as a Social Problem   198
EILEEN BARKER

14 Other Religions as Social Problem: The Universal Church of the
Kingdom of God and Afro-Brazilian Traditions   213
STEVEN ENGLER

15 Islam and Integration in German Media Discourse   229
YASEMIN EL-MENOUAR AND MELANIE BECKER

Contributors   245
Index   249

Tables

2.1   Descriptive Statistics for Variables Included in the Analysis 20

2.2   Mediators for Explaining the HIV/AIDS and Muslim Relationship 23

2.3   Mediators for Explaining the HIV/AIDS and Muslim Relationship, Continued 25

2.4   The Suppressing Role of Contraceptive Prevalence; and Polygyny for Explaining the HIV/AIDS and Muslim Relationship 26

3.1   Immigrant Statistics 38

3.2   Demography (in %) 40

3.3   Identified as Muslim (in %) 41

3.4   Existential Religiosity (in %) 43

5.1   Objective Programs (OP) in Finland and Number of Parishes Taking Part in the Years 2000–2006 69

5.2   OP3 Sub-Programs in Which Parishes Have Participated 70

5.3   Social Problems in the Projects 70

10.1   Participant Characteristics by Gender (N=1000) 164

10.2   Gender Differences towards Select Attitudinal Statements 168

10.3   Having Muslim Friends by Attitudes 169

Figures

3.1   Employment and religion.   45

7.1   Orientation map and places of worship (churches) in a
        Western Cape community: The town of Paarl.   104

7.2a   Orientation map and places of worship (churches) in a
        Western Cape community: The city of George.   105

7.2b   Prevalence of one particular social problem in a Western
        Cape community: HIV and Aids in the city of George.   105

7.3   People's perceptions about the church's involvement
        with a particular social problem in a Western Cape
        community: Sexual and violent crime in the town of
        Paarl.   106

7.4   The degree of assistance to victims of a particular
        social problem in a Western Cape community through
        direct involvement: Sexual violence and crime in the
        town of Paarl.   107

7.5a   Areas of high service need concerning a particular
        social problem in a Western Cape community: Sexual
        and violent crime in the town of Paarl.   108

7.5b   Areas ready for church intervention with regard to a
        particular social problem in a Western Cape community:
        Sexual and violent crime in the town of Paarl.   109

7.6a   Community profile (C-Index) of needs satisfaction in a
        Western Cape community: Lwandle in the Helderberg
        Basin.   110

7.6b   Community profile (C-Index) of needs satisfaction in a
        Western Cape community: Eastridge in Mitchell's Plain. 111

7.6c   Community profile (C-Index) of needs satisfaction in a
Western Cape community: Milky Town in Paarl.   111

10.1   Response to "What are the first words that come into
your mind when . . . 'Muslim' is mentioned?"   165

10.2   Response to "What do you like most about Muslims?"   166

10.3   Response to "What do you like least about Muslims?"   167

10.4   Proportion of respondents, by most Australians have
good feelings for Muslims.   167

Preface and Acknowledgments

Many of the chapters in this collection have their origins in papers presented at the 2007 conference of the International Society for the Sociology of Religion (ISSR/SISR) in Leipzig, Germany. Some of the original presentations didn't make it to the book and some new people became involved as the project developed, including presenters from the second "Religion and Social Problems" thematic session that convened at the 2009 ISSR meeting in Santiago De Compostela, Spain. The balance of chapters in this book does not therefore reflect only my personal tastes, but discussions from these meetings.

I would like to thank all the people who have been involved in conference discussions and the creation of this book in different ways. You all have contributed to the recognition of religion and social problems as an important field of research. First and foremost this includes the contributors to this volume, but also the following people: Mohammed Ababou, Amy Black, Bogdan Blaga, Peter Clarke, Iraj Faizi, Arthur E. Farnsley, Chang-gang Guo, Mark Hanshaw, Guénolé Labey-Guimard, Shawn Landres, David Machacek, Richard McCallum, Päivi Pöyhönen, Heinrich Schäfer, Hossein Serajzadeh, Nuri Tinaz, and Richard Wood. Ben Holtzman and Max Novick from Routledge have been a great support throughout the process. Finally, special thanks to Steven Engler for joining the project at a very short notice, for expert advice, and for friendship.

1 Religion and Social Problems
Three Perspectives

Titus Hjelm

In our modern, media-saturated world we are confronted by a myriad of social problems every day. From local fear of neighborhood crime through national interest in poverty alleviation to global concerns over rapid climate change, social problems are omnipresent. In many ways—at least if we take media representations as our yardstick—our social reality is defined by the social problems we face in our particular social contexts.

A glance at the development of modern societies shows that religious communities have historically had a central place in defining and responding to social problems. In the western context, before the emergence of the welfare state in its different forms, care of the poor and the sick was mainly the function of local parishes. Later, organizations such as the Salvation Army were established on religious principles to combat social problems. It was only in the twentieth century that the state assumed many of the functions that religious communities have traditionally had. In the midst of the global economic crises of the early twenty-first century, it seems that religious communities are increasingly reclaiming some of the functions the struggling welfare state cannot adequately provide. It is safe to say, then, that religion's role as a *solution* to social problems is firmly established in public consciousness.

The flipside of the coin is to see religion as the *source* of social problems. While it could be argued that this perspective has a long history as well, it is especially relevant in the post-9/11 world. Although religious communities have from time immemorial perceived other religious communities as heretical and deviant, and while sometimes secularist states have proclaimed *all* religion a menace, the awareness of religion's destructive potential has reached new global heights after international terrorism has become synonymous with religious fanaticism. The "deviant beliefs" of religious people may or may not become a social problem; it is the actions putatively inspired by these beliefs that have created global social problems such as religious terrorism.

In light of this widespread awareness of religion as both a solution for and a source of social problems, it is somewhat surprising that the study of religion and social problems has not emerged as an independent sub-field of research either in the sociology of social problems or in the sociology of religion. Except for the "impact" tradition discussed below, both sub-disciplines have been mostly ignorant of theoretical developments in their respective fields (see Chapter 4). Of the few examples available, the use of contemporary social problems theory has been most evident in the study of new religious movements. The constructionist approach to social problems (see below; Spector and Kitsuse 2001) has proved to be an especially useful tool in analyzing the widespread public labeling of alternative religions as dangerous "cults" (e.g. Beckford 1985; Robbins 1985; 1988; Swanson 2002). Research on the Satanism scare that gripped the USA in the late 1980s and early 1990s (Richardson et al. 1991) has most explicitly anchored itself in contemporary social problems theory. Among the contributors to this work is Joel Best, one of the leading figures in the sociology of social problems (see Best 1991). Alongside some other examples—notably Hadden's (1980) and Beckford's (1990) important articles—sociology of religion has flirted with social problems theory but, as mentioned above, a systematic approach or anything comparable to a "school" is yet to emerge.

This is mostly the case with this collection as well. Although many of the authors draw explicitly from social problems theory, others highlight the intersection of religion and social problems through concepts such as social capital and theories of cultural practice. Instead of making an exclusive statement of how religion and social problems should be studied, the aim of this book is to display a variety of approaches, in hopes that something might emerge that is more than the sum of its parts, and yet characteristic of this sub-field in particular.

The chapters in this book are organized thematically. The first part discusses what I refer to as the "impact" tradition. This approach looks at the effects—the impact—of religion on a variety of social problems. It is also distinctive in its methodologically quantitative approach. The second part discusses religion as a solution to social problems and the final part examines how religion has been understood as a social problem in itself. Before a fuller discussion of the different parts, I will briefly outline the epistemological approaches underlying the three perspectives.

THREE PERSPECTIVES, TWO EPISTEMOLOGIES

The organization of the chapters in this book into three thematic parts nicely illustrates the different perspectives or "points of entry" into the study of religion and social problems. On a broader epistemological and theoretical level, however, the chapters can be divided between what social problems research has usually referred to as the objective and subjective approaches. A look at the development of social problems theory illuminates the differences between the two.

Contemporary social problems theory is largely an American affair.[1] Many later renowned sociologists and departments of sociology—the sociology department of the University of Chicago in particular—got the impetus for their research and theories from the rapid social changes of the early twentieth century and the problems that accompanied urbanization, mass immigration and ethnic and racial conflict. The early sociologists who studied the emerging urban society saw themselves as "impartial and trained observers" (Fuller and Myers 1941, 320) whose job was to observe the objective conditions in which social problems arose. This early period produced sociological classics such as *The City* (Park and Burgess 1984) and *Street Corner Society* (Whyte 1993).

Although the early sociology of social problems acknowledged that social problems also have a subjective element, that is, an "awareness of certain individuals that the condition is a threat to certain cherished values" (Fuller and Myers 1941, 320), this subjective side was largely left unexamined until the 1960s. At that point, a definitive break from earlier research occurred, with several important publications endorsing a completely revised approach that became known as "labeling theory." Howard Becker, often quoted as one of the main representatives of the approach, wrote in his influential book *Outsiders*:

> [S]*ocial groups create deviance by making the rules whose infraction constitutes deviance*, and by applying those rules to particular people and labeling them as outsiders. From this point of view, deviance is not a quality of the act the person commits, but rather a consequence of the application by others of rules and sanctions to an "offender". (Becker 1991[1963], 9; emphasis in original)

The culmination of this development came with the publication of Spector and Kitsuse's *Constructing Social Problems* (2001), which soon became the standard work in the field. Their definition of social problems radically subjectivized the study of social problems, by stating that "social problems [are] the activities of individuals or groups making assertions of grievances and claims with respect to some putative conditions" (Spector and Kitsuse 2001, 75; emphasis in original). In effect, Spector and Kitsuse took a completely disinterested stance towards any claims regarding the reality of the phenomenon in question. What matters are the public claims made regarding what is seen as a social problem, and this is what sociologists should study. Therefore, the process of making claims about problematic conditions becomes the focus of constructionist study of social problems.

The individual chapters in this book fall on different points of the objective-subjective continuum. By virtue of its methodology, the impact approach is by definition "objectivist" in the above sense. However, the discussions of religion as a solution to social problems and religion as a social problem approach the topic from both objective and subjective viewpoints. It is to these various discussions that I now turn.

THE IMPACT PERSPECTIVE

In an earlier article (Hjelm 2009) I referred to the impact perspective as the "traditional approach." This is because it is, simply, the oldest and most significant perspective on religion and social problems—thus no evaluative meaning should be read into the term. The progenitor of this perspective was, of course, Emile Durkheim. In his *Suicide* (1897) Durkheim compared statistical data from different European countries in order to analyze the impact of social and cultural factors on the voluntary taking of one's life. His famous conclusion was that Protestants were more prone to commit suicide than followers of other confessions in all of the countries he compared (Durkheim 1979[1897], 154). Although fiercely criticized by many (see especially Stark and Bainbridge 1996), Durkheim's basic premise continues to inspire research. If not in other respects, the one feature this perspective has retained from Durkheim is the focus on statistical data. Thus, religion often appears in the form of a variable in quantitative assessments with titles examining "the impact of religion on X" and "the effects of religion on X" (e.g. Evans et al. 1995; Johnson et al. 2001; Shields et al. 2007).

Chapter 2, authored by Amy Adamczyk, is a prime example of the impact perspective. In her study, Adamczyk examines the reasons for the lower prevalence rate of HIV/AIDS in Muslim countries. HIV/AIDS is a globally recognized health problem that has had devastating consequences for the developing world, especially Africa. Using cross-national data Adamczyk shows how behavior related to Islamic beliefs and norms has an effect on the spread of HIV/AIDS. Factors such as proscriptions against extramarital sex, restrictions on alcohol use and circumcision all seem to have an impact on the prevalence of HIV/AIDS infections in the countries studied.

In Chapter 3 Peter Andersen and Peter Lüchau examine Max Weber's famous theses about the work ethic in world religions and apply them to the case of Denmark, with a special reference to Muslim immigrants and their position in the labor market. The issue of unemployment in general and the apparent high levels of unemployment among immigrants in particular are one of the most pressing social problems in countries with a comprehensive welfare state system, such as Denmark. The question is whether religion—in this case Islam—has an effect in contributing to unemployment and sustaining a situation perceived as a social problem. Andersen and Lüchau conclude that "it is highly unlikely that the higher unemployment rate among non-Western immigrants in Denmark is the product of a particular Muslim work ethic." Instead, current factors, such as education and gender are more likely to have an impact on the employment rate.

RELIGION AS A SOLUTION TO SOCIAL PROBLEMS

One of the few scholars that have previously discussed the intersection between religion and social problems is James Beckford, who here returns to the topic of his presidential address for the 1989 meeting of the Association for the Sociology of Religion, titled "The Sociology of Religion and Social Problems" (Beckford 1990). Beckford outlines the importance of mutual recognition for both sociology of religion and sociology of social problems and discusses the effects of increasing religious diversity on the perception of social problems. He acknowledges that religion has been mostly considered as a solution to social problems, but increasingly as a possible source of social problems. Drawing from both approaches, Beckford then focuses on what he calls "religion as expedient," that is, the ways in which governments—in this case the British government—have appropriated religion in both combating social problems and in ensuring that religions do not become deviant, but rather contribute to social cohesion. These formal policies of supporting and working with faith communities represent a "new—and not unproblematic—phase in the intertwining of religion and social problems." Although Beckford's examples are from the UK, they may offer a potential lesson for other national contexts where religious diversity is creating government responses.

The next chapter by Sanna Lehtinen looks at some aspects of Beckford's idea of religion as expedient at the level of the European Union. She examines the role of the Evangelical Lutheran Church of Finland in solving social problems in the intersection between the EU, the public sector, and the third sector. She shows how the church actively raises awareness of social problems and coordinates with other welfare agents, thus participating in the active definition of problems and solutions. At the same time the role of the parish—and by extension, the church—is being constantly renegotiated. Is it a religious institution that is relegated by definition to a particular religious sphere of public life, or is it an alternative to the failing welfare state? Lehtinen's chapter is an interesting example of the dynamic between the "function" and "performance" of religious actors, as discussed by Peter Beyer (1994, 80).

While ecumenical responses to global social problems have received some attention in research, social work within the Orthodox Church has been rather under-studied. In a study that is the first of its kind, Lina Molokotos-Liederman discusses religion as a solution to social problems, with a focus on the specific characteristics of Orthodox charity work. She examines how Orthodox social theology has been translated into action by Orthodox Non-Governmental Organizations around the world. Orthodox responses to social problems are especially pressing in the context of post-1989 Eastern Europe, where rapid social change has resulted in poverty and other socio-economic problems. As governments struggle with providing welfare, the role of religious NGOs has become increasingly important.

"Social capital" has become a very fashionable concept in contemporary sociology in general and sociology of religion in particular. Although theorization on the concept can be traced back to Pierre Bourdieu (e.g. Bourdieu 1986), it became especially important after Robert Putnam's influential *Bowling Alone* (2000). The concept has been since re-evaluated and redefined many times both theoretically and by applying it to different social contexts. Ignatius Swart's chapter discusses the role of churches in social capital formation in the South African province of Western Cape. While churches provide a platform for tackling many of the social problems affecting the poorest part of the population, in terms of social capital formation, the role of religious actors seems to be inconclusive. While preaching values and building trust is in many ways the main "business" of churches, the tangible results of social capital formation often remain thin. Swart's chapter discusses the ways in which research can conceptualize and analyze social capital in relation to a practical aim of solving and alleviating pressing social problems.

Moving to another continent and also toward a more constructionist approach, Gastón Espinosa examines how church leaders in the United States have responded to the labeling of Latin American immigrants as "illegal aliens" and as a social problem. By engaging in active claims-making through religious ritual, social activism and political lobbying, leaders such as Cardinal Roger Mahony and Reverend Samuel Rodríguez have harnessed the language of religion and compassion and managed to deconstruct some of the prevailing images of Latin American immigrants. The religious discourse of the above leaders and others have provided the Latin American community with moral authority to counter claims made by politicians and the media, for example. This religious discourse, in turn, Espinosa argues, has been adapted by politicians looking for the support of the growing Latino/a community in the United States. In effect, religious discourse has proved to be a "solution," a counterforce to claims that portray the Latin American community in a negative light.

In the most explicitly constructionist chapter of this section, Marian Burchardt analyses the processes in which HIV/AIDS is "problematized" by religious actors in South Africa. Burchardt examines how faith-based "life skills education" constructs HIV/AIDS as a social problem and how religious actors construct solutions to the problem. Burchardt identifies two types of actors and discourses: the missionary and the social worker. With the former the "concern with social issues such as AIDS is subordinated to, and part of, a much broader religious project," and sexual behavior becomes part of a discourse of sin. For the latter, "concerns with social justice, health and wellbeing clearly override efforts to mission." The prevalence of AIDS has changed the whole idea of intimate relationships in countries like South Africa and, as a result, the range of solutions offered takes on great significance.

RELIGION AS A SOCIAL PROBLEM

As many of the authors in this part of the book argue, 9/11 had a huge influence on pushing religion back into the center of public discussion and debate. However, tones that were previously reserved mostly for dangerous "cults" were now used in describing a legitimate "world religion", namely Islam, as well. After 9/11 *all* religion became a potential social problem and few traditions have been spared from the effects of this public refocusing of the connection between religion and social problems. The chapters in this section examine how religion has become to be seen increasingly as the *source* of social problems.

In Chapter 10, Abe Ata analyzes survey data on the attitudes of Australian secondary school students towards Islam and Muslims. Although Ata works with survey data, his study is less about the impact of religion on attitudes (see section one) than the influence that secondary education might have on the perception of religion, in this case Islam. While official government policy in Australia endorses intercultural development and interfaith interaction, knowledge of Islam and Muslims among non-Muslim students is still severely lacking. The attitudes of non-Muslim students towards Islam and Muslims often follow the stereotyped portrayals of the media, where Islam is mainly discussed in a problem framework. Although knowledge of Islam (in the sense of curriculum development) does not emerge as a primary path to attitude change, simply promoting the awareness of Islam in the context of schools does seem to have a positive impact on attitudes.

As Michiaki Okuyama argues in his chapter, religion has been often perceived in a social problem framework in the Japanese context. This has been pronouncedly so after the 1995 Aum Shinrikyo affair, where the followers of founder Shoko Asahara released deadly nerve gas in the Tokyo subway system, killing thirteen people and injuring hundreds (see Reader 2002). Okuyama discusses two "religious problems" that have been the center of public attention after 1995, namely the so-called "cult problem" and the case of the Yasukuni shrine, which became an international issue after then prime minister Junichiro Koizumi visited the shrine in an official capacity, seemingly paying respect to convicted WWII war criminals. Both cases illuminate the ways in which religion can become a social—constitutional, legal, and cultural—problem in the Japanese context.

On the surface, Derek H. Davis's chapter analyzes how the Bush administration—with the sympathy of the United States Supreme Court—strongly constructed religion as an important, even crucial, solution to social problems. Using this analysis as a starting point, however, Davis goes further and presents a legal critique of Bush's Faith-Based Initiatives. From a legal point of view the "discrimination against religion" policies and court cases present a threat to the constitutional interpretation of state–church relations that is at the heart of American understanding of religion. Although

Bush's Faith-Based Initiatives have not yet been constitutionally challenged and many programs continue—albeit in slightly amended forms—under the Obama administration, the situation is perceived as a social problem for those who see the separation of church and state as a crucial element of U.S. society. Although Davis limits his discussion to the constitutional aspects of the case, some research—especially the supply side explanations of rational choice theorists—supports the idea that government funding of religion through Faith-Based Initiatives might turn out to be a social problem *for* religion and religious institutions in particular, by paradoxically reducing participation, if not belief (Fox and Tabory 2008; Stark and Finke 2000).

In Chapter 13 Eileen Barker, whose work has been instrumental in defining the study of new religious movements (NRMs), tackles a question that has been central to the field since its inception: how is it that so-called "cults" are so often seen as deviant and portrayed as a social problem? Drawing from the constructionist approach of Berger and Luckmann (1967) and her own extensive studies, Barker concludes that both NRMs and the so-called anti-cult movement are to blame. She discusses how on the one hand the newness of the movements itself can lead to behaviors easily condemned by the broader society. On the other hand, the anti-cult movement—for various reasons—wants to project NRMs as harmful to society. The result is what Barker terms "cult wars" where constructions on both sides of the divide struggle for attention and legitimacy in the public sphere.

Steven Engler picks up and expands Barker's ideas and, explicitly applying social problems theory, examines how religions construct other religions as a social problem. His fascinating case involves the Brazilian Universal Church of the Kingdom of God (UC) and their constructions of Afro-Brazilian religions (primarily Candomblé and Umbanda)—their practices of healing in particular—as "demonic." By using the UC as a case for tackling the "social" part in social problems theory, Engler shows that defining problems also contributes to identity formation. In this sense his analysis comes close to Kai Erikson's brilliant observation: "One of the surest ways to confirm an identity, for communities as well as for individuals, is to find some way of measuring what one is *not*" (Erikson 1966, 64; original emphasis).

While Ata's chapter looked at the attitudes towards Muslims based on survey research and an "objective" approach, Yasemin El-Menouar and Melanie Becker turn their gaze to the media in order to examine the possible sources of these attitudes in the German context. In the final chapter of this volume, El-Menouar and Becker analyze the discursive construction of Islam and integration in the highly influential German magazine *Der Spiegel*. Like many others, they note how 9/11 marked a significant change in the media discourse on Islam. While controversial issues, such as the veiling of women and forced marriage, were treated—no differently from many other countries—mainly in a problem framework in the German media before 2001, the different discourses started to converge during the first years of the new millennium into a discussion on so-called "parallel societies." The authors note that if the agenda-setting example of *Der Spiegel* is any measure, integration is seen mainly as a cultural issue and "failed integration on various levels is mainly associated with a lack of cultural integration instead of other factors such as socioeconomic deprivation, injustice of the educational system, recursive processes of discrimination and retreat, or the like." It could be safely said that this issue is relevant for Muslim immigrants in *any* country.

THE FUTURE OF RELIGION AND SOCIAL PROBLEMS RESEARCH

The chapters in this book demonstrate how religion and social problems are—perhaps increasingly so—intertwined in the modern world. The media thrives on problem discourse and religion brings an extra element of fascination to the portrayal of problematic events around the world. One of the aims of this book has been to draw attention to this omnipresent overlapping of religion and social problems and to provide a framework through which these intersections might be explored. However, despite the agenda-setting undertone, this book is not intended as a final word on the issue. As noted above, the variety of approaches utilized by the contributors is living proof of the variety of paths that religion and social problems research can take. It is up to future research to refine and expand these discussions.

In addition to making a strong case for religion and social problems as a legitimate field of study in its own right, the chapters in this volume show how the intersection between the two has implications for broader issues both in the sociology of social problems and the sociology of religion. For example, social problems theory has to seriously start considering the role of "supernatural" or "transcendent" actors in the formation of social problems discourse in order to fully grasp the diversity of claims-making activities. Similarly, the study of religion and social problems provides a lens through which many of the central issues in the sociology of religion, such as religious pluralism, secularization, and resacralization, can be examined.

Erik Allardt (1990, 66) has said (speaking of the sociology of religion) that the strength and significance of a sub-discipline is measured by the ways in which it contributes to discussions in the general discipline and other sub-disciplines. I believe the study of religion and social problems can have a lasting impact not only on the sociology of social problems and the sociology of religion, but also on broader discussions in sociology and the study of religion.

NOTE

1. It should be noted that the "moral panics" tradition emerged in the UK in the 1960s and 1970s (see Cohen 2002; Hall et al. 1978). Although it has affinities with the subjective/constructionist approach in American social problems theory, it should be considered as a separate tradition (see Critcher 2003).

REFERENCES

Allardt, Erik. 1990. Commentary on James Beckford's and Emile Poulat's Papers on the Predicament of the Sociology of Religion. *Social Compass* 37 (1): 65–69.

Becker, Howard S. 1991[1963]. *Outsiders: Studies in the Sociology of Deviance.* New York: The Free Press of Glencoe.

Beckford, James. A. 1985. *Cult Controversies: The Societal Response to the New Religious Movements.* London: Tavistock.

———. 1990. The Sociology of Religion and Social Problems. *Sociological Analysis*, 51 (1): 1–14.

Berger, Peter. L., and Luckmann, Thomas. 1967. *The Social Construction of Reality: A Treatise in the Sociology of Knowledge.* Garden City, NY: Anchor Books.

Best, Joel. 1991. Endangered Children and Antisatanist Rhetoric. In *The Satanism Scare*, edited by J. T. Richardson, J. Best, and D. G. Bromley. 95–106. New York: Aldine deGruyter.

Beyer, Peter. 1994. *Religion and Globalization.* London: Sage.

Bourdieu, Pierre. 1986. Forms of Capital. In *Handbook of Theory of Research for the Sociology of Education*, edited by J. E. Richardson. 241–258. New York: Greenwood Press.

Critcher, Chas. 2003. *Moral Panics and the Media.* Buckingham: Open University Press.

Durkheim, Emile 1979[1897]. *Suicide.* New York: The Free Press.

Evans, D. T., Cullen, F. T., Dunaway, R. G., and Burton, V. S. 1995. Religion and Crime Reexamined: The Impact of Religion, Secular Controls, and Social Ecology on Adult Criminality. *Criminology*, 33 (2): 195–224.

Erikson, Kai T. 1966. *The Wayward Puritans: A study in the Sociology of Deviance.* New York: John Wiley and Sons.

Fox, Jonathan, and Tabory, Ephraim. 2008. Contemporary Evidence Regarding the Impact of State Regulation of Religion on Religious Participation and Belief. *Sociology of Religion* 69 (3): 245–271.

Fuller, Richard. C., and Myers, Richard. R. 1941. The Natural History of a Social Problem. *American Sociological Review*, 6 (3): 320–8.

Hadden, Jeffrey K. 1980. Religion and the Construction of Social Problems. *Sociological Analysis*, 41 (2): 99–108.

Hall, Stuart, Critcher, Chas, Jefferson, Tony, Clarke, John, and Roberts, Brian. 1978. *Policing the Crisis: Mugging, the State, and Law and Order.* Basingstoke: Macmillan.

Hjelm, Titus. 2009. Religion and Social Problems: A New Theoretical Perspective. In *The Oxford Handbook of the Sociology of Religion*, edited by P. Clarke. Oxford: Oxford University Press.

Johnson, B. R., Jang, S. J., Larson, D. B., and De Li, S. 2001. Does Adolescent Religious Commitment Matter? A Reexamination of the Effects of Religiosity on Delinquency. *Journal of Research in Crime and Delinquency*, 38 (1): 22–44.

Park, Robert E., and Burgess, Ernest W. 1984 [1925]. *The City.* Chicago: University of Chicago Press.

Putnam, Robert D. 2000. *Bowling Alone: The Collapse and Revival of American Community.* New York: Simon & Schuster.

Reader, Ian. 2002. Dramatic Confrontations: Aum Shinrikiyo Against the World. In *Cults, Religion and Violence*, edited by J. G. Melton and D. G. Bromley. 189–208. Cambridge: Cambridge University Press.

Richardson, James T. , Best, Joel, and Bromley, David G. (eds). 1991. *The Satanism Scare.* New York: Aldine deGruyter.

Robbins, Thomas. 1985. Nuts, Sluts, and Converts: Studying Religious Groups as Social Problems. *Sociological Analysis*, 46 (2): 171–178.

———. (1988). *Cults, Converts and Charisma: The Sociology of New Religious Movements*. London: Sage.

Shields, J., Broome, K. M., Delany, P. J., Fletcher, B. W., and Flynn, P. M. 2007. Religion and Substance Abuse Treatment: Individual and Program Effects. *Journal for the Scientific Study of Religion*, 46 (3): 355–371.

Spector, M., and Kitsuse, J. I. 2001[1977]. *Constructing Social Problems*. New Brunswick, NJ: Transaction Publishers.

Stark, Rodney, and Bainbridge,William S. 1996. *Religion, Deviance, and Social Control*. New York: Routledge.

Stark, Rodney, and Finke, Roger. 2000. *Acts of Faith: Explaining the Human Side of Religion*. Berkeley: University of California Press.

Swanson, Paul. L. 2002. Religion as a Social Problem. *Bulletin of the Nanzan Insitute for the Study of Religion & Culture*, 26: 8–18.

Whyte, William Foote. 1993 [1943]. *Street Corner Society: The Social Structure of an Italian Slum*. 4th Edition. Chicago: Chicago University Press.

Part I

The Impact of Religion on Social Problems

2 The Indirect Result of Religious Norms and Practices
Explaining Islam's Role in Limiting the Spread of HIV/AIDS

Amy Adamczyk

Across the world the Human Immunodeficiency Virus (HIV) has continued to spread, particularly in Africa, which has the highest prevalence rates of HIV/AIDS in the world (UNAIDS 2006). From the beginning of the AIDS epidemic, researchers noted a lower HIV/AIDS prevalence rate in countries that had a high proportion of Muslims (Drain et al. 2006; McIntosh and Thomas 2004). In his multivariate analysis of 38 sub-Saharan African nations Gray (2004), for example, shows that the percentage of Muslims within countries negatively predicted HIV prevalence. Likewise, in their analysis of over 94 countries McIntosh and Thomas (2004) found that along with Orthodox Christian nations, predominantly Muslim nations had a lower prevalence of HIV/AIDS.

Although researchers have found a cross-national relationship between proportion Muslim and HIV/AIDS, the reasons for this cross-national relationship are not clear. Most religions provide their adherents with behavioral guidelines (Stark and Finke 2000). Rather than discourage religious belief, strict religions, which make a lot of behavioral demands of their members, are often quite successful at getting their adherents to abide by religious precepts (Iannaccone 1994; Stark and Finke 2000). The many behaviors (e.g. marital fidelity, male circumcision) that Islam either requires or inspires may have the indirect effect of limiting HIV/AIDS transmission amongst residents of Muslim-majority nations.

While many Islamic-inspired behaviors, like circumcision, may limit the spread of HIV/AIDS, there may be some Islamic-inspired behaviors, like polygyny, which could weaken the otherwise inverse relationship between proportion Muslim and HIV/AIDS. Understanding which Islamic-inspired behaviors limit HIV/AIDS and which behaviors may be suppressing the otherwise inverse relationship between proportion Muslim and HIV/AIDS would add some important insight into why countries in similar regions of the world have lower HIV/AIDS prevalence rates, and what researchers and policy makers might do to further the positive health influence of many Islamic-inspired behaviors. Using cross-national data that includes several Islam-inspired norms and behaviors, this study examines the ways through which the Muslim faith may either decrease the risk of HIV/AIDS, or encourage behaviors that contribute to the epidemic.

PERSONAL RELIGIOUS BELIEFS AND NATIONAL RELIGIOUS CONTEXTS

Much research in the sociology of religion has found that religion can have a powerful effect on behaviors, like substance use (Adamczyk and Palmer 2008), delinquency (Regnerus 2002), abortion decisions (Adamczyk and Felson 2008), and the timing of premarital sex (Meier 2003; Adamczyk and Felson 2006). In addition to religious affiliation and personal religious beliefs, living in a place where there is a high proportion of religious people can also shape the attitudes and behaviors of people who are highly religious and share the same religious beliefs. Referred to as the "moral communities" hypothesis, researchers (Scheepers, Te Grotenhuis, and Van Der Slik 2002; Finke and Adamczyk 2008) have found that when religious people regularly interact with other religious people their religious beliefs are more likely to influence their behaviors. Whereas some support has been found for the moral communities hypothesis, some research has also found that in more religious contexts religious and secular people alike are likely to behave in ways that are consistent with religious norms (Adamczyk and Palmer 2008; Regnerus 2002).

For Muslims and non-Muslims alike, an Islamic religious culture could shape attitudes and behaviors associated with the spread of HIV/AIDS. In countries with a high proportion of Muslims, residents should get more exposure to Islamic inspired media and government policies, which may strengthen norms and encourage behaviors, like marital fidelity, that are consistent with Islamic religious precepts. Opportunities to participate in Islamically-proscribed behaviors, like extramarital sex, might be expected to be more limited in Muslim majority countries. Finally, access to drugs and alcohol, which Islam discourages, should be less available. As a result of these macro influences, the behaviors of people living in a country with a high proportion of Muslims may be influenced by Islamically inspired behaviors and norms.

To date much of the research on religion's influence has been conducted in Europe and North America, where there are relatively small Muslim populations. As a result, little research attention has been given to the way Islamic beliefs may shape individuals' attitudes and behaviors (for exceptions see Yuchtman-Yaar and Alkalay 2007; Finke and Adamczyk, 2008).

Below, I discuss the many attitudes and behaviors through which macro-level Islamic contexts could influence the prevalence of HIV/AIDS within a country.

ISLAM AND RISK REDUCING BEHAVIORS

Circumcision[1]

A common explanation for the relationship between Islam and lower rates of HIV/AIDS is male circumcision (Drain et al. 2006). While male circumcision is practiced by many non-Muslims around the world, it is obligatory for Muslim males (Drain et al. 2006; UNAIDS 2007). Early into the AIDS crisis researchers noticed that circumcised men were less likely to contract HIV/AIDS than uncircumcised men (Fink 1987). Since HIV/AIDS infection may occur through trauma to or lesions on the foreskin (Aral and Holmes 1999), eliminating the foreskin can decrease the likelihood of infection amongst people who have heterosexual sex[2] (Smith et al. 2010; Weis, Hankins, and Dickson 2009). Likewise, because other STD's can increase the risk of HIV/AIDS transmission, circumcision can indirectly reduce the risk of HIV/AIDS by lowering the probability of contracting an STD (Fleming and Wasserheit 1999).

Research on Muslims and HIV/AIDS suggests that circumcision may partially explain the relationship, yet little research has specifically tested for or found that it fully explains the relationship (i.e. Drain et al. 2006; Quigley et al. 1997; Kelly et al. 1999). Circumcision is not the only Islamic practice that may limit the spread of HIV. As discussed in the following section, Islam may indirectly influence rates of HIV/AIDS by limiting substance use and extramarital sex in countries with a high proportion of Muslims.

Sex with Multiple Partners and Sex for Pay

In Africa, which has the highest proportion of people infected with HIV/AIDS, 93% of all adult cases have been spread through heterosexual sex (Mann, Tarantola, and Netter 1992: 32). The likelihood of transmission increases drastically if the individual's health is poor or he /she has another STD (Chen et al. 2007). Sex with many partners or with a partner who has had many other partners not only increases the likelihood of contracting HIV, but also other STDs, making it easier for HIV to pass between individuals when one of them is infected (Chen et al. 2007; Caldwell and Caldwell 1993). If a husband and wife minimize their number of extramarital sex partners, they drastically decrease the probability that either of them will contract HIV.

Within Muslim society, close liaisons between unmarried members of the opposite sex are strongly discouraged and acts of adultery can include severe punishments like stoning or lashings (McDermott and Ahsan 1980). Muslim proscriptions regarding sex outside of marriage also apply to sex with prostitutes, whose many clients can drastically increase the likelihood that she has HIV or another STD infection (Chen et al. 2007). Islamic beliefs regarding extramarital sex may influence all residents in countries with a high proportion of Muslims by drastically increasing the social, legal, and physical costs to having an extramarital affair and limiting the supply of willing extramarital sex partners.

Alcohol and Drug Use

Islamic law also forbids alcohol (Al-Qaradawi 1985) and research conducted in Africa (Bailey et al. 1999; Mbulaiteye et al. 2000) has found that Muslims are less likely than non-Muslims to drink. There also appears to be a relationship between increased alcohol consumption and HIV transmission (Mbulaiteye et al. 2000). Alcohol consumption may raise the risk of HIV infection by increasing sexual activity, the number of sexual partners, or by increasing a couple's willingness to have sex without a condom. High alcohol use could also disrupt marital relations, which could increase the number of lifetime sexual partners.

Muslim proscriptions against alcohol use extend to other substances, including intravenous drug use (Al-Qaradawi 1985). While HIV is typically transmitted through heterosexual sex in Africa, in Eastern Europe and parts of Asia HIV/AIDS is more likely to be spread through injecting drug use (Aceijas et al. 2004). If Muslims are more likely to follow religious proscriptions against substance use, then a high proportion of Muslims may increase anti-substance use norms for all residents. The contextual effect should limit the number of social occasions that include drinking, reduce the number of bars and supply of alcohol and drugs, and limit the availability of friends with whom one can drink and use drugs.

ISLAM AND RISK INCREASING BEHAVIORS

While a number of Islam-inspired behavioral proscriptions may explain lower prevalence rates of HIV/AIDS in Muslim majority countries, behaviors like polygyny may limit the otherwise risk-reducing effect of Islamic religious beliefs. Unlike Judeo-Christian traditions, the Muslim faith allows polygyny (Gatrad and Sheikh 2004), which is the practice of having more than one wife at the same time. On the condition that they receive equal privileges, a maximum of four wives is allowed (Al-Qaradawi 1985). Most husbands in Islamic countries do not have four wives and the majority typically has one.

Nevertheless, by increasing the number of lifetime sexual partners, polygynous relationships may encourage the spread of HIV amongst members of the same household. Some regional studies done in Africa have found higher incidence rates of HIV amongst people in polygynous marriages (Reniers and Tfaily 2008; Gausset 2001). Additionally, some studies have suggested that the institution of polygyny may endorse the belief that men require more than one woman for sexual satisfaction (Caldwell et al. 1993; Caldwell and Caldwell 1993). Indeed, when they tested the relationship between adultery and marriage type, Reniers and Tfaily (2008) found that men in polygynous marriages were 50% more likely to self-report extramarital affairs than men in monogamous unions. Rather than appease men's sexual desires, polygyny may contribute to norms that encourage multiple sex partners outside of marriage and, as a result, contribute to the spread of HIV/AIDS.

In sum, the practice and acceptance of polygyny may limit the otherwise risk-reducing influence of Islamic norms and behaviors. Conversely, there are several behaviors (i.e. circumcision, extramarital sex, and substance use) that could explain the inverse relationship between HIV prevalence rates and proportion Muslim within a country. Below, I test which of these behaviors can help explain why nations with higher proportions of Muslims have lower HIV/AIDS rates, and which behaviors may suppress the otherwise inverse relationship between proportion Muslim and HIV/AIDS.

DATA AND METHODS

Researchers are just starting to conduct multivariate analysis to explain cross-national variation in the spread of HIV/AIDS. Part of the problem has been that measures for many countries, particularly in Africa, are not available due to difficulties in conducting survey research and a lack of centralized sources from which to obtain information. Although data is still somewhat sparse, enough has become available to test some competing ideas for the inverse association between the proportion Muslim and HIV/AIDS prevalence rates. Descriptive statistics are presented in Table 2.1. Below is a description of the variables that will be used in this study.

Key Variables

HIV/AIDS: The measure of HIV/AIDS prevalence rates is taken from the Central Intelligence Agency's World Factbook (2005), which was accessed through the Association of Religion Data Archives (ARDA). It measures the prevalence of HIV/AIDS among adults (age 15 to 49) in 2003. Because it is highly skewed, the variable is logged, which is the typically way this variable tends to be used (McIntosh and Thomas 2004).

Proportion Muslim: The measure of proportion Muslim within a country is taken from the World Christian Database (2005). The measure indicates the proportion Muslim within each country.

Table 2.1 Descriptive Statistics for Variables Included in the Analysis[1]

Variable name	N[2]	Mean	SD	Min	Max
Variables included in every model					
Percent of adults with HIV/AIDS[3]	157	2.61	6.08	0.01	38.80
Logged percent of adults with HIV/AIDS	157	-0.66	1.75	-4.72	3.66
Proportion Muslim	157	0.25	0.36	0.00	0.99
Human Development Index (HDI)	157	0.70	0.18	0.28	0.96
Date of first reported HIV/AIDS case	157	1985	2.88	1978	1993
Mediators					
Male circumcision prevalence	150	1.81	0.93	1.00	3.00
Percentage of females reporting higher risk sex in the last year	55	11.09	10.14	0.60	51.80
Percentage of men reporting commercial sex in the last 12 months	53	4.38	4.54	0.00	23.40
Percentage of female sex workers	59	1.09	1.27	0.09	7.40
Per capital alcohol consumption (liters)	147	6.69	4.69	0.01	18.57
Percentage of injecting drug users (IDU)	115	0.39	0.42	0.00	2.05
Percentage of women in polygynous marriages	52	19.90	15.86	1.00	57.70
Acceptance of polygamy[4] (country mean)	115	0.34	0.42	0.00	1.00

1. Whenever data was provided for more than one year, I selected data that was as close as possible to 2003, which is the year when the dependent variable was developed.
2. A total of 157 countries had data on HIV/AIDS, proportion Muslim, HDI, and date of first reported HIV/AIDS case. All analyses are conducted with a subset of these countries and the subset is determined by the availability of the mediator being examined. The following list indicates which countries are included in each set of models, where 2=included in Table 2, Models 1 and 2; 3=included in Table 2, Models 5 and 6; 4=included in Table 2, Models 7 and 8; 5=included in Table 2, Models 9 and 10; 6=included in Table 1 and 2; 7=included in Table 3, Models 3 and 4; 8=included in Table 4, Models 1 and 2; and 9=included in Table 3, Models 1 and 5. Algeria [2,6,7,8,9], Angola [2,6,8], Argentina [6,7,8], Armenia [2,3,4,5,6,7,8], Australia [2,4,5,6,7,8], Austria [2,6,7,8], Azerbaijan [2,5,6,7,8], Bahamas [2,6,7,8,9], Bangladesh [2,6,7,8,9], Barbados [6], Belarus [2,5,6,7,8], Belgium [2,5,6,7,8], Belize [2,5,6,7,8], Benin [2,3,4,5,6,8,9], Bhutan [2,6], Bolivia [2,4,5,6,7,8], Bosnia and Herzegovina [2,5,6,7,8], Botswana [2,6,8], Brazil [2,3,4,6,7,8], Brunei [6,7], Bulgaria [2,3,4,6,7,8], Burkina Faso [2,3,4,5,6,8,9], Burma [2,7,8], Burundi [2,3,6], Cambodia [2,5,6,7], Cameroon [2,3,4,5,6,8,9], Canada [2,3,6,7,8], Central African Republic [2,4,8,9], Chad [2,3,4,6,8,9], Chile [2,3,4,6,7,8,9], China [2,6,7,8], Colombia [2,3,5,6,7,8], Comoros [2], Democratic Republic of the Congo [2], Republic of the Congo [2,4], Costa Rica [2,3,6,7,8], Cote d'Ivoire [2,3,4,5,6,7,8,9], Croatia [2,5,6,7,8], Cuba [2,5,6,7], Cyprus [6,7], Czech Republic [2,3,5,6,7,8], Denmark [2,5,6,7,8], Djibouti [2,3,6], Dominican Republic [2,3,4,5,6,7,8], Ecuador [2,6], Egypt [2,6,7,8,9], El Salvador [2,6,7,8], Equatorial Guinea [2,6,8], Eritrea [2,4,6,8,9], Estonia [2,5,6,7,8], Ethiopia [2,3,4,5,6,8,9], Fiji [2,6,7,8], Finland [2,5,6,7,8], France [2,5,6,7,8], Gabon [2,3,4,6], Gambia [2,6], Georgia [2,3,4,6], Germany [2,3,5,6,7], Greece [2,3,4,5,6,7,8], Guatemala [2,6,7], Guinea [2,3,4,6,7,8], Guinea-Bissau [2,4], Haiti [2,3,4,5,6,8,9], Honduras [2,4,6,7,8], Hungary [2,5,6,7,8], Iceland [2,6,7,8], India [2,3,5,6,7,8,9], Indonesia [2,5,6,7,8], Iran [2,6,7,8,9], Ireland [2,6,7,8], Israel [2,6,7,8], Italy [2,4,5,6,7,8], Jamaica [2,6], Japan [2,6,7,8,9], Jordan [2,6,7,8,9], Kazakhstan [2,3,4,5,6,7], Kenya [2,3,4,5,6,8,9], Kuwait [2,6,7,8,9], Kyrgyzstan [2,5,6,7], Laos [2,6,7], Larvia [2,3,5,6,7], Lebanon [2,6,7,8,9], Lesotho [2,6,7,8,9], Libya [2,6,7,8,9], Lithuania [2,5,6,7], Luxembourg [2,5,6,7], Madagascar [2,5,6,7,8], Malawi [2,3,4,6,8,9], Malaysia [2,5,6,7,8], Maldives [2,6], Mali [2,4,6,8,9], Malta [2,6,8,9], Mauritania [2,6,7,8], Mauritius [2,6,8,9], Mexico [2,6,7,8], Moldova [2,7], Mongolia [2,4,6,8,9], Morocco [2,6,7,8], Mozambique [2,6,8,9], Namibia [2,4,6,8,9], Nepal [2,4,5,6,7,8], Netherlands [2,3,4,5,6,7,8], New Zealand [2,6,7,8], Nicaragua [2,6,7,8,9], Niger [2,3,4,5,6,7,8], Nigeria [2,4,6,7,8,9], Norway [2,4,6,7,8,9], Oman [2,6,7,8,9], Pakistan [2,6,7,8,9], Panama [2,6,7,8,9], Papua New Guinea [2,3,6,7], Paraguay [2,6,7,8], Peru [2,3,4,5,6,7,8], Philippines [2,3,4,5,6,7,8], Poland [2,5,6,7,8], Portugal [2,4,6,7,8], Qatar [2,6,7], Romania [2,5,6,7,8], Russia [2,5,6,7,8], Rwanda [2,3,4,6], Saudi Arabia [2,6,7,8], Senegal [2,3,4,5,6,7,8,9], Singapore [2,6,7], Slovakia [2,3,5,6,7,8], Slovenia [2,3,5,6,7], South Africa [2,3,5,6,7], Spain [2,3,4,6,7,8,9], Sri Lanka [2,3,4,6,7,8], Sudan [2,3,6,7,8,9], Suriname [2,3,6,8,9], Swaziland [2,3,6], Sweden [2,5,6,7,8], Switzerland [2,3,5,6,7], Syria [2,6,7,8,9], Tajikistan [2,5], Tanzania [2,4,6,7,8,9], Thailand [2,3,4,6,7,8], Togo [2,4,6,8,9], Trinidad and Tobago [2], Tunisia [2,6,7,8], Turkey [2,6,7,8], Turkmenistan [2,3,5,6,7], Uganda [2,3,4,6,8,9], Ukraine [2,3,5,6,7], United Arab Emirates [2,6,7,8,9], United Kingdom [2,3,4,5,6,7,8,9], United States [2,4,5,6,7], Uruguay [2,6,7,8], Uzbekistan [2,4,5,6,7], Venezuela [2,6,7,8,9], Vietnam [2,5,6,7,8], Yemen [2,6,7,8,9], Zambia [2,3,4,5,6,7,8,9], and Zimbabwe [2,3,4,6,8]. To determine which countries are included in the remaining models look at the region (e.g. Africa) indicated in the model or the availability of country data, as determined from the above list, on the mediators included in a given model (e.g. Table 3, Models 5 through 8).
3. This variable is included for descriptive purposes only. Logged percent is used in all models.

Mediators and Suppressors

Circumcision: The prevalence of male circumcision is taken from UNAIDS (2007). The UNAIDS report provides estimates of circumcision at three different levels: 1 "<20% prevalence", 2 "20–80% prevalence," and 3 ">80% prevalence."

Women's risky sex: The percentage of women who engage in riskier sex behaviors is taken from UNAIDS (2002a), which provides countrywide percentages of females (age 15–49) who reported higher risk sex in the last year.

Sex workers: For estimating prostitution prevalence, the percentage of female sex workers and the percentage of men who frequent them are used. Vandepitte et al. (2006) provide the percentage of adult (15–49) females who are sex workers within each country. For the percentage of men reporting commercial sex in the last 12 months, I use Carael et al.'s (2006) more conservative measure, which does not include women who had sex with men in exchange for gifts or favors. [3]Alcohol: Country estimates of alcohol use are taken from WHOSIS (http://www.who.int/whosis/en/index.html). The level of alcohol use indicates a country's total adult per capital alcohol consumption in liters for 2002.

Intravenous drug use: The level of intravenous drug use is taken from Aceijas et al. (2004) and indicates the percentage of people within a country who are intravenous drug users.

Polygamy Acceptance: The measure of polygamy acceptance was obtained from Jütting et al. (2006) and was accessed through Swivel (http://www.swivel.com/data_sets/show/1007377). The variable ranges from 0 to 1 where "1" indicates complete acceptance of polygamy within a given society.

Polygyny: Several sources were used to develop the measure of polygyny, which is the percentage of women who report having one or more co-wives. First, I used the estimates provided by Tertilt (2005, 1367). I then used data from the Demographic and Health Surveys (DHS), accessed through the DHS STATcompiler (http://www.statcompiler.com/) for all of the countries that had available information. Finally, I used Tertilt's (2005, 1346) estimates of the percent of polygynous relationships in Iran (1%) and Jordan (3.8%).

Control Variables

On the basis of previous research (McIntosh and Thomas 2004), I considered including a variety of control variables related to economic development, gender inequality, military and health expenditures, and population size. To conserve degrees of freedom only control variables that were significant or changed key relationships were included in the final analyses. Duration of the AIDS epidemic and the Human Development Index (HDI) fit this criterion.

Date of the first reported HIV/AIDS case provides a measure of the duration of the epidemic in each country. UNAIDS (1998) and UNAIDS (2002b) provide estimates of when the epidemic started. The United Nations

Development Programme (2005) provided the 2003 HDI, which is a composite index that includes measures of life expectancy at birth; the adult literacy rate and the combined gross enrollment ratio for primary, secondary, and tertiary schools; and GDP per capita in purchasing power parity using U.S. dollars. Higher scores indicate higher levels of development.

ANALYSIS

Because the number of countries with information on all the mediators is relatively small, it was not possible to listwise delete across all models and still have enough power to detect significant effects. Rather, before and after a given mediator or suppressor is tested, the case base remains the same so that any changes in the Muslim coefficient can be attributed to the mediator or suppressor, rather than a change in the number or composition of countries. After all of the mediators have been tested, all the significant mediators are included in the same model. Because the case base in this final model will be limited to only countries that have information on all significant variables, the power to detect significant effects will be vastly reduced. Nevertheless, even with the smaller casebase, it is possible to find significant effects for variables that are particularly robust.

Significant mediation is determined using a test derived by Sobel (1982; 1986), and carried out with the STATA command "sgmediation." The purpose of the Sobel mediation test is to assess whether the mediator carries the influence of the independent variable (i.e. Muslim proportion) to the dependent variable (i.e. HIV/AIDS percent).

In order to detect significant mediation, more power is required than is typically needed to detect significant relationships among variables. Since previous research has shown that the effect of the Muslim rate variable on HIV is negative when the mediators or suppressors are included, I rely on a one-tailed significance test for determining significant mediation. For the relationships between coefficients, I continue to rely on the standard two-tailed test since the hypothesized direction of the relationships for some of the control variables is less certain. Whenever enough countries are available to produce power that is greater than .70,[4] the analysis is carried out for smaller case bases of interest (i.e. African countries and when applicable, countries that allow polygyny).

FINDINGS

In Table 2.2, Models 1 and 2 test whether male circumcision significantly mediates the relationship between the proportion Muslim and percentage of people with HIV/AIDS. Somewhat surprisingly, the prevalence of male circumcision in Model 2 is not significantly associated with the percent of people

Table 2.2 Mediators for Explaining the HIV/AIDS and Muslim Relationship Unstandardized OLS Regression Coefficients

	Model 1	Model 2	Model 3	Model 4	Model 5	Model 6	Model 7	Model 8	Model 9	Model 10
	All countries		Africa only		All countries		All countries		All countries	
Muslim proportion	-2.01**	-2.38**	-3.03**	-2.43**	-1.98**	-1.49*	-2.91**	-2.68**	-2.00**	-1.87**
Male circumcision prevalence		0.20		-0.59**						
Females reporting higher risk sex (%)						0.04*				
Men reporting commercial sex (%)								0.06*		
Female sex workers in each country (%)										0.19+
Human Development Index	-7.38**	-7.15**	-4.79**	-4.59**	-7.79**	-7.17**	-7.99**	-7.77**	-7.27**	-6.51**
Date of first reported AIDS/HIV case	-0.10**	-0.10**	-0.06	-0.05	-0.08	-0.07	-0.07	-0.08+	-0.08*	-0.06+
Constant	213.43**	210.74**	127.72	102.35	160.30	144.36	144.98	170.00+	159.00*	132.77+
Observations	150	150	47	47	55	55	53	53	59	59
R-squared	0.62	0.62	0.69	0.75	0.71	0.75	0.73	0.75	0.69	0.71
Sobel test: p-value with a one-tailed test		0.10		0.01		0.04		0.20		0.20

+<.10, *<.05, **<.01 (two-tailed test)

who have HIV/AIDS. However, in Models 3 and 4, the sample is confined to only countries in Africa. With 47 African nations, a higher prevalence of circumcision is significantly associated with a decrease in HIV/AIDS, and circumcision partially mediates the relationship between proportion Muslim and HIV/AIDS. Specifically, in an African country where 80% or more of the males are circumcised, the percent of people with HIV/AIDS is 2.24%, compared to 7.32% in an African nation where less than 20% of the males are circumcised, holding all other variables constant. Because Africa has the highest HIV prevalence in the world and the circumcision rate of countries in Africa is twice as high compared to other countries in the sample, the relationship between circumcision and HIV/AIDS prevalence is strengthened when the analysis focuses only on African nations.

As expected, Model 6 shows that as the percentage of females who report higher risk sex increases, so does the percent of people with HIV/AIDS. Additionally, the Sobel test shows that higher risk sex partially mediates the relationship between the proportion Muslim and HIV/AIDS.

Models 7 through 10 examine commercial sex work as a potential mediator. Model 8 shows that although the percentage of men reporting commercial sex in the last year is positively associated with HIV/AIDS, it does not significantly mediate the relationship. Model 10 shows that the relationship between the percent of females who are sex workers is not significantly related to the percent of people with HIV/AIDS.

Table 2.3 examines the mediating role of alcohol and injecting drug use. Model 2 shows that alcohol use partially mediates the relationship between proportion Muslim and HIV/AIDS. Model 4 shows that increases in intravenous drug use are associated with HIV/AIDS, but intravenous drug use does not significantly mediate the relationship between proportion Muslim and HIV/AIDS.

Models 5 and 6 include all of the variables that the previous models found significantly mediate the relationship between proportion Muslim and HIV/AIDS. With 54 countries the power to detect significant effect for six variables is quite small. Nevertheless, alcohol use and the percent of females who reported higher risk sex in the last year are both significant. Additionally, the Sobel test shows that even after controlling for alcohol use and male circumcision, the percentage of females who reported higher risk sex helps to significantly explain the relationship between proportion Muslim and HIV/AIDS.

In Models 7 and 8 the sample is limited to the 22 African nations that have information on the prevalence of male circumcision, percentage of females who reported higher risk sex, and alcohol use. Even with this very small sample size the prevalence of male circumcision is significant and the Sobel test shows that male circumcision significantly mediates the relationship between proportion Muslim and HIV/AIDS. This finding makes clear that in Africa countries with a high proportion of Muslims have lower levels of HIV/AIDS in part because a higher proportion of men are circumcised.

Table 2.3   Mediators for Explaining the HIV/AIDS and Muslim Relationship,[1] Continued Unstandardized OLS regression coefficients

	Model 1	Model 2	Model 3	Model 4	Model 5	Model 6	Model 7	Model 8
	All countries		All countries		All countries		Africa only	
Muslim proportio[n]	-1.95**	-1.57**	-1.51**	-1.52**	-2.00***	-0.66	-2.03**	-0.72
Alcohol consumption (liters)		0.06*				0.08*		-0.01
IDU (%)				0.57**				
Male circumcision prevalence								-0.66*
Females reporting higher risk sex (%)						0.04*		0.03+
Human Development Index	-7.25**	-7.63**	-6.05**	-6.54**	7.87***	-7.78**	0.23	0.09
Date of first reported AIDS/HIV case	-0.10**	-0.09**	-0.11**	-0.13**	-0.08	-0.06	0.00	-0.04
Constant	198.29**	185.79**	231.93**	271.53**	169.82	122.22	8.41	77.68
Observations	147	147	115	115	54	54	22	22
R-squared	0.60	0.61	0.47	0.50	0.70	0.78	0.45	0.66
Sobel test[2]: p-value with a one-tailed test		0.02		0.45		alcohol: 0.07 high risk sex: 0.03 circumcision: 0.20		alcohol: 0.43 high risk sex: 0.10 circumcision: 0.04

+<.10, *<.05, **<.01 (two-tailed test)

1. The African nations included in Models 7 and 8 are: Benin, Burkina Faso, Burundi, Cameroon, Chad, Cote d'Ivoire, Djibouti, Ethiopia, Gabon, Guinea, Kenya, Lesotho, Madagascar, Malawi, Niger, Rwanda, Senegal, Sudan, Swaziland, Uganda, Zambia, and Zimbabwe. These countries are also included in Models 5 and 6, along with: Armenia, Brazil, Canada, Chile, Colombia, Costa Rica, Cuba, Czech Republic, Dominican Republic, France, Georgia, Germany, Greece, Haiti, India, Japan, Kazakhstan, Latvia, Netherlands, Norway, Papua New Guinea, Peru, Philippines, Slovenia, Spain, Sri Lanka, Sweden, Switzerland, Thailand, Turkmenistan, Ukraine, and the United Kingdom.

2. P-values are provided for the new variable that has been added. When more than one variable is added, the variable name along with the p-value is indicated.

Table 2.4   The Suppressing Role of Contraceptive Prevalence; and Polygyny for
Explaining the HIV/AIDS and Muslim Relationship
Unstandardized OLS regression coefficients

	Model 1	Model 2	Model 3	Model 4	Model 5
	All countries		Countries with Polygyny		
Muslim proportion	-2.15***	-3.05**	-3.01**	-3.06**	-3.55**
Acceptance of polygamy (mean)		1.36**			1.08*
Polygyny (%)				0.02*	0.02+
Human Development Index	-7.53***	-6.11**	-4.44**	-3.05**	-2.86**
Date of first reported HIV/AIDS case	-0.09***	-0.10**	-0.15**	-0.13*	-0.14**
Constant	186.35**	193.37**	300.76**	253.71*	288.87**
Observations	115	115	45	45	45
R-squared	0.67	0.70	0.83	0.85	0.87
Sobel test: p-value with a one-tailed test		0.00		0.35	acceptance of polygamy: 0.02 polygyny: 0.32

+<.10, *<.05, **<.01 (two-tailed test)

The Models in Table 2.4 examine whether the prevalence of polygyny
and attitudes about polygamy suppress the risk-reducing influence of living in a country with a higher proportion of Muslims. Model 2 shows that
an increase in polygamy acceptance significantly mediates the relaitonsip
between proportion Muslim and HIV/AIDS.

Models 3 and 4 examine the percent of women in polygynous relationships for explaining the relationship between proportion Muslim and HIV/
AIDS. Whereas the percent of women in polygynous relationships is significant, the small increase in the Muslim coefficient is not significant,
indicating that it does not significantly mediate the relationship between
proportion Muslim and HIV/AIDS.

To see if polygamy acceptance continues to have an effect, even after
accounting for the practice of polygyny, Model 5 includes both polygamy
acceptance and the percentage of women in polygynous relationships. While
the percentage of women in polygynous relationships is no longer significantly associated with HIV/AIDS cases, acceptance of polygamy remains significant. Moreover, the Sobel test shows that even with this relatively small
sample size and controlling for the percentage of women in polygynous relationships, polygamy acceptances significantly suppresses the otherwise risk
reducing influence of proportion Muslim for explaining HIV/AIDS.

DISCUSSION AND CONCLUSION

This study examined several of the mediators that could explain the cross-national relationship between proportion Muslim and the percentage of people with HIV/AIDS. A large body of research has confirmed a relationship between adherence to Islam at the national level and lower rates of HIV/AIDS. However, few studies have comprehensively examined the mechanisms that may explain the cross-national relationship. This study shows that countries with a higher proportion of Muslims have a smaller percentage of women engaging in riskier sex, lower rates of alcohol use, and higher prevalence of circumcision, all of which limit the transmission of HIV/AIDS. The proportion of women engaging in higher risk sex is the most robust mediator of the relationship between proportion Muslim and HIV/AIDS. Conversely, while commercial sex and injecting drug use also contribute to the spread of HIV, they do not help explain the cross-national relationship between the proportion Muslim and HIV/AIDS.

This study also examined the role of attitudes about and the practice of polygyny in suppressing the risk-reducing influence of Islam on HIV/AIDS. The practice of polygyny did not statistically mediate the relationship between Islam and HIV/AIDS. However, a country's acceptance of polygamy was a significant mediator, even after accounting for the practice of polygyny. Some research (Caldwell et al. 1993; Caldwell and Caldwell 1993) has suggested that where polygamy is accepted, there may be more support for the belief that men require more than one woman for sexual satisfaction. The lower risk of HIV/AIDS for people living in a country with a higher proportion of Muslims may be even lower, if attitudes toward polygamy were less accepting.

There are three processes through which living in a country with a high proportion of Muslims may limit HIV/AIDS. Individuals who adhere to Islam may have a lower risk of contracting HIV/AIDS because they have more conservative sex behaviors, lower alcohol use, and are more likely to be circumcised. Secondly, the alcohol use and sex behaviors of all people, Muslims and non-Muslims alike, who live in a country with a high proportion of Muslims, may be influenced by conservative Islamic norms and behaviors. Finally, a Muslim religious context may bolster personal religious beliefs, further limiting the likelihood of Muslims drinking alcohol and participating in riskier sex behaviors. Because survey research remains a challenge in Africa and the Middle East, the data are not yet available to conduct cross-national multi-level models, which would permit the examination of separate individual and country-level effects on individuals' risk of HIV/AIDS.[5] Although this study can confirm that one of these processes is at work, more data is needed to unravel the specifics.

There are primarily three ways through which HIV/AIDS is transmitted -heterosexual sex, homosexual sex, and intravenous drug use. While this study examined mediators related to heterosexual sex and intravenous drug use, it did not consider attitudes and behaviors related to homosexuality. Anti-homosexual sentiment is particularly high in Africa and the Middle East. In some countries (e.g. Iran) homosexual acts are punishable by death. As a result, we have very little information on the rate of people with homosexual or bisexual histories. (For some regional estimates see Cáceres et al. 2008). Anti-homosexual sentiment may, in part, help explain the inverse relationship between Muslim rates and HIV/AIDS transmission through homosexual sex. However, heterosexual sex is the most common way through which HIV/AIDS is spread in Africa where the epidemic is greatest. As a result, attitudes and laws related to homosexuality may have a minimal effect.[6]

There are other limitations related to the data that warrant discussion. First, with so many challenges to collecting data in Africa, the validity of the national-level estimates undoubtedly vary and some of the measures used were not ideal. Second, within countries, regional estimates of HIV/AIDS and other variables of interest, like circumcision, may vary drastically, making it difficult to find significant cross-national relationships. Finally, while the temporal sequence of events for the national-level relationships are likely correct (i.e. a high proportion of Muslims influences overall rates of circumcision, which limit HIV/AIDS), the temporal sequence of events for individuals is not clear from this macro analysis. For example, circumcision for some males may not be done until adolescence when sexual activity may have already been initiated (Bailey et al. 1999).

A number of studies have reported a relationship between a country's proportion Muslim and HIV/AIDS, but few have been able to provide specifics about the mechanisms that may explain the relationship. This is the first study to examine the mediators that might explain the relationship between a high proportion of Muslims and HIV/AIDS. National-level data, particularly those collected in less research friendly countries, presents some challenges. But because it is *more* difficult to find significant effects with small sample sizes and inconsistent reporting, significant findings should be taken as conservative estimates of a given behavior's role in explaining the relationship between proportion Muslim and HIV/AIDS. In other words, with individual-level data and/or more countries we should be even more likely to find effects.

While the HIV/AIDS epidemic has continued to spread, nations with a high proportion of Muslims appear to have lower prevalence rates of HIV/AIDS. These nations may not have intended to limit HIV/AIDS transmission by encouraging adherence to Islamic beliefs. Yet, they are experiencing some of the indirect effects of beliefs that strongly encourage circumcision, marital fidelity, and limit alcohol consumption. Likewise, people who live in countries with a high proportion of Muslims may be experiencing some of the religion's risk reducing effects, even if they are not Muslim. This study shows the power of religious beliefs measured at the macro level to influence behaviors that have indirectly shaped the spread of HIV/AIDS.

NOTES

1. Because homosexuality is illegal in a number of African nations and countries with a high proportion of Muslims, the current study largely focuses on the spread of HIV/AIDS through heterosexual sex and intravenous drug use. In a separate analysis the potential mediating roles of anti-homosexual sentiment and laws were examined, but the data quality was questionable. Nevertheless, there were no significant mediating effects of anti-homosexual sentiment or laws.

2. Research is still unclear about whether or not there is a protective effect of male circumcision on the spread of HIV/AIDS for men who have sex with men (Smith et al. 2010).

3. Some of the estimates used in Carael et al. (2006) were taken from the Demographic and Health Surveys (DHS). In many earlier DHS surveys in sub-Saharan Africa, an extended definition of sex worker relationships was used: "In the last year, have you had sex in exchange for gifts, favors or money?" In later surveys, men were asked "Did you have sex in exchange for money in the last 12 months?", "Did you pay for sex in the last 12 months?", or "Did you have sex with a sex worker?" Whenever both phrasings of the question were available, I relied on the more conservative definition. In a separate analysis I found that estimates that incorporated the more liberal definition did not significantly predict logged HIV/AIDS prevalence, suggesting that they may be less accurate since several studies have established that sex work can increase HIV/AIDS transmission.

4. A power of .70 and greater is a liberal estimate of the power needed to reject the null hypothesis. To estimate power I rely on Stata's "powerreg," command, which uses information about the sample size, number of covariates, number of new variables, and the R-squared for the reduced and full model to estimate the amount of power needed to detect a "true" effect, if there is one. The R-squared for the reduced model is determined by the R-squared given when all variables, but the potential mediator or suppressor, is entered into the model. The R-squared for the full model is determined by adding .01 to the R-square of the reduced model.

5. For multi-level analysis the power to detect significant effects is determined by the number of level-2 units. Hence, while studies like the Demographic and Health Surveys provide a large number of individual survey respondents, the number of countries where this survey is collected is quite small.

6. In a separate analysis I used data from the World Values Survey to examine the influence of public opinion on HIV/AIDS. The relationship was not significant.

REFERENCES

Aceijas, Carmen, Stimson, Gerry V., Hickman, Matthew, and Rhodes, Tim. 2004. Global Overview of Injecting Drug Use and HIV Infection Among Injecting Drug Users. *AIDS* 18: 2295–2303.

Adamczyk, Amy, and Palmer, Ian. 2008. Religion's Contextual Influence on Marijuana Use. *Journal of Drug Issues* 38: 717–742.

Adamczyk, Amy, and Felson, Jacob. 2006. Friends' Religiosity and First Sex. *Social Science Research* 35: 924–947

Adamczyk, Amy and Felson, Jacob. 2008. Fetal Positions: Unraveling the Influence of Religion on Premarital Pregnancy Resolution. *Social Science Quarterly* 89: 17–38.

al-Qaradawi, Yusuf. 1985. *The Lawful and the Prohibited in Islam*. Indianapolis: American Trust Publications.

Aral Sevgi O., and Holmes, King K. 1999. Social and Behavioral Determinants of the Epidemiology of STDs: Industrialized and Developing Countries. In *Sexually Transmitted Diseases*, edited by K. K. Holmes, P. A. Mardh, and P. F. Sparling et al. New York: McGraw-Hill.

Bailey, Robert C., Neema, Stella, and Othieno, Richard. 1999. Sexual Behaviors and Other HIV Risk Factors in Circumcised and Uncircumcised Men in Uganda. *Journal of Acquired Immune Deficiency Syndromes* 22: 294–301

Cáceres, Carlos F., Konda, Kelika, Segura, Eddy, and Lyerla, Rob. 2008. Epidemiology of Male Same-Sex Behavior Associated with Sexual Health Indicators in Low- and Middle-Income Countries: 2003–2007 Estimates. *Sexually Transmitted Infections* 84: i49i56–.

Caldwell et al. 1993. African Families and AIDS: Context, Reactions and Potential Interventions. *Health Transition Review* 3: 1–14.

Caldwell, John, and Caldwell, Pat. 1993. The Nature and Limits of the sub-Saharan African AIDS Epidemic: Evidence from Geographic and Other Patterns. *Population and Development Review* 19: 817–848.

Carael, Michel, Slaymaker, Emma, Lyerla, Rob, and Sarkar, Sawarup. 2006. Clients of Sex Workers in Different Regions of the World: Hard to Count. *Sexually Transmitted Infections* 82 (Supplement III): iii26–iii33.

Central Intelligence Agency. 2005. *World Factbook*. CIA: Washington D.C.

Chen et al. 2007. Sexual Risk Factors for HIV Infection in Early and Advanced HIV Epidemics in Sub-Saharan Africa: Systematic Overview of 68 Epidemiological Studies. *PloS One* 2(10): 1–14.

Drain, Paul K. et al. 2006. Male Circumcision, Religion and Infectious Diseases: An Ecologic Analysis of 118 Developing Countries. *BMC Infectious Diseases*. Available: http://www.ncbi.nlm.nih.gov/pmc/articles/PMC1764746/pdf/1471–2334–6-172.pdf. Accessed July 11, 2010.

Fink, A. J. 1987. Circumcision and Heterosexual Transmission of HIV Infection to Men [Letter]. *New England Journal of Medicine* 316: 1546–1547.

Finke, Roger, and Adamczyk, Amy. 2008. Explaining Morality: Using International Data to Reestablish the Macro/Micro Link. *Sociological Quarterly* 49: 615–650.

Fleming D. T. and J. N. Wasserheit. 1999. From Epidemiological Synergy to Public Health Policy and Practice: The Contribution of Other Sexually Transmitted Diseases to Sexual Transmission of HIV Infection. *Sexually Transmitted Infections* 75: 13–17.

Gatrad, A., Sheikh Rashid, and Sheikh, Aziz. 2004. Risk Factors for HIV/AIDS in Muslim Communities. *Diversity in Health and Social Care* 1: 65–69.

Gausset, Quentin. 2001. Aids and Cultural Practices in Africa: The Case of the Tonga (Zambia). *Social Science and Medicine* 52: 509–518.

Gray, Peter B. 2004. HIV and Islam: Is HIV Prevalence Lower Among Muslims? *Social Science and Medicine* 58: 1751–1756.

Iannaccone, Laurence R. 1994. Why Strict Churches Are Strong. *American Journal of Sociology* 99: 1118–1211.

Jütting, Johannes P., Morrisson, Christian, Dayton-Johnson Jeff, and Drechsler, Dennis. 2006. *Measuring Gender (In)Equality: Introducing the Gender, Institutions and Development Data Base*. (Working Paper No. 247). Organisation for Economic Co-operation and Development, Paris.

Kelly, Robert et al. 1999. Age of Male Circumcision and Risk of Prevalent HIV Infection in Rural Uganda. *AIDS* 13: 399–405.

Mann, Jonathan M., Tarantola, Daniel J. M., and Netter Thomas W. (eds). 1992. *AIDS in the World*. Cambridge, MA: Harvard University Press.

Mbulaiteye, et al. 2000. Alcohol and HIV: A Study among Sexually Active Adults in Rural Southwest Uganda. *International Journal of Epidemiology* 29: 911–915.

McDermott, Mustafa Yusuf, and Ahsan, Muhammad Manazir. 1980. *The Muslim Guide for Teachers, Employers, Community Workers, and Social Administrators in Britain.* Leicester: The Islamic Foundation.
McIntosh, William Alex and John K. Thomas. 2004. Economic and Other Societal Determinants of the Prevalence of HIV: A Test of Competing Hypotheses. *Sociological Quarterly* 45: 303–324.
Meier, Ann M. 2003. Adolescents' Transition to First Intercourse, Religiosity and Attitudes about Sex. *Social Forces* 81: 1031–1052.
Quigley M. et al. 1997. Sexual Behaviour Patterns and Other Risk Factors for HIV Infection in Rural Tanzania: A Case Control Study. *AIDS* 11: 237–248.
Regnerus, Mark D. 2002. Friends' Influence on Adolescent Theft and Minor Delinquency: A Developmental Test of Peer-Reported Effects. *Social Science Research* 31: 681–705.
Reniers, Georges, and Tfaily, Rania. 2008. *Polygyny and HIV in Malawi.* (Working paper). Boulder: University of Colorado at Boulder, Institute of Behavioral Science.
Scheepers, Peer, Te Grotenhuis, Manfred, and Van Der Slik, Frans. 2002. Education, Religiosity and Moral Attitudes: Explaining Cross-National Effect Differences. *Sociology of Religion* 63: 157–176.
Smith, Dawn K. et al. 2010. Male Circumcision in the United States for the Prevention of HIV Infection and Other Adverse Health Outcomes: Report from a CDC Consultation. *Public Health Reports Supplement* 125: 72–82.
Sobel, Michael E. 1982. Asymptotic Confidence Intervals for Indirect Effects in Structural Equation Models. *Sociological Methodology,* 13: 290–312.
Sobel, Michael E. 1986. Some New Results on Indirect Effects and their Standard Errors in Covariance Structure Models. *Sociological Methodology,* 16: 159–186.
Stark, Rodney and Roger Finke. 2000. *Acts of Faith: Explaining the Human Side of Religion.* Berkeley: University of California Press.
Statcompiler. (http://www.statcompiler.com/). Measure DHS: Calverton, Maryland.
Swivel. 2007. Acceptance of Polygamy by Country. (http://www.swivel.com/data_sets/show/1007377).
Tertilt, Michèle. 2005. Polygyny, Fertility, and Savings. *Journal of Political Economy,* 113: 1341–1371.
UNAIDS 1998. *Report on the Global HIV/AIDS Epidemic.* June 1998. Geneva: UNAIDS.
UNAIDS 2002a. *Report on the Global HIV/AIDS Epidemic.* Geneva: UNAIDS
UNAIDS 2002b. *AIDS Epidemic Update.* December 2002. Geneva: UNAIDS.
United Nations Development Programme. 2005. *Human Development Report.* New York: United Nations Development Programme.
UNAIDS 2007. *Male Circumcision: Global Trends and Determinants of Prevalence, Safety and Acceptability.* Geneva: UNAIDS
Vandepitte Judith, Lyerla, Rob, Dallabetta, Gina, Crabbé, Francois, Alary, Michel, Buvé, Alary. 2006. Estimates of the Number of Female Sex Workers in Different Regions of the World. *Sexually Transmitted Infections* 82: iii18–iii25.
Weiss, Helen A., Hankins, Catherine A., and Dickson, Kim. 2009. Male Circumcision and Risk of HIV Infection in Women: A Systematic Review and Meta-Analysis. *Lancet Infectious Diseases,* 9 (11): 669–677.
WHO Statistical Information System (WHOSIS). 2009. (http://www.who.int/whosis/en/index.htm).
World Christian Database. 2005. (http://worldchristiandatabase.org). Brill: Boston.
Yuchtman-Yaar, Ephraim, and Alkalay, Yasmin. 2007. Religious Zones, Economic Development and Modern Value Orientations: Individual versus Contextual Effects. *Social Science Research* 36: 789–807.

3 Islam and Labor Market Integration in Denmark

Peter B. Andersen and Peter Lüchau

Denmark has a comprehensive welfare state with a wide range of services including universal healthcare and poor relief. Such a system is expensive and is one of the reasons why taxes in Denmark are so high (at least compared to the other European countries). The welfare system can only be upheld so long as the unemployment rate is relatively low; otherwise tax revenue will be too low. The unemployment rate for ethnic Danes was around 3% in the year 2006, but around 9% among first- and second-generation immigrants living in Denmark. Among non-Western immigrants the unemployment rate was around 12%.[1] Such a high unemployment rate is a problem that needs to be addressed in a welfare system like Denmark's. Addressing the problem requires an understanding of the factors that contribute to the relatively high unemployment rate among non-Western immigrants. One interpretation, voiced in political debates, is that it is the religious belonging of the immigrants that is to blame for the high unemployment rate. Hence this article will analyze if there is a connection between immigrant religion and unemployment.

The history of immigration in Denmark has been similar to that of the rest of Europe, at least, as reflected in reports from the Danish Home Ministry. Initially there was a strong emphasis on the rights of "guest workers" in 1970 to establish family reunions where the migrants' wives and children settled in Denmark in so far as the immigrants were interested (Simonsen 1990, 25), but no one expected that any "real immigration" would be the result. No one expected the gradual shift towards the expectation of settlement that occurred later among immigrants. A 1983 report stated that facilities should be created in order to integrate the immigrants into Danish society through initiatives regarding education, social communities, and housing policy (Simonsen 1990, 31). In their reports from 1980 and 1983, successive governments (first a Social Democratic government and later a coalition of the Conservative, Liberal, Centre Democrats, and Christian People's party) explicitly aimed at integrating the immigrants. This should be done with "reasonable consideration" to their particular background, but the report stated that it would make "considerable demands toward [the immigrants'] effort to adapt to the conditions in Danish society" (Simonsen 1990, 31). As the historian Simonsen sombrely notes, "the report did not forward any specific directions on how the reasonable considerations were to be understood." In the Danish context of those days this hould be taken as indicating that the immigrants would be allowed to sustain their own culture in so far as it did not clash with the laws and regulations of the host country, and that no one would interfere with the religion of immigrants, as safeguarded by the Danish constitution. It was also evident that immigrants were considered individuals and were not seen as parts of a collective whole.

The Danish government has tried to create advisory bodies in a top-down manner. The "Immigrant Council" ("Indvandrerrådet"), presently the "Council for Ethnic Minorities" ("Rådet for Etniske Minoriteter") has been an advisory body under the Home Ministry since 1983 (presently under the Ministry of Refugee, Immigration and Integration). But as with the bottom-up organisations, the council has had only minor impact, and with the creation of elected "Integration Councils" in the municipalities in 1999 the Council for Ethnic Minorities was appointed by the elected councils and no longer by the immigrants' own organisations (Togeby 2003, 148–149). This process may be seen as a way to legitimate the representation of the Council for Ethnic Minorities, but it is still an open question whether the council will give the minorities a voice to such an extent that the state will listen to it.

Immigrants in Denmark are by no means a homogeneous group. The many different immigrant organisations are to a large extent the product of the distinct differences between immigrant groups residing in Denmark. These groups differ with regard to immigration histories, ethnicity, social status, demography, and religious identification (see Gundelach and Nørregård-Nielsen 2007). To analyze immigrants residing in Denmark as a single group, even if only those from non-Western countries are considered, would be an analytical fallacy. One way to compensate for this could be to narrow the number of immigrant groups to be analyzed using common criteria like immigrations history, country of origin or religious identification.

CULTURE AND EMPLOYMENT IN DENMARK

The high unemployment rate among, in particular, non-Western immigrants in Denmark has been noticed in the media and among politicians. It is important to note that the difference between ethnic Danes and immigrants is not the product of differences in age (e.g. number of pensioners) or working ability (e.g. disabled or ill). The percentage is the number of unemployed among those in the workforce, those able to work. That the high unemployment rate has become a topic in public discourse is not surprising taken the economic strain imposed by high unemployment rates in the Danish welfare system into consideration. But the discussions have quickly changed into a discussion not about the traditional causes of unemployment, e.g. education, structural factors, the economy etc., but about the perceived cultural differences between ethnic Danes and non-Western immigrants.

One example of this is the Danish Minister for Employment (the Liberal party) who has expressed his worry about whether the migrants possess the same "tough" approach to work as "Danes" in a statement where he considered the implementation of economic incentives to motivate them to take up vacant jobs. [2] According to the Danish Minister of Employment immigrants would only work if there was a monetary incentive as opposed to Danes who work because it is the "right thing to do." Here a phenomenon that is normal in economic theory (the more money individuals can earn the more they are motivated to work) is turned into something negative and basically unnatural (or un-Danish). What should influence employment is not economic gain but a particular (Danish) work ethic.

This statement on the work ethic (or lack hereof) of immigrants in Denmark must be seen within the broader frame of the debates on immigrants in Denmark. Political discussions on immigrants have turned from being primarily about the labor market situation of immigrants to being primarily about culture (Madsen 2000) and this culture is overwhelmingly defined as Muslim. In present Danish political discourse Muslims and immigrants have become more or less synonymous (Hussein 2000; Hussein, Yilmaz, and O'Connor 1997). To talk about immigrants (or at least non-Western immigrants) is to talk about Muslims. As the discussions on immigrants are now focused on cultural differences, rather than structural, economic, or social factors, they have become, among other things, discussions about the special properties of Islam in relation to labor market participation. This is of course off the mark because far from *all* non-Western immigrants are Muslims (Lüchau 2004, 52) but the consensus in political discussions nevertheless seem to be that all non-Western immigrants are Muslims. This means that in political discourse the higher unemployment rate of non-Western immigrants in Denmark, to certain extent, becomes a product of Islam and being a Muslim. This points toward the theme of work ethic that has been an important issue in social science for more than 100 years.

THE WORK ETHIC OF WORLD RELIGIONS

With non-Western immigrants being interpreted as Muslims and their unemployment rate being so high as to (at least formally) be a problem for the Danish welfare system one way to interpret the situation is to say that religion has been turned into a social problem in so far as religion comes to explain poor labor market integration (see Hjelm in this volume). This makes it relevant to consider whether it is possible to identify a work ethic which is specific to Islam and different from that of the work ethic of the majority of the Danish population.

The most famous study regarding work ethics in the world religions is the series of works on the economic ethics in the world religions which Max Weber undertook from the beginning of the twentieth century to his death in 1920.[3] In many regards these studies were a large scale attack on materialist (Marxist) economic theory[4], so Weber added a number of themes to the materialist considerations of various kinds of feudal and prebendal societies[5]. A major issue against the materialist approaches to economic history was his search for explanations of why people acted as they did, and it is here that the work ethic became so important for Weber's argument.

If the development of capitalism in one place and not in another place could be explained by differences in work ethic it would undermine the historical materialist approach's focus on formal structures. As the work ethic had to come from somewhere outside the economic sphere Weber devoted much consideration to identify how the differences of the (religious) salvation systems resulted in different attitudes towards work. Among the considerations was also the rationality of the religion in case as some level of rationality was necessary for the calculated planning of capitalist enterprises. In general Weber considered magic and mysticism as irrational. One important example of mysticism is the Catholic interpretation of the Eucharist as a complete transformation compared to the more rational interpretation of the Puritans who only saw it as symbolic[6]. As this paper concerns the resulting work ethic we do not need to consider the origins of different work ethics, but can restrict ourselves to look at the ethics as they are present in the world religions.

In his study of Hinduism and Buddhism (Weber 1923) Weber cautiously considered the prebendal structures in comparison to the situation in China (e.g. Weber 1934), but the chapters on Hinduism stress Hindu mysticism and the lack of rationality among Hindu ascetics; aspects which under certain circumstances might have led to the growth of a capitalist work ethic. To Weber's mind the chances for the growth of such a situation were not large, however, as no Hindu or Buddhist monk carried any work out (Weber 1923:161). And it was especially the transfer of the work ethics of the ascetics (the Catholic monks) to the secular world which was so important in his study *The Protestant Ethic and the Spirit of Capitalism* (Weber 2003) that one may say it constituted an important precondition for the growth of the capitalist spirit in parts of Europe.

Weber never wrote any comprehensive study of Islam, so Bryan S. Turner's book on *Weber and Islam* (1974) is the most systematic consideration of Weber's thoughts on Islam. Here Turner has collected Weber's stray considerations on Islam into an attempt to consider the approach for the study he never finalised. Turner stresses that Weber gave little consideration to Islamic work ethic, but that he argued that an Islamic warrior ethic and the prebendal economic structure in Islamic societies were obstacles to the development of capitalism (Turner 1974)[7]. We will never know if Weber would have stressed the rational aspects of the teaching of the Koran or the non-magic aspects of Sufi mysticism if he had been able to carry through his plans. Turner (1974) thinks not, as he underscores the problems and prejudice in these aspects of Weber's approach. Sukidi (2006) agrees with Turner in her reading of Weber, but adds that recent Islamic reform movements such as the Muhammadiyah in Indonesia manifest a number of the rational features found in Puritanism. But instead of carrying out a new study of the work ethic in the history of Islam, it is more apt for the present paper to consider how historical studies have tried to see Weber's general study of *The Protestant Ethic and the Spirit of Capitalism* on the background of the specific social transformations of European society.

Here it is relevant to consider the critique of Weber's *The Protestant Ethic and the Spirit of Capitalism* forwarded by historians. They make it clear that it was not the Puritan Protestant ethic which laid the basis of the ethics in business capitalism, but specific historical circumstances in British society from the seventeenth to the nineteenth century (Tawney 1961, 197–270). And it has been documented by Trevor-Roper in his study of social changes after the Reformation that it was not religious belonging but migrant status which determined the development of business capitalism. He stresses the fact that the "entrepreneurial class of the new 'capitalist' cities of the seventeenth century [. . .] the whole class is predominantly formed by immigrants" (Trevor-Roper 1968, 28).

If Trevor-Roper's findings were to be turned into a general sociological rule it should be expected that immigrants were the ones who would do better in all kinds of economic endeavours, but at least in the current Danish context this is not the case. This could be caused by too simple a view of immigrants or rather too broad a generalization about immigrants. With Bauman one can make a distinction between two types of migrants: Tourists and Vagabonds (Bauman 2000). Some migrants move voluntarily and stay within the upper strata of society usually earning extremely well, while others move out of necessity (be it poverty or war) in the lowest strata of society with all the problems, sickness, exploitation and restrictions they meet there. All this only to suggest that migrant status in itself does not carry much predictive value and hence it might be more analytically fruitful to return to the idea that cultural and/or religious background may be a factor in the degree of labor market integration.

In Europe there are several examples of how cultural or religious background or a combination of both has influenced the situation for individuals in different groups. The "merchant ethos" or "merchant ideology" which Tambs-Lyche found in his Weberian study of Hindu Patidars in London in the 1970s may be part of their original background in Gujarat society (Tambs-Lyche 1980: 32; see also Warrier 1994), as opposed to Punjabis. But as most of the Punjabis in London were also Sikhs it could also have been the difference in religious belonging between the two groups that was the determining factor. In Denmark the higher than average education and socio-economic status of the Jewish community could also be interpreted as a consequence of a particular religiously defined group ethos (Blum 1973). Again it could also be that the relative high position of the members of the Danish Jewish community is the result of long term integration in Danish society as the first Jews were allowed to settle in the seventeenth century.

It is important to note that the hypothesis here is that it is religious belonging or a particular religiosity which is the determining factor in labor market integration. It is not ethnicity, gender composition, immigrations history or other factors such as social marginalization. The idea is that Islam as a religion has certain traits that work against labor market participation. Therefore Muslims will tend to have a higher unemployment rate than non-Muslims (be they Christian or religiously unaffiliated).

METHOD AND THE DANISH FRAMEWORK

The data used in the following analyzes comes from a survey on labor market experience, gender roles, and religion among immigrant from three immigrant groups in Denmark[8]. The survey was conducted between February and November 2006. Telephone interviews were used with face-to-face follow up interviews if needed. If at all possible, the interviews were conducted over the phone (around 72%), but if this was for some reason not possible the interviewer would visit respondents in their homes. Interviews could be conducted in the native language of the respondent although Danish was preferred and around 72% of the interviews ended up being conducted in Danish. It is important to note that the interviews started just as the so-called Muhammad Cartoon Crisis began to unfold (see Christoffersen 2006; Rothstein 2007). The crisis originated in the publication of several cartoon drawings of the Prophet in the national Danish newspaper *Jyllandsposten*. After some public debate in Denmark the Muhammad cartoons garnered the attention of large Muslim groups in the Middle East leading to boycotts of Danish goods, diplomatic difficulties, and rioting including the burning down of a Danish embassy building. The Muhammad cartoon crisis was a very visible topic in the media while the interviews for the survey were conducted. Chances are that the Muhammad cartoon crisis may have resulted in a few more refusals to participate while at the same time sharpening opinions thereby reducing the number of missing answers in the interviews conducted.

Since immigrants in Denmark are a very diverse group it was decided to sample three immigrant groups and only first-generation immigrants. The three groups were immigrants from Iran, Pakistan, and Turkey. The countries of origin were selected because they are all predominantly Muslim countries but with three very different national histories and located in three very different parts of the world. Also the immigration histories of the three groups were different. They have arrived in Denmark at different times and for different reasons, some were migrant workers while others were refugees. Finally Iranians, Pakistanis, and Turks represent some of the largest single immigrants groups in Denmark.

Only 1st generation immigrants from the three groups were sampled which should maximise the impact of their original (country of origin) culture which tend to become transformed among 2nd generation immigrants. Since one of the aims of the survey was to analyze the job situation among immigrants the sample was skewed so as only to include people ages 18 to 45. This maximises the chances of having able bodied respondents, people in the workforce. Respondents were selected using simple random sampling on data from the government databases at Statistics Denmark, the samples are therefore representative of 1st generation immigrants, ages 18 to 45, coming from Iran, Pakistan, and Turkey.

The drop-out rate was just under 50 per cent making the survey just acceptable according to Mangione's considerations (1995). An investigation of skewedness was conducted, using data from Statistics Denmark, comparing the respondents to those who refused to participate or could not be reached on a number of variables. Significant differences between participants and drop outs were found but weighting the data accordingly in analyzes of labor market attitudes made no difference for the results (Deding et al. 2008). The final number of usable responses was 1662.

Denmark does not have a particularly large immigrant population. The actual percentage depends on the way "immigrant" is defined. The easiest way to delineate between ethnic Danes and immigrants would be citizenship but taking the political discussions on immigrants into consideration this is not a useable option. As noted above, political discussions

Table 3.1   Immigrant Statistics

Entire Population	5427459
Ethnic Danes	4964224
Western Immigrants	139427
Non-Western Immigrants	323808
Sample taken from	
1st gen. from Turkey	31008
1st gen. from Pakistan	10591
1st gen. from Iran	11689

Source: Statistics Denmark
Data from 2006

on immigrants have turned from being primarily about the labor market situation of immigrants to being primarily about culture (Madsen 2000). This way it can be argued that even though immigrants may have obtained Danish citizenship they are still culturally different from ethnic Danes. If a cultural definition is used then it could be argued that only those who are born in Denmark by Danish parents are Danes. Such a definition has been used by Statistics Denmark and with this method a little over 450,000 people or around 9% of the Danish population are immigrants.

Political discussions on immigrants tend to focus on cultural differences and hence tend to ignore immigrants from Western countries like Europe and the United States. If immigrants from Western countries (as defined by Statistics Denmark[9]) are ignored, a little over 300,000 people or around 6% of the Danish population are immigrants of a sort that is culturally different from ethnic Danes (see Table 3.1)—not a particularly large group. Since the sample only incorporated 1st generation immigrants from three countries of origin the population sampled is even smaller. The sample therefore represents only a little over 53,000 people. They are nonetheless three groups that have had plenty of media coverage in recent years and they represent the majority of their immigrant group since there are more than twice as many 1st generation immigrants as there are 2nd generation immigrants among non-Western immigrants in Denmark.

Before the analysis it is important to remember that the groups analyzed are not representative of immigrants in Denmark in general. They are however all groups from predominantly Muslim countries which makes it possible to analyze the influence of Islam itself. If being a Muslim has an influence upon the behavior of immigrants, it should be found here. The aim is therefore to analyze whether being a self-reported Muslim and/or being religious have an influence upon labor market integration among selected immigrants in Denmark. As stated above, the basic idea is that religiosity or belonging to a specific religious tradition has an influence upon the motivation for seeking a job and hence the chance of actually holding a job. This of course ignores the impact of factors external to the immigrants such as discrimination, etc.

The relatively high unemployment rate of non-Western immigrants was mentioned above. This is, of course, the percentage of the work force who are not currently employed. To keep the analysis comparable to the official numbers the following analyzes will only include people who are in the work force. Respondents who are on early retirement or taking an education are excluded. For the purpose of comparing the ethnic groups sampled, only respondents identifying as belonging to one of the four ethnic groups shown below are included. This leaves 1274 respondents out of the original 1662.

A cursory look at the survey data reveals a striking stratification among the immigrants sampled with regard to employment as gender seems to be an important determinant of unemployment. Among females around 37% are unemployed against around 14% of the men (Table 3.2). The overall unemployment rate in the sub-sample was around 24%. This was higher

Table 3.2   Demography (in %)

	Employed	Un-employed	total	
Female	63	37	100	***
Male	86	14	100	
Residence				
1–10 years	67	33	100	***
11–20 years	78	22	100	
21–45 years	83	17	100	
Highest Education				
None	62	38	100	***
Elementary School	77	23	100	
High School	93	7	100	
Vocational	86	14	100	
Short further	85	15	100	
Medium further	92	8	100	
Long further	92	8	100	
Turk	74	26	100	*
Kurd	73	27	100	
Iranian	81	19	100	
Pakistani	73	27	100	

Stat. sig.: * $p < 0.05$, ** $p < 0.01$, *** $p < 0.001$

than for all non-Western immigrants (where it was around 12%) but this is most likely a product of the sampling (only immigrants from three countries of origin were included and a the age distribution was purposely constricted). The rather large discrepancy between the unemployment rate of females and males is probably an expression of a more conservative family pattern where females tend to stay at home and take care of the children while the husband serves as the provider. Not surprisingly the number of years an immigrant has stayed in Denmark has a positive influence upon employment. The more years in Denmark the lower the unemployment rate (Table 3.2). Another determinant of employment is the highest education taken in Denmark, the higher the educational level the higher the probability of holding a job. Dividing the sample into four ethnic groups (people originating from Turkey and Iran can be either Iranians, Kurds, or Turks) reveals that Iranian respondents are less likely to be unemployed than respondents from the three other groups.

Respondents were asked to identify their religious affiliation. To simplify the analysis this variable has been reduced to a dummy dividing the sample into Muslims and "other." Around 77% of the sub-sample identified as Muslim, around 13% identified as non-affiliated, and a little under 9% identified as religious but not Muslim. All the variables seen in Table 3.3 are stratified by religious affiliation. As is generally the case among Christians in Europe, females were more likely than males to identify as Muslim (Table 3.3). There was a slight tendency for people who had stayed in Denmark for ten years or less to be more likely to identify as Muslims. It is difficult to discern whether this means that Muslim immigrants tend to become secularized (in the sense of becoming less religious) over time

Table 3.3 Identified as Muslim (in %)

	Muslim	Non-Muslim	total	
Female	81	19	100	*
Male	76	24	100	
Residence				
1-10 years	85	15	100	*
11-20 years	79	21	100	
21-45 years	78	22	100	
Highest Education				
None	88	12	100	***
Elementary School	85	15	100	
High School	65	35	100	
Vocational	78	22	100	
Short further	67	33	100	
Medium further	59	41	100	
Long further	56	44	100	
Turk	84	16	100	***
Kurd	89	11	100	
Iranian	54	46	100	
Pakistani	97	3	100	
Employed	76	24	100	***
Unemployed	87	13	100	

Stat. sig.: * $p < 0.05$, ** $p < 0.01$, *** $p < 0.001$

in Denmark at this point. For that a multivariate analysis is needed which will be done below. Another explanation could be that the differences are due to the different ethnic groups in the sub-sample arriving in Denmark at different points in history.

There was a strong inverse relationship between identifying as a Muslim and education (taken in Denmark). Those with either no education, elementary school, or a vocational education were much more likely to identify as Muslims compared to those with at least a high school diploma. In general the higher the educational level the fewer respondents identified as Muslims. It should be noted, however, that even among those with a university degree almost 60% identified as Muslim, which is comparable to the little under 60% among the Danes that identified as Protestant in the European Social Survey 2006.[10]

There were significant differences among the four ethnic groups with regard to religious affiliation. The least Muslim group was the Iranians where around 54% identified as Muslim. The most Muslim group was the Pakistanis where around 97% identified as Muslim. Among Turks and Kurds between 85 and 89% identified as Muslim. That there were so relatively few Muslims among the Iranians is probably explained by the Iranians' unique immigration history. Most Iranian immigrants in Denmark were intellectuals who fled after the Islamic Revolution in 1979. Many of them fled in part because they belonged to non-Muslim religious communities or were left wing with an atheist stance. This does not seem to have influenced their employment rate however.

Finally, there was a strong tendency for respondents identifying as Muslim to have a higher unemployment rate than non-Muslims. Around 76% of respondents with employment identified as Muslim while the number was around 87% among the unemployed.

The differences between Muslims and non-Muslims in Table 3.3 suggest that being a Muslim may have an influence upon unemployment. Not only were respondents identifying as Muslim more likely to be unemployed, they were also less likely to hold a degree above high school level. This seems to support the idea of a Muslim work ethic among the immigrants sampled. Looking at the differences with regard to religious affiliation, residence and ethnic belonging, however, suggest that the higher unemployment rate of Muslims in the sub-sample may be the product of ethnic differences. Iranians were less likely to be unemployed but also less likely to identify as Muslim. If education and residence is controlled for, the differences in unemployment rate among Muslims and non-Muslim s may disappear.

It could be argued that identifying as Muslim is as much a question of ethnic identity as it is a question of existential (or inner) religiosity. It is a way of identifying what make the members of your group unique but it is also a special way of relating to the transcendent. The two need not be related in any particular way. In an attempt to separate the two a separate table has been produced with religious affiliation being replaced by subjective religiosity (Table 3.4).

Table 3.4 Existential Religiosity (in %)

	Not at all religious	A little religious	Somewhat religious	Very religious	total	
Female	14	24	39	23	100	***
Male	27	28	31	13	100	
Residence						
1–10 years	15	23	43	19	100	***
11–20 years	23	28	31	19	100	
21–45 years	27	23	35	15	100	
Highest Education						
None	14	24	39	23	100	***
Elementary School	16	24	44	16	100	
High School	18	33	30	18	100	
Vocational	24	32	33	10	100	
Short further	29	24	33	14	100	
Medium further	46	25	19	9	100	
Long further	43	32	16	9	100	
Turk	8	30	42	19	100	***
Kurd	21	26	40	13	100	
Iranian	48	31	15	6	100	
Pakistani	4	16	49	32	100	
Employed	24	26	34	16	100	***
Unemployed	15	26	37	22	100	

Stat. sig.: * $p < 0.05$, ** $p < 0.01$, *** $p < 0.001$

Respondents were asked "regardless of whether you belong to a religious denomination or not how religious would you say you are" and given four Likert-type answer categories. The results regarding religiosity are almost identical to the ones regarding religious affiliation seen in Table 3.3. In general females were more religious than males. Respondents who had had residence in Denmark for ten years or less were more religious than the rest. The higher the educational level the less religious respondents were. Again the Iranians were significantly less religious than the other ethnic groups. Finally, there was a slight tendency for the unemployed to be more religious than the employed. Again this could be seen as support for the idea of a particular religious work ethic among the immigrants sampled, but again it could also be argued that it is the result of differences in education and length of residence in Denmark.

ISLAM AND LABOR MARKET INTEGRATION

Because most of the variables to be analyzed are either nominal or ordinal level the most suitable multivariate approach is a chain graph model (see Whittaker 1993). Chain graph models make for easily interpreted models in the form of graphs. Circles represent variables and lines or arrows between the circles represent relationships. If the relationship goes both ways, i.e. there is a lack of causality, it is represented by a line and if one variable influences another, but not vice versa, it is represented by an arrow. If there is no relationship between two variables then there is no line or arrow connecting them which means that they are unrelated when controlling for the other variables in the model (they are conditionally independent). The variables in the model are tied together in a causal structure consisting of causal blocks; some variables can influence others but not be influenced themselves. This makes for a chain of variables, hence the name chain graph model.

The following chain graph model has eight variables, seven control variables and one dependent variable. The first block is made up by age, gender, and ethnicity. These variables are given beforehand and cannot be influenced by the other variables. They were chosen because they could all influence employment. The second block is made up by highest education taken in Denmark, length of residence, religiosity, and religious affiliation (identifying as Muslim). Finally the dependent variable is employment. All variables used in the chain graph model are the same as seen in Tables 3.2, 3.3, and 3.4 except for age which was collapsed into four equal seven-year intervals for the sake of simplicity.

The chain graph model clearly shows that the idea that religiosity and Islam (or perhaps Muslim identity) have an influence upon labor market integration is wrong. Neither identifying as Muslim nor subjective religiosity have an influence upon employment or unemployment. Hence there are no arrows between the circles representing the two religious variables and the circle representing employment (Figure 3.1). There may still be some kind of cultural impact upon the labor market integration of the four ethnic groups but neither religious identity nor existential religiosity are part of this.

Out of the seven control variables in the model, three influenced employment. When controlling for the other variables employment was determined by gender, education taken in Denmark, and age. The strongest influences were exerted by gender (partial gamma = -0.55) and highest education

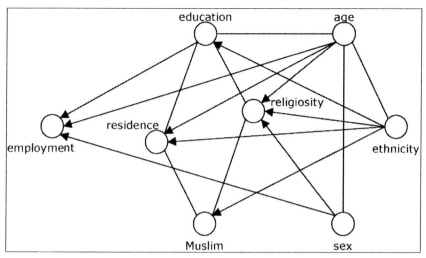

Figure 3.1   Employment and religion.

taken in Denmark (partial gamma = 0.56). The influence of age was much smaller than that of gender and education and can basically be ignored. This means that respondents were more likely to be employed if they were men and were better educated.

It is maybe just as interesting to note what variables did not influence employment in the multivariate model compared to the bivariate comparisons in Tables 3.2, 3.3, and 3.4. When controlling for the other variables there were no longer any differences in employment between the four ethnic groups. This means that the lower unemployment rate of the Iranians in the sub-sample was most likely the product of a generally higher level of education within this group. Length of residence in Denmark also had no influence upon employment in the multivariate model. There is a strong relationship between length of residence and education in the multivariate model which suggests that the bivariate relationship between employment and length of residence was really the product of differences in educational level. It is also interesting to note that there was no relationship between the two most influential variables, gender, and education. This means that females and males were equally likely to have a Danish education and yet females were much more likely than males to be unemployed. It could be argued that females in the four ethnic groups have the same qualifications for holding a job as the males but they either choose not to use them or are held back by factors not included in the chain graph model. Most likely females choose to stay home and build a family at least until the children are old enough to be sent to school. Chances are that had the age range of the respondents not been artificially constrained to between ages 18 and 45 more females would have been employed. The perception of gender roles, which is most likely the cause of the lower employment among females, is of course a cultural phenomenon, but it is impossible to say whether it is related to religiosity and religious identity. For this an analysis focusing on perceptions of gender roles would have to be conducted.

With regard to religion the model shows some interesting patterns. In the bivariate comparisons females were more likely than males to identify as Muslim but when controlling for other variables this relationship disappears. When females were more likely to identify as Muslim it most likely had to do with differences between the ethnic groups and not gender as such. The tendency for respondents who had stayed in Denmark a relatively short time to be more likely to identify as Muslim compared to those who had had residence for a longer period persisted even when controlling for other variables. This relationship was not the product of differences between the ethnic groups. Something happens with the religious identity of immigrants in the four ethnic groups over time. It could be argued that being a (Muslim) minority in a (nominally) Christian majority culture would strengthen the religious identity of the minority but instead the opposite seems to be the case. [11] Existential (or inner) religiosity on the other hand was not related to length of residence. This means that the 1st generation immigrants surveyed here do not become more or less religious over time living in a supposedly secular country (Denmark has a national church and most holidays are Christian in origin but the Danes themselves are among the least religious in Europe). It is only the religious identity of the immigrants sampled that was affected over time and not their existential (or inner) religiosity.

The fact that religiosity (identity and existential) and length of residence did not influence employment among the respondents explains why belonging to a certain ethnic group makes no difference for labor market integration. Looking at the chain graph model (Figure 3.1) it is obvious that the four ethnic groups analyzed have very different immigration histories and different compositions. The four ethnic groups are different with regard to age, religiosity, religious affiliation, and length of residence. They have come to Denmark at different times in history, for different reasons, and from different religious traditions (although all nominally Muslim). Even though all four groups come from countries with a Muslim hegemony they are different with regard to religiosity and Muslim identity. It is not their past (immigration history and ethnicity) but their present (education in Denmark) that is the key to their employment situation. The other factor that influenced employment, gender, seems to be the same regardless of ethnic belonging although it is difficult to analyze in detail using the current multivariate model.

The main conclusion from the multivariate analysis is that neither religious identity nor existential religiosity had an influence upon labor market integration for the four ethnic groups sampled. Immigrants were not more likely to be unemployed if they identified as Muslim or were very religious. In this sense the immigrants in the survey were secularized in that their religiosity was unrelated to their work life. There is no crossover between the religious sphere and the work sphere. Since neither the religious identity nor the existential religiosity of the immigrants sampled had any influence upon their employment (or lack thereof) it is highly unlikely that the higher unemployment rate among non-Western immigrants in Denmark is the product of a particular Muslim work ethic. It may be added that the fact that the participants in the survey were first-generation immigrants gives even more force to this conclusion because the migrants had not been brought up by parents socialized for years into a Danish (perhaps Lutheran, but definitely not Puritan) work ethic.

Looking at the variables influencing employment among particular groups of immigrants (people originating in Iran, Pakistan, and Turkey) the higher unemployment rate among immigrants was most likely caused by two things: a generally lower level of education and a conservative view of gender roles. Immigrants were more likely to be unemployed because their general level of education was lower than that of the Danes (or at least their employment rate could be raised if their educational level was raised, as it is evident by the positive effect on employment by education in Denmark). They were also more likely to be unemployed because immigrant women were less likely to hold a job than women who were ethnic Danes. This was most likely because the immigrant women preferred to stay home and build a family. In this sense it could be argued that there was a cultural difference between ethnic Danes and immigrants but it was not specifically religious. If it had been then religion would have had an influence upon employment in the multivariate model. It would be better to call it a product of tradition, a tradition that may be influenced by religion as well as national and ethnic histories. Religion does not seem to be a social problem as far as integration on the employment market in Denmark among first generation Iranians, Pakistanis, and Turks is concerned.

NOTES

1. Statistics Denmark define Western immigrants as people coming from any of the countries of the European Union, Andorra, Iceland, Liechtenstein, Monaco, Norway, San Marino, Switzerland, the Vatican state, Canada, the United States, Australia, or New Zealand. An immigrant coming from a country other than these is considered a non-Western immigrant.
2. Claus Hjort Frederiksen to *Deadline*, broadcast on television on April 18, 2007, quotes also found by Birgitte Romme Larsen,"Ministerens dovne flygtninge," readers opinion in *Weekendavisen* 1, June 2007.
3. One may consider *The Protestant Ethic and the Spirit of Capitalism* published 1904–1905 (Weber 2003) as the first important study in this line, but

social ethics was not included in the name before the publication of later works 1915 (Weber 1934: 237), and the original study was not included among these works, but stands independent in front of them in the publication of the *Gesammlte Aufsätze aur Religionssoziologie* (Weber 1934).

4. For references to the discussion regarding the work of Weber in relation to Marx see for instance Turner 1974.

5. The difference between feudal and prebendal systems is based on rights of ownership. In feudal system the rights to land depend on personal inheritance, in prebendal systems the king owns the lands and allocate to landlords in return for military services. Turner (1981: 203–233, especially 208–210) rightly stresses that the differences between feudal and prebendal structures may be vague and that it was overstated by the economic historians in the nineteenth early twentieth centuries even if Turner upholds that it carries some explanatory power for the understanding of the development of capitalism. A recent non-essentialist approach to some of these problems is found in Zubaida (2006).

6. This distinction lie implicit behind much of Weber's (2003) argument regarding the origin of the spirit of capitalism.

7. Turner distinguishes between (a) the Protestant Ethics thesis which includes the work ethics and rationality in the interpretation of the growth of a capitalist spirit in Europe, versus (b) the Weber thesis which regards the lacking growth of capitalism in the non-Christian civilisations where Weber according to Turner did not consider the work ethics (Turner 1974). As it is evident from our summery of Weber's studies on the world religions, we do not agree with Turner in this clear-cut division between the different studies. It is a fact, however, that Weber never offered us the study on Islam where he could have expanded his considerations of the relation between warrior ethic and other kinds of work ethic.

8. The survey was the product of a joint effort involvement researcher from AKF, the Danish Institute of Governmental Research, SFI, The Danish National Institute of Social Research, the University of Copenhagen, and the University of Aarhus. The survey was financed by a research grant from The Danish Council for Strategic Research and by a grant from the Danish Ministry of Immigrants, Refugees, and Integration.

9. Western countries are specified in note 1.

10. Again, this can be compared to the fact that around 80% of the Danish population are members of the Danish national church. There is a large discrepancy between religious belonging and formal membership in Denmark. Due to the way the item on religious affiliation was worded in the immigrant questionnaire compare it to belonging rather than formal membership would be the most correct thing to do.

11. Schiffhauer (1988), for example. An ethnic approach to the analysis of a related development is proposed by Ballard (1994) in his overview of the emergence of South Asian communities in the United Kingdom.

REFERENCES

Ballard, Roger. 1994. Introduction: The Emergence of *Desh Pardesh*. *Desh Pardesh: The South Asian Experience in Britain*, edited by Roger Ballard. 1–34. London: Hurst & Company.

Bauman, Zygmunt. 2000 [1998]. *Globalization: The Human Consequences*. Cambridge: Polity Press.

Blum, Jacques. 1973. *Dansk og/eller jøde: En kultursociologisk undersøgelse af den jødiske minoritet i Danmark*. København: Gyldendals Samfundsbibliotek.

Christoffersen, Lisbet (ed.). 2006. *Gudebilleder: Ytringsfrihed og religion i en globaliseret verden.* København: Tiderne Skifter.

Deding, Mette, Fridberg, Torben and Jakobsen, Vibeke. 2008. Non-response in a survey among immigrants in Denmark. *Survey Research Methods* 2(3): 107–121.

Gundelach, Peter and Nørregård-Nielsen, Esther. 2007. *Etniske gruppers værdier—Baggrundsrapport.* København: Ministeriet for Flygtninge, Indvandrere og Integration.

Hussain, Mustafa. 2000. Islam, Media and Minorities in Denmark. *Current Sociology* 48(4): 95–116.

Hussein, Mustafa, Yilmaz, Ferruh, and O'Connor, Tim. 1997. *Medierne, Minoriteterne og Majoriteten—en Undersøgelse af Nyhedsmedier og den Folkelige Diskurs i Danmark.* København: Nævnet for Etnisk Ligestilling.

Lüchau, Peter. 2004. Kristendom og tolerance i Danmark. *Dansk Sociologi* 15(4): 41–54.

Madsen, Jacob Gaarde. 2000. *Mediernes konstruktion af flygtninge- og indvandrerspørgsmålet.* Århus: Magtudredningen.

Mangione, T. W. 1995. *Mail Surveys: Improving the Quality.* Thousand Oaks, CA: Sage.

Murakami, Annelise. 1997. *Én hånd klapper ikke alene—Det psykiske arbejdsmiljø som 12 indvandrerkvinder med etnisk minoritetsbaggund oplever det.* DRC.

Rothstein, Mikael. 2007. Weapons of Mass Defamation: Aspects of the 2006 "Cartoons Crisis." *Temenos* 43(1): 115–134.

Schiffauer, Werner. 1988. Migration and Religiousness. In *The New Islamic Presence in Western Europe,* edited by Tomas Gerholm and Yngve Georg Lithman. London: Mansell.

Simonsen, Jørgen Bæk. 1990. *Islam I Danmark, muslimske institutioner I Danmark 1970–1989.* Århus: Aarhus Universitetsforlag.

Sukidi. 2006. Max Weber's Remarks on Islam: The Protestant Ethic among Muslim Puritans. *Islam and Christian-Muslim Relations* 17(2): 195–205.

Tambs-Lyche, Harald. 1980. *London Patidars: A Case Study in Urban Ethnicity.* London: Routledge & Kegan Paul.

Tawney, Richard H. 1961 [1922]. *Religion and the Rise of Capitalism: A Historical Study.* Harmondsworth: Penguin.

Trevor-Roper, Hugh. R. 1977 [1956]. *Religion, the Reformation and Social Change and other Essays.* London and Basingstoke: Macmillan.

Togeby, Lise. 2003. *Fra fremmedarbejdere til etniske minoriteter.* Århus: Aarhus Universitetsforlag.

Turner, Bryan S. 1974. *Weber and Islam.* London: Routledge & Kegan Paul.

Turner, Bryan S. 1981. *For Weber: Essays on the sociology of fate.* London: Routledge & Kegan Paul.

Warrier, Shrikala. 1994. Gujarati Prajapatis in London: Family Roles and Socability Networks. In *Desh Pardesh: The South Asian Presence in Britain,* edited by Roger Ballard. 191–212. London: Hurst & Company.

Weber, Max. 2003 [1904–1905]. *The Protestant Ethic and the Spirit of Capitalism.* Translated by Talcott Parsons with a foreword by R. H. Tawney. Mineola, NY: Dover Publications.

Weber, Max. 1923. *Hinduismus und Buddhismus: Gesammelte Aufsätze aur Religionssoziologie,* Vol II (Zweite Auflage).

Weber, Max. 1934. *Die Wirtschaftsethik der Weltreligionen: Gesammelte Aufsätze zur Religionssoziologie,* Vol I: 237–257. (Zweite Auflage).

Whittaker, Joe. 1993. Graphical Interaction Models: A New Approach for Statistical Modelling. In *Population Health Research: Linking Theory and Methods,* edited by Kathryn Dean. 160–180. London: Sage Publications.

Zubaida, Sami. 2006. Max Weber's *The City* and the Islamic City. *Max Weber Studies* 6(1–2): 111–118.

Part II

Religion as a Solution to Social Problems

4 Religious Diversity and Social Problems
The Case of Britain

James A. Beckford

Sociological studies of religion are no different in most respects from sociological studies of other social and cultural phenomena. They all try to make sense of phenomena that display change—as well as continuity—over time and space. Their target is a moving one. At the same time, sociological ways of thinking about religion also undergo change. The frameworks of theories, concepts and methods of investigation are constantly under critical review. In other words, the apparatus for examining religion as a social or cultural phenomenon is subject to just as much change as is religion itself. The question of whether the rate of change is similar for the apparatus *and* for the object of investigation is not only interesting in itself but also a digression from the central point of this chapter.

The main aim of this chapter is to consider some of the changes that have occurred in the intersection between religion and social problems. This involves considering changes in three interrelated topics: religion, social problems, and the points at which they cut across each other. The discussion begins with the context in which my ideas about this topic first took shape. The central section of the chapter examines the factors that have affected each topic, drawing mainly on examples from England. Special attention will be given to the importance of two particular factors: on the one hand, the rapid growth of religious diversity and, on the other, the development of British government policies that seek to strengthen links between the state and faith communities.

At this point, however, I need to be specific about the two terms at the centre of my argument. In order to make the discussion as inclusive as possible, I shall use "religion" in a broad sense to refer to any pattern of beliefs, emotions, practices and organization that derives from perceptions of the ultimate significance of the human and natural worlds. It is essential for my purposes to think of religion in terms that do not obscure the fact that its conceptual boundary is unclear. The line between religion and non-religion is actually contested and fuzzy in everyday social life. It would be a mistake, then, to impose a sharp distinction between them for the purposes of sociological analysis. Similarly, the meaning that I attribute to "social problem" recognizes that the concept is used in a wide range of different ways—by social scientists as well as by the person-in-the-street. But in general terms, social problems are features of social life that are widely identified as causing harmful but avoidable and possibly remediable difficulties to significantly large numbers of people—if not entire societies or the whole of humanity. These problems are blamed for damaging their victims' health and material circumstances as well as causing feelings of despair, pain and misery. Nevertheless, the political process of identifying and combating social problems—as social constructions of putatively harmful conditions (Kitsuse and Spector 1987)—can also generate doubt, contestation and rejection. Consequently, social problems are never fixed: they vary across time and place in the degree to which they are recognized, validated and tackled. Thus, agreement may be widespread on the political desirability of combating social problems such as poverty, disease, lack of education, poor housing and mass unemployment, but there is much less agreement on considering environmental degradation, global warming, obesity, abortion or infractions of human rights as "real" social problems.[1]

THE CONTEXT

The historical context for this chapter goes back to 1989. That was the year in which "Religion and Social Problems" was the theme of the annual conference of the Association for the Sociology of Religion in San Francisco. It was my privilege, as President of the association, to choose the conference theme and to deliver a presidential address on "The sociology of religion and social problems" (Beckford 1990).[2] My intentions, in choosing that particular theme for the meeting, were predominantly to express my own intellectual and political interests and partly to honor the work of earlier generations of sociologists who had first mapped out the territory where religion and social problems were intertwined.

This area of investigation began in the 1920s with the many surveys conducted by H. Paul Douglass and others at the short-lived Institute for Social and Religious Research in New York City (Hadden 1980). It subsequently included contributions from founding members of the American Catholic Sociological Society (forerunner of today's Association for the Sociology of Religion). In Europe the lead was taken by various Catholic institutes that collaborated on the publication of the journal *Social Compass* in the early 1950s. Early issues of this journal focused extensively on such social problems as juvenile delinquency, industrial unrest, poverty and the fragility of some inner-city communities. Both the American and the European contributions threw light on current social problems and the responses that Christian churches offered to them.

Nevertheless, my argument in 1989 was that the promise of these early years was never fully realized. The main reason was that the dominance of normative functionalism in American sociology from the 1950s until the 1980s effectively marginalized any serious concern with religion and social problems. This was mainly because the normative functionalist perspective constructed religion as the institution whose systemic function was to integrate societies and thereby to solve their problems. By contrast, analyses of religion as the source of problems or as a medium for formulating and giving expression to problems were relatively rare. Important exceptions included studies of the role of religious professionals and organizations in combating racism (Wood 1981) and militarism (Zahn 1968).

The original context of my interest in the intersection between religion and social problems prompts two reflections. First, relatively few discussions of religion and social problems have been published since 1989, although some of the exceptions to this generalization merit special recognition (Robbins 1985; Nason-Clark 2001; Nesbitt 2001; Barnes 2004; Wallace et al. 2007; Agadjanian and Menjívar 2008; Hjelm 2009). Despite the undoubted growth of interest—both social scientific and popular—in religion since 1989, the intersection between religion and social problems does not feature prominently in the literature. I shall argue below that this omission or neglect represents a failure to do justice to one of the most interesting aspects of religion in the present-day.

Second, it is clear to me that my understanding of religion and social problems in 1989 is now out-dated. Indeed, it was something of a shock recently to re-read the text of my 1990 article. It would certainly be untrue to say that I now disagree with everything I wrote then, but many subsequent developments and complications have modified the relation between religion and social problems. Nevertheless, I have not changed my view that the role played by religion in relation to social problems has grown in importance at a time when secularization is widely assumed to be a dominant force, at least in technologically advanced societies.

The main reasons that I gave in 1989 for religion becoming more important in relation to social problems had to do with globalization and new social movements. Taking my inspiration jointly from Jürgen Habermas (1981; 1987) and Roland Robertson (1985; Robertson and Chirico 1985), I argued that the global circumstance imparts a religious significance to the distinctively modern perception of social problems articulated by the new social movements for ecology, peace, justice, gender equality and human rights. These movements attack social problems that all have complicated associations with religion.

The nexus between religious movements, new social movements and globalization is particularly interesting because it reveals some of the new settings in which social problems intersect with religion (Beckford 2000;

2001). Using Habermas's formulation, this nexus illustrates the conflicts and problems of advanced industrial societies which "are not sparked by problems of distribution, but concern the grammar of forms of life" (Habermas 1981, 35). Many expressions of religion are therefore relevant to the perception and treatment of social problems associated with what Habermas called "the organic foundations of the life-world" and the "criteria of livability." Indeed, many new—and ostensibly secular—social movements are host to forms of "free-floating religious phenomena" (Beckford 2001). This means that social movements are increasingly likely to draw on religious and spiritual resources in order to frame their grievances and make their claims.

On the other hand, religion is not simply a resource for movements that aim to combat social problems. It can also be a social problem in itself. Indeed, "Religious discourse has . . . become more of a problem to the forces of established order, especially when characterized as extremist or fanatical" (Beckford 1990, 10). The cases that I cited in my 1989 presidential address included Northern Ireland and Lebanon, but nowadays the list is much longer and certainly includes Afghanistan, Iraq, Palestine/Israel, Sri Lanka, Indonesia, the Philippines and India, to say nothing of the USA and Western Europe. I also had in mind the problems associated with "cults" or new religious movements, some of which were extremely controversial in the closing decades of the twentieth century (Beckford 1985; Robbins 1985; Richardson 1997). These days, "cult controversies" have abated in many countries but are still considered a major social problem in countries such as France, Belgium, and China (Beckford 2004; Edelman and Richardson 2005).

RE-FRAMING RELIGION AND SOCIAL PROBLEMS

The reasons for thinking that the intersection between religion and social problems should be of growing importance to social scientists arise in relation to two relatively new issues. The first concerns the link between globalization and religious diversity. The second—which is possibly unique to the UK—concerns the way in which governments since 1997 have used religion as an expedient for dealing with social problems.

Religious Diversity

It would not be helpful to spend time deconstructing the concept of globalization here.[3] Considering all the complexities, subtleties and unresolved ambiguities, let me just note that, for my purposes, the term "globalization" carries a wide range of meanings and that it is heavily contested. Nevertheless, when I use the term, my focus is principally on "the growing frequency, volume and interconnectedness of flows of ideas, materials, goods, information, pollution, money and people across national boundaries and between regions of the world" (Beckford 2000, 170). This means that religious ideas, practices, personnel, and organizations now circulate relatively quickly around the world and that, as a result, levels of religious diversity in many countries have increased. The global flows of religion can present many advantages, but equally they can give rise to suspicion and hostility. In some cases they are also implicated in social problems.

For example, my research on religion in prisons has brought to light some of the problems that arise when rapidly growing numbers of prisoners identify with faith traditions other than the dominant tradition or traditions in the country where they are imprisoned (Beckford and Gilliat 1998; Beckford, Joly and Khosrokhavar 2005). Some of these prisoners are active in global networks of crime; others have been convicted of committing crimes outside their countries of origin. The result is that the prison population of England and Wales is religiously more diverse than the British population outside prison. Taking the case of Muslims, they amounted to about 12% of the total prison population of 82,319 in April 2008 but only 3% of the general population, according to the UK Census of 2001.[4] Nevertheless, the category of "Muslim" is highly heterogeneous in the prison population. Two examples will serve to underline the extent of the diversity of Muslim inmates. First, in terms of what the Prison Service of England and Wales calls "ethnic groups," 14% of Muslim prisoners were classified in June 2007 as "White," 6% as "Mixed," 34% as "Black or Black British," 42% as "Asian or Asian British."[5] Second, there are big differences between male and female Muslim inmates: the 208 Muslim women inmates fell into the following ethnic groups: 19% White, 9% Mixed, 23% Asian or British Asian, and 46% Black or Black British. The intersection of religion, ethnicity, and gender is complex and sensitive in many spheres of life these days but is particularly so in prisons where levels of religious and ethnic diversity are higher than in the outside world.

The relatively high level of religious diversity in prisons creates the technical difficulty for administrators of knowing how to categorize correctly each prisoner's religious identity for administrative purposes. This is important against the background of legislation and regulations designed to protect prisoners' rights to practice the religion of their choice. Questions about the degree of even-handedness with which such protection can be provided loom especially large in the social setting of prisons, where competition for all resources is often intense. As the level of religious diversity among prisoners has increased, members of prison staff have faced more and more issues about rights and equality in relation to religious activities, resources, personnel, and so on. Further complications have arisen since the 1990s from widespread anxiety about the role that the experience of imprisonment has allegedly played in encouraging and facilitating violent extremism among serving and released Muslim prisoners—another social problem (Khosrokhavar 2004).

Wider difficulties associated with the relatively rapid growth of religious diversity have to do with the fear among some religious minorities that not only prison systems but also other institutional structures and organizations are hostile to them. Schools, health care institutions, the military and the police in many western countries, for example, are all struggling to come to terms with the implications of rapidly growing religious diversity. The problems are refracted through each country's framework of laws, political structures, culture, and public media. From a sociological point of view, religious diversity is not a problem in of itself. But it can be associated with problems linked to the resentment experienced by sections of previously dominant religious majorities as well as to the feelings of oppression experienced by some religious minorities (Weller, Feldman, and Purdam 2001). And, although there are good reasons for questioning the usefulness of the term "Islamophobia," it is undeniable that Muslims in Britain and elsewhere in the western world are subject to discrimination, exclusion and violence (Commission on British Muslims and Islamophobia 1997, 2001; Vertovec 2002; O'Beirne 2004; Weller 2006). The social scientific literature on social problems is largely silent on this topic, but sociologists of religion are in a good position to study this new intersection between religion and the processes that create social problems instead of regarding it as merely a result of the clash of civilizations.

Indeed, social scientists have produced extensive evidence of the critical role played by the western mass media in framing material about Muslims and Islam as particular kinds of problem (Agha 2000; Poole 2000; Abbas 2001; Poole and Richardson 2006; Moore and Mason 2008). In addition, the capacity of the mass media to shape public opinion concerning new religious movements has been particularly well documented (Wright 1997; Richardson and Van Driel 1997; Beckford 1999; Lehmann and Birman 1999; Hill and Hickman 2001; Ownby 2008). Nevertheless, with the important exceptions of Richardson (1997) and Richardson, Best, and Bromley (1991), few such studies exploit to the full the analytical power of the concepts widely employed to explain the social construction of social problems.

Let me conclude this section on the social problems associated with the rapid growth of religious diversity by suggesting that one of the reasons for the relatively small number of studies in this area is that until recently—with the exception of the USA—neither the scholarly literature, nor campaigning organizations nor courts of law have tended to regard discrimination against minorities on the grounds of religion as a central aspect of discrimination or inequality. For example, it took the European Court of Human Rights many years to find the first violation of Article 9 of the European Convention Concerning Human and Civil Rights (guaranteeing religious freedom) in 1993 (Richardson 2006; Beckford and Richardson 2007).

Religion as Expedient

The focus of most of the social scientific literature on religion and social movements is on two central topics: the first is the impact of religion on the identification and resolution of social problems, and the second is the contribution of religion to creating or aggravating social problems. I want to argue here that a new, third topic also calls for sociological analysis. It concerns the ways in which governments and other public authorities use religion as a device or resource in their policies for combating social problems. My use of the term "expedient" to cover both "device" and "resource" does not imply cynicism on my part or on that of public authorities. It merely refers to policies and practices that acknowledge the potential advantages of drawing on religious resources to solve problems. Let me now suggest why the term "expedient" is appropriate in the context of some of the policies recently implemented by British governments.

Some of the policies implemented by the New Labour governments that have been in power continuously since 1997 have had the effect of enlisting "faith" as a political resource. In other words, religion has served—and not for the first time in the UK—as an expedient for the implementation of government policies. It is no accident that this political strategy has coincided with the diversification of religion in the UK. Nor is it coincidental that most of this attempt to "use" religion for the purpose of public policy has been categorized as part of the broader strategy for achieving "social cohesion" in the face of growing diversity and divisions.

The results of the 2001 UK Census showed that, although 77% of British people reported that they had a religion,[6] there were significant differences between England, Scotland, Wales, and Northern Ireland.[7] Identification with religions other than Christianity also varied between these different parts of the UK.[8] Moreover, religious differences overlapped strongly with ethnic diversity. In short, the UK is characterized by extensive—but uneven—religious and ethnic diversity. The British government's response has been two-fold. On the one hand, it emphasizes the value of diversity in itself, although this response has been muted since 2001. And on the other, it insists on managing diversity in such a way that it contributes towards the promotion of social cohesion.

The first Blair government began to use religion as an expedient for facilitating preparations for the millennium celebrations. Following the events of September 11, 2001 and consultation with leading representatives of faith communities, it created a Faith Communities Unit in the Home Office in 2003 and put in place formal procedures by means of which all government departments were to consult faith communities about policy.[9] An Interdepartmental Group on Faith then began to co-ordinate consultations across all government departments. A Home Office (2004, 8) report confirmed that "Government Departments are increasingly coming to realize the importance of engaging with the faith communities just as much as they do with other sections of society." A follow up report from the Department for Communities and Local Government (2005, 2), reviewing the progress of engagement between government and faith communities, found that "good progress is being made in engaging faith communities in the development of policy in a number of areas." These developments, not all of which apply in the partly devolved administrations of Scotland and Wales include:

- training civil servants in "faith literacy and other skills relevant to working with faith communities"
- funding capacity-building projects in faith communities[10]; and developing a "Religion and belief toolkit"
- ensuring that policies on culture, media and sport take account of "people of all faiths and none"
- encouraging collaborative working between faith schools and other schools
- addressing the health needs of "disadvantaged faith communities"
- strengthening legislation against discrimination and the incitement to hatred on religious grounds
- identifying faith groups as targets for fostering awareness of international development policies
- commissioning research on the intersection between faith communities and the strategic priorities of government departments
- orienting the Women and Equality Unit towards "outreach work with Muslim women"
- understanding the public transport needs of "visible religious communities," and
- improving the representation of faith communities on the boards of public bodies.

The work of the Faith Communities Unit—now relocated in the Department for Communities and Local Government—is complemented by that of such other organizations as The Faith Based Regeneration Network, the Faith Communities Consultative Council and the UK Inter Faith Network. With government funding they, along with other agencies, have translated the broad policies into a wide range of practical outcomes. Some examples include a report on "Empowering Muslim women: case studies" (Department for Communities and Local Government 2008a), an academic research programme on Religion and Development,[11] a "Muslim Scholars Roadshow" to dissuade young Muslims from taking extremist positions, a report on the contributions that faith-based organizations can make towards preventing released prisoners from re-offending (National Offender Management Service 2007), a comprehensive strategy for partnership between Government and faith communities (Department for Communities and Local Government 2008b) and guidance on how faith communities could alleviate an influenza pandemic[12] (Department for Communities and Local Government 2008c).

The report of a project funded by the former Office of the Deputy Prime Minister (Beckford et al. 2006) showed that the government was not seeking to make policies specifically for the "emergent faith communities" of Hindus, Muslims, and Sikhs. But it was definitely interested in obtaining answers to two questions: first, were public policies succeeding or failing to meet the needs of Hindus, Muslims and Sikhs? And, second, how far could minority faith communities help government departments to achieve success for their policies? In other words, the British government wanted to know how faith communities could be "used" in their framing and implementation of public policy.

The report showed that public policies were not systematically putting Hindus, Muslims and Sikhs at a disadvantage but that the intended impact of some policies was less successful with these groups than with the rest of the population. For example, many families with South Asian origins prefer to look after their elderly, chronically sick or disabled members at home, thereby making it difficult for professionals in health and social services departments to deliver appropriate services. Similarly, Muslims who preferred to finance house purchases without incurring interest payments on mortgages incurred higher rates of taxation than did other purchasers. This inequity prompted the Treasury to change its rules on the taxation of house purchases. Again, policies aimed at revitalising some economically deprived, inner-city neighborhoods have met with opposition from Muslims who wish to continue living in communities where they form the clear majority. Government is therefore interested in the factors that might persuade significant numbers of Muslim families to relocate to other residential areas. Finally, a large proportion of the material and social deprivation experienced by Muslims—especially Bangladeshis—is attributable to their low levels of female participation in the labor market after marriage.

At the same time, the British government has invested heavily in various initiatives for involving minority faith communities in consultation processes, usually through the intermediary of the UK Inter Faith Network or the Faith Communities Consultative Council and its two predecessor organizations. Fostering the participation of minority faith communities in the voluntary and charitable sector of civil society is another of the government's aims. The government's expectation is that all these schemes will enable it to make effective use of faith communities in achieving its policy objectives. At the level of local government, policies and processes for involving faith communities in consultations are already in place.[13]

On the other hand, criticism of Government policies for closer cooperation with faith communities has been growing in some places. The British Humanist Association and other secularist groups, for example, are highly critical of what has been called "the increasingly central position the Government is awarding religion in much of its social policies, and particularly in its policy to contract out public services to religious organisations" (British Humanist Association 2007, 1). Other critics of Government policy have questioned "the explicit promotion of social cohesion as a policy objective, marking as it does the significant shift away from the long-standing promotion of multicultural race relations" (Zetter 2006). And the National Council for Voluntary Organisations (2007) fears that Government policies targeting faith communities will alienate other sectors of civil society. Nevertheless, these critical voices are not often heard in the mainstream media.

CONCLUSIONS

Social problems such as poverty, homelessness, unemployment, crime, and racism are common in many societies. The rapid growth of religious and ethnic diversity in the UK, in the context of global flows of people and resources, is not a problem in itself but it has given a new twist to some old problems; and it has prompted some unprecedented strategies for partnerships between Government and faith communities at local, regional and national levels. The rationale given for these strategies is that they are expedient for achieving the Government's policy objectives— particularly in relation to social cohesion and the prevention of extremism. The UK is not unique in this respect among European states, but the strength of the British government's investment in a formal policy of supporting and working with faith communities for political reasons is unparalleled elsewhere in Europe. It represents a new form of public response to social problems that goes much further than the traditionally tacit support shown by governments throughout the twentieth century for religiously-inspired program to alleviate social problems. It also outstrips the scope and the achievements of the USA's faith-based initiatives (Farnsley 2007). There is good reason, then, to consider these developments as a new—and not unproblematic—phase in the intertwining of religion and social problems.

NOTES

1. These problems are the "five giants" blocking the road to the post-World War II reconstruction of the UK, according to William Beveridge (1942), the principal architect of the British welfare state.
2. The occasion was memorable for me not only because it was my presidential year but also because a powerful earthquake struck San Francisco at 3 o'clock in the morning midway through the conference.
3. But for some widely differing guides to the arguments, see Beyer 1994; Cohen and Rai 2000; Rosenberg 2000; Waters 2001; Lechner and Boli 2005; Stiglitz 2002; and Juergensmeyer 2006.
4. According to figures given on behalf of the Government by Lord Hunt of Kings Heath in a written answer dated June 26, 2008 to a question raised in the House of Lords. Online document at: http://www.publications.parliament.uk/pa/ld200708/ldhansrd/text/80626w0002.htm.
5. Ministry of Justice 2008, Offender Management Caseload Statistics 2007, *Ministry of Justice Statistics Bulletin*. London: Ministry of Justice.

Online document at: http://www.justice.gov.uk/docs/omcs2007.pdf (10.01.09).

6. The Census question about religion was voluntary and took different forms in Scotland, N. Ireland, England and Wales.
7. 86% of people in Northern Ireland identified themselves with a religion on the Census form, but the percentages were lower for England and Wales (77%) and Scotland (67%). The percentage of people who stated that they had no religion was 15% in England and Wales and 28% in Scotland.
8. 3% of people in the UK as a whole identified their religion as Islam, but Muslims amounted to only 0.84% in Scotland and 0.75% in Wales (most Muslims in Wales lived in the three largest cities of South Wales—Cardiff, Newport and Swansea). All the religious minorities together in Northern Ireland amounted to only 0.3% of the total for the province.
9. It was located in the Directorate for Race, Cohesion, Equality, and Faith.
10. £7.5 million were allocated to "faith-based groups whose work promotes understanding or dialogue" between communities. See: http://press.homeoffice.gov.uk/press-releases/boost-faith-communities-society?version=1.
11. The Religion and Development Research Programme, University of Birmingham, is funded by the Department for International Development. See http://www.rad.bham.ac.uk/index.php?section=1.
12. Circulation of this leaflet was quickly halted. It is no longer available.
13. See, for example, Birmingham City Council's "Corporate Religion and Belief Equality Scheme 2007–2010". Online document at: http://www.birmingham.gov.uk/ELibrary?E_LIBRARY_ID=565.

REFERENCES

Abbas, Tahir. 2001. Media Capital and the Representation of South Asian Muslims in the British Press: an Ideological Analysis. *Journal of Muslim Minority Affairs* 21(2): 245–257.

Agadjanian, Victor, and Menjívar, Cecilia. 2008. Talking about the "Epidemic of the Millennium": Religion, Informal Communication, and HIV/AIDS in Sub-Saharan Africa. *Social Problems* 55(3): 301–221.

Agha, Olfar Hassan. 2000. Islamic Fundamentalism and Its Image in the Western Media: Alternative Views. In *Islam and the West in the Mass Media: Fragmented Images in a Globalizing World*, edited by Kai Hafez. 219–233. Cresskill, NJ:Hampton Press.

Barnes, Sandra L. 2004. Priestly and Prophetic Influences on Black Church Social Services. *Social Problems* 51(2): 202–221.

Beckford, James A. 1985. *Cult Controversies. The Societal Response to New Religious Movements*. London: Tavistock.

Beckford, James A. 1990. The Sociology of Religion and Social Problems. *Sociological Analysis* 51(1): 1–14.

Beckford, James A. 1999. The Mass Media and New Religious Movements. In *New Religious Movements: Challenge and Response*, edited by Bryan R. Wilson and Jamie Cresswell. 103–119. London: Routledge.

Beckford, James A. 2000. Religious Movements and Globalization. In *Global Social Movements*, edited by Robin Cohen and Sirin Rai. 165–183. London: Athlone Press.

Beckford, James A. 2001. Social Movements as Free-floating Religious Phenomena. In *The Blackwell Companion to Sociology of Religion*, edited by Richard K. Fenn. 229–248. Oxford: Blackwell.

Beckford, James A. 2004. "Laïcité," "Dystopia," and the Reaction to New Religious Movements in France. In *Regulating Religion: Case Studies from around the Globe*, edited by James T. Richardson. 27–40. New York: Kluwer/Plenum.

Beckford, James A. and Gilliat, Sophie. 1998. *Religion in Prison: Equal Rites in a Multi-Faith Society*. Cambridge: Cambridge University Press.

Beckford, James A., and Richardson, James T. . 2007. Religion and Regulation. In *The SAGE Handbook of the Sociology of Religion*, edited by James A. Beckford and N. J. Demerath III. 396–418. London: Sage.

Beckford, James A., Joly, Danièle, and Khosrokhavar, Farhad. 2005. *Muslims in Prison: Challenge and Change in Britain and France*. Basingstoke: Palgrave Macmillan.

Beckford, James A., Gale, Richard, Owen, David, Peach, Ceri, and Weller, Paul. 2006. Review of the Evidence Base on Faith Communities. London: Office of the Deputy Prime Minister. Online document at: http://www.communities.gov. uk/publications/communities/review.

Beveridge, William. 1942. *Social Insurance and Allied Services*. CMD 6404. London: HMSO.

Beyer, Peter. 1994. *Religion and Globalization*. London: Sage.

British Humanist Association. 2007. *Quality and Equality: Human Rights, Public Services and Religious Organisations*. London: British Humanist Association.

Cohen, Robin and Rai, Shirin M. (ed.) 2000. *Global Social Movements*. London: Athlone Press.

Commission on British Muslims and Islamophobia. 1997. Islamophobia. Its Features and Dangers. London: Runnymede Trust.

Commission on British Muslims and Islamophobia. 2001. Addressing the Challenge of Islamophobia. London: Commission on British Muslims and Islamophobia.

Department for Communities and Local Government. 2005. *Working Together: Co-operation between Government and Faith Communities*. Progress Report. Online document at: http://www.communities.gov.uk/index.asp?id=1502454.

Department for Communities and Local Government. 2008a. *Empowering Muslim Women: Case Studies*. London: Department of Communities and Local Government.

Department for Communities and Local Government. 2008b. *Face to Face and Side by Side: A Framework for Partnership in Our Multi Faith Society*. London: Department for Communities and Local Government.

Department for Communities and Local Government. 2008c. *Faith Communities and Pandemic Flu: Guidance for Faith Communities and Local Influenza Pandemic Committees*. London: Department for Communities and Local Government.

Edelman, Bryan, and Richardson, James T. 2005. Imposed Limitations on Freedom of Religion in China and the Margin of Appreciation Doctrine: A Legal Analysis of the Crackdown on the Falun Gong and other "Evil Cults". *Church and State* 47(2): 243–246.

Farnsley, Arthur E. II. 2007. Faith-Based Initiatives. In *The SAGE Handbook of the Sociology of Religion*, edited by James A. Beckford and N. J. Demerath III. 345–356. London: Sage.

Habermas, Jürgen. 1981. New Social Movements. *Telos* 49(Fall): 33–37.

Habermas, Jürgen. 1987. *The Theory of Communicative Action, vol. 2: Lifeworld and System*. Boston: Beacon Press.

Hadden, Jeffrey K. 1980. H. Paul Douglass: His Perspective and His Work. *Review of Religious Research* 22(1): 66–88.

Hill, Harvey, Hickman, John, and McLendon, Joel. 2001. Cults and Sects and Doomsday Groups, Oh My: Media Treatment of Religion on the Eve of the Millennium. *Review of Religious Research* 43(1): 24–38.

Hjelm, Titus. 2009. Religion and Social Problems: A New Theoretical Approach. In *The Oxford Handbook of the Sociology of Religion*, edited by Peter B. Clarke, 924–941. Oxford: Oxford University Press.

Home Office, The. 2004. *Working Together: Co-operation between Government and Faith Communities*. Online document at: http://www.communities.gov.uk/index.asp?id=1502626.

Juergensmeyer, Mark (ed.) 2006. *Religion in Global Civil Society*. New York: Oxford University Press.

Khosrokhavar, Farhad. 2004. *L'Islam dans les prisons*. Paris: Balland.

Kitsuse, John I., and Spector, Malcolm. 1987. *Constructing Social Problems*. New York: Aldine De Gruyter.

Lechner, Frank and Boli, John. 2005. *World Culture: Origins and Consequences*. Oxford: Blackwell.

Lehmann, David. 2002. Religion and Globalization. In *Religions in the Modern World*, edited by Linda Woodhead, Paul Fletcher, Hiroko Kawanami, and David Smith. 299–315. London: Routledge.

Lehmann, David, and Birman, Patricia. 1999. Religion and the Media in a Battle for Ideological Hegemony: The Universal Church of the Kingdom of God and TV Globo in Brazil. *Bulletin of Latin American Research* 18(2): 145–164.

Moore, Kerry, Mason, Paul and Lewis, Justin. 2008. Images of Islam in the UK. Cardiff: Cardiff School of Journalism, Media and Cultural Studies.

Nason-Clark, Nancy. 2001. Woman Abuse and Faith Communities: Religion, Violence, and the Provision of Social Welfare. In *Religion and Social Policy*, edited by Paula D. Nesbitt. 128–145. Walnut Creek, CA: Alta Mira Press.

National Council for Voluntary Organisations. 2007. *Faith and Voluntary Action*. London: NCVO.

National Offender Management Service. 2007. *Believing We Can: Promoting the Contribution of Faith-Based Organisations Can Make to Reducing Adult and Youth Re-Offending*. London: National Offender Management Service.

Nesbitt, Paula D. (ed.) 2001. *Religion and Social Policy*. Walnut Creek, CA: AltaMira Press.

O'Beirne, Maria. 2004. Religion in England and Wales: Findings from the 2001 Home Office Citizenship Survey. Home Office Research Study 274. London: Home Office.

Ownby, David. 2008. *Falun Gong and the Future of China*. New York: Oxford University Press.

Poole, Elizabeth. 2000. Framing Islam: An Analysis of Newspaper Coverage of Islam in the British Press. In *Islam and the West in the Mass Media*, edited by Kai Hafez. 157–179. Cresskill, NJ: Hampton Press.

Poole, Elizabeth, Richardson, John E. (eds). 2006. *Muslims and the News Media*. Oxford: I.B. Tauris.

Richardson, James T. 1997. The Social Construction of Satanism: Understanding an International Social Problem. *Australian Journal of Social Issues* 32(1): 61–85.

Richardson, James T. 2006. The Sociology of Religious Freedom: a Structural and Socio-Legal Analysis. *Sociology of Religion* 67(3): 271–294.

Richardson, James T., and Van Driel, Barend. 1997. Journalists' Attitudes toward New Religious Movements. *Review of Religious Research* 39(2): 116–136.

Richardson, James T., Best, Joel, and Bromley, David G. 1991. Satanism as a Social Problem. In *The Satanism Scare*, edited by James T. Richardson, Joel Best, and David G. Bromley. 3–17. New York: Aldine de Gruyter.

Robbins, Thomas. 1985. Nuts, Sluts and Converts: Studying Religious Groups as Social Problems. *Sociological Analysis* 46(2): 171–178.

Robertson, Roland. 1985. The Sacred and the World System. In *The Sacred in a Secular Age*, edited by Phillip E. Hammond. 347–358. Berkeley, CA: University of California Press.

Robertson, Roland and Chirico, Jo Ann. 1985. Humanity, Globalization and Worldwide Religious Resurgence: A Theoretical Exploration. *Sociological Analysis* 46(3): 219–242.

Rosenberg, Justin. 2000. *The Follies of Globalisation Theory: Polemical Essays.* London: Verso.

Stiglitz, Joseph. 2002. *Globalization and its Discontents.* London: Penguin.

Vertovec, Steven. 2002. Islamophobia and Muslim Recognition in Britain. In *Muslims in the West: From Sojourners to Citizens*, edited by Y. Haddad. 19–35. New York: Oxford University Press.

Wallace, John M., Yamaguchi, Ryoko, Bachman, Jerald G., O'Malley, Patrick M., Schulenberg, John E., and Johnston, Lloyd D. 2007. Religiosity and Adolescent Substance Use: The Role of Individual and Contextual Influences. *Social Problems* 54(2): 308–327.

Waters, Malcolm. 2001. *Globalization.* London: Routledge.

Weller, Paul, Feldman, A., and Purdam, Kingsley. 2001. Religious Discrimination in England and Wales. *Home Office Research Study* no. 220. London: Home Office.

Weller, Paul. 2006. Addressing Religious Discrimination and Islamophobia: Muslims and Liberal Democracies. The Case of the United Kingdom. *Journal of Islamic Studies* 17(3): 295–325.

Wood, James R. 1981. *Legitimate Leadership in Voluntary Organizations: The Controversy over Social Action in Protestant Churches.* New Brunswick, NJ: Rutgers University Press.

Wright, Stuart A. 1997. Media Coverage of Unconventional Religion: Any "Good News" for Minority Faiths? *Review of Religious Research* 39(2): 101–115.

Zahn, Gordon. 1969. *Chaplains in the RAF: A Study in Role Tension.* Manchester: Manchester University Press.

Zetter, Roger, Griffiths, David, Sigona, Nando, Flynn, Don, Pasha, Tauhid, and Beynon, Rhian. 2006. *Immigration, Social Cohesion and Social Capital.* York: Joseph Rowntree Foundation.

5 Fighting Against Unemployment

Finnish Parishes as Agents in European Social Fund Projects

Sanna Lehtinen

The European Union (EU) has created a common internal market aiming at full employment and social development. In the Treaty on the Functioning of the EU, it also takes formal authority over the social policies of its member states (ratified Deember 1, 2009). With the European Social Fund (ESF), the EU attempts to co-ordinate national labor market policies for increased efficiency and employment by handing out project funding through structural funds. By offering incentives through the ESF, the EU manages affairs and groups of people that it sees as connected to marginalization and social problems (European Communities 2007, 3). Both secular welfare organizations and church-related groups such as Evangelical Lutheran parishes in Finland have responded to the social problems defined by the EU, acting through projects funded by the ESF.

Historically, European religious development has been characterized by the differentiation of state and church and decreasing church membership. The differentiation of sectors within society and the privatization of religion have weakened the institutional standing of mainstream churches (Dobbelaere 2000). The weakening of the institutional position of the church can be seen also in Finland, where the church is an independent public corporation (Heikkilä et al. 2005, 523, 527). The church membership has decreased from 84.1% in 2003 to 79.7% in 2009 (Niemelä 2004, 89; Kirkko numeroina 2010). However, social issues have kept the churches involved in public debate (Hadden 1980; Casanova 1994; Pessi 2009). Since the 1990s, churches have taken on new public roles, for example in defending the rights of marginalized and ignored groups (Casanova 1994; Davie 2000; Yeung 2003).

In this article I will examine, first, how parishes have responded to eradicating problems related to unemployment in the ESF projects they participated in, and second, what kinds of roles parishes have in ESF projects related to unemployment and labor-market accession problems on the local level in Finland. Finnish parishes fight against unemployment both administratively in the social networks and in practice with the unemployed. Since the welfare responsibility is in transition in Finland, the role of the local parishes in the ESF projects is unclear leading to severe expectations towards parishes such as complementing the public social work, supporting unemployed and working as an employer. At the same time, in these processes parishes gain opportunities to become visible actors in local networks.

FINNISH PARISH SOCIAL WORK IN THE NATIONAL AND THE EU CONTEXT

In Nordic welfare states such as Finland, the state and the authorities have extensive comprehensive responsibility for people's welfare. Finnish legislation on social welfare applies to everyone incapable of securing basic subsistence. After Finland's accession to the EU in 1995, other policy areas such as taxation and labor legislation began to affect Finnish national social policy (Kari 1998). Finnish labor policy also began to reflect OECD and EU employment strategies. Instead of the basic principle of the welfare state, political decisions started to become motivated by the idea of activation policy, i.e. the concept of incentive (Björklund 2008). Responsibility for people's welfare is now transferred gradually from the public to the private sector, non-governmental organizations (NGOs) and to the people themselves (Julkunen 2006). As the EU policy emphasizes the role of local actors, as a result, people have begun to seek economic and social support also from local parishes.

The Constitution of Finland stipulates that the organization and the administration of the Evangelical Lutheran Church are to be laid out in the Church Act (CA). The church has a right to collect tax from its members to finance its activities. This has brought responsibilities to the church also in social questions. However, even if at national level the Finnish Lutheran church is a public actor, at the EU level all churches belong to the third sector and non-profit community economy when it comes to the ESF-project funding.

The third sector can be defined as voluntarily organized non-profit action and institutions that are not part of the public sector, i.e. the state and municipalities. The public sector aims at general well-being and its tasks are laid out in legislation and funded with taxes. The interests of third-sector actors are usually specialized and limited to a specific group or issue. The third-sector actors are usually characterized by flexibility, mutual support, communality and caring (Rönnberg 2000, 72; Helander 2002; Möttönen and Niemelä 2005). In contrast to the private sector, the public and third sectors are non-profit. However, in some European countries, like Sweden, the church and other religious organizations appear as legal personae having a status of a private organization (Friedner 2005, 544). On the national level, the European churches are not purely private-, public- or third-sector institutions, but can be defined as "para-public" institutions (Minkenberg 2003). Local parishes in Finland are organizationally and economically self-governing. This is the reason why at the national church level there is no information about the funding parishes have received from the EU.

According to the CA, the purpose of the social work of the church is to help those most in need and who are not helped by others (Kirkkojärjestys 2005, 4:3). Due to economic recession in the 1990s, the social work of the Finnish parishes changed its focus from the elderly to working-age people. Because of historical reasons, parishes in Finland have a close partnership with local municipalities. They both have similar institutional structures, covering the same geographical areas and often sharing elected trustees. The parish social work in Finland is unique from an international perspective because it covers the entire country and employs a huge number of paid trained employees who occupy a central position in the organization of the church and the CA.[1] Even if the main responsibility for the well-being of citizens belongs to the state and the municipalities, a lot of social work is performed in parishes with unemployed people and through different cooperation projects with other local actors. The ESF has been one of the funding bodies of these projects (Lehtinen 2007). From the EU perspective, parish social work is the biggest third-sector agent in Finland.

STUDIED PROJECTS

On its website the ESF states that it is the most important tool the EU has for turning its labor policy goals into practical interventions in Member States. The EU funded 5,059 ESF projects in Finland in 2000–2006, of which 4,888 have been documented.[2] The EU has specific objective programs (OP) for implementing unemployment policies in Member States.

Table 5.1　Objective Programs (OP) in Finland and Number of Parishes Taking Part in the Years 2000–2006

OP	Projects	Parishes
OP1A: Regional development programs in Eastern Finland	803	2
OP1B: Regional development programs in Northern Finland	638	3
OP2A: Regional development programs in Western Finland	694	3
OP2B: Regional development programs in Southern Finland	427	7
OP3: Seeking, testing and producing new perspectives and mainstreaming good practices in Finnish labor, industry and education policies	2317	19

Table 5.2   OP3 Sub-programs in which Parishes have Participated

Sub-programs	Projects	Parishes
3.1.1. Employing unemployed people in open labor markets and safeguarding the availability of labor for companies	205	1
3.2.2. Promotion of vocational education and training and reducing drop-outs	253	8
3.2.3. Supporting disadvantaged groups in the labor market	136	9
3.4.2. Developing skills and coping at work for employees	393	1

Parishes participated in 34 projects of these OP's during the program period.[3] In this chapter, the focus is on the OP3, the largest ESF program in Finland, covering over 80% of the Finnish population. The OP3 was divided into sub-programs, and parishes have participated in four of these.

The specific focus here is on sub-program 3.2.3, which aimed at supporting exceptionally disadvantaged groups in the labor market (ESR Suomessa 2008). In this sub-program, parishes took part in nine projects (7%). In seven of the projects, the parishes participated in the steering group, and they acted as administrators in two of them. In two of the projects, they participated as cooperation partners. All the projects were implemented in the largest cities and parish federations. The sub-program 3.2.3 ESF projects studied here focus on people with the greatest risk of marginalization.

SOCIAL PROBLEMS IN THE PROJECTS

According to final reports, the projects studied here have reached at least 2,798 people.[4] The immediate or indirect target groups of all the projects were people with difficulties finding employment. The social problems concerning the projects are presented below.

For the long-term unemployed, the projects promoted employability through organizing supported employment, traineeships and tryouts. New employment opportunities were also sought, for example, in the NGO

Table 5.3   Social Problems in the Projects

Social problems	Projects	Code
Long-term unemployed	2	LT
Immigrants	2	I
Prisoners	3	P
People working with marginalized persons	2	PW

sector. It was important to find facilities where unemployed people could work, participate in activities, and do work-related practice. People participating in the employment actions of the project, for example, ran a cafeteria. One project evolved into a social enterprise.[5]

The immigrant projects were motivated by the low level of employment among immigrants in Finland. Both projects focused on integrating them into Finnish society. Integration is the legal duty of a municipality. However, parishes have their own immigrant activities. Immigrant projects organized courses in Finnish language and society as well as leisure activities and visits to NGOs and workplaces. The projects combined theoretical studies and simultaneous traineeships. Most of the participants went on to employment or further studies after the project.

Ex-convicts have substantially worse access the labor market or to education than any other citizens. In the projects, the idea was to offer convicts a seamless transition from prison to freedom. Attempts were made to integrate them into society while still in prison and immediately after release. The projects offered counseling in life management, self-responsibility for oneself and training and work tryouts for improving employability.

The parishes and third-sector agents that worked with unemployed people were the target of the project actions in two of the projects. These projects focused on developing a new culture of cooperation and aimed at offering professional tools for handling and preventing unemployment in a certain group or area. In this innovative work parishes seem to have a special role. For example, problems faced by young people and factors that contribute to marginalization were identified with the *Textari-helppi* ("SMS-help") service initiated by local parish.[6] In these projects local actors made broad-based cooperation efforts to promote employment interventions arising from local needs and initiatives, and to provide businesses with employees. The indirect target groups in these projects consisted of people with serious difficulties in finding employment. In the following, I will examine the role of parishes in solving social problems.

PARISHES TAKE RESPONSIBILITY FOR THE UNEMPLOYED

In the ESF projects studied, the project partners saw parishes as reliable partners because they followed the rules of public administration and were subject to supervision. In some of these projects, the parish functioned as an "other public" funding body. Especially solid parish federations were able to take part in resource-intensive project cooperation. Projects have become the new official mode of cooperation (see also Lehtinen 2007, 155), which facilitate and create a new kind of dialogue between different agents. In addition to the conventional social and health care sector, state job-center officials became close partners with parishes.

In Finland, parishes have created modes of action that are specialized in meeting the needs of certain groups in society. Modes of action that surfaced in the projects studied, such as working with prisoners, immigrants, young people, and the long-term unemployed, already part of the parish work, had been included in ESF projects as they were. The work done by a parish in eradicating social problems arising from unemployment can be seen as filling in the gaps left by the public sector. The parish helped unemployed people with finding accommodation, offered debt counseling, paid off unpaid rents and helped them in different ways to get back on their feet.

Participating in projects increased but also alleviated the work of parish staff. New ways of helping the unemployed were discovered. As we can see here, parish staff looked to projects for solutions when they were faced with insurmountable challenges.

LT parish social worker: *"There are hopeless cases. If I could get them some kind of a place where they could be secure, the clients with drinking problems who, on the other hand, were also unemployed; I can't find any solution for these kinds of cases."*

Some people had such big problems, such as huge debts and severe mental health issues, that parish social workers were unable to help them. In those cases, the staff directed clients to other services through the projects. This was an administrative way of helping people in difficult situations.

Project managers saw parishes as public agents in the projects, as they thought that the comprehensive welfare duty pertained also to the parish. A municipal representative working as a project manager said that taking part in the project was exactly what the parish should be doing. There was also great demand for parish involvement in prison social work.

P project manager: *From the viewpoint of the prison I cannot think of areas of work in which the parish couldn't participate."*

Parish social work contributes to welfare together with other agents by taking responsibility and acting in society. Parish representatives felt that they received recognition for their work through project cooperation. In the projects the parish staff took a lot of responsibility, and it was given to them, too.

Helping the unemployed seems to have become a permanent part of the work done by parishes in Finland. With their involvement, parishes emphasized with their involvement that all issues related to unemployment pertained to the church as well. Parish staff felt that their particular duty in authority networks was to emphasize the importance of holistic encounters and a human perspective (Lehtinen 2008). Taking part in projects was also justified by saying that parish social work cannot do enough on its own.

LT parish social worker: *"What we can do in parish social work is not enough. I should know all sorts of people from the job center and the social services, people who could help this one person, and it is always a different social worker and a different job centre clerk; it gets really complicated."*

Like public administration, the imperative of efficiency and cost-efficient management bind the work of parishes. Attempts were made to avoid overlaps with municipalities and the state in project actions.

Through parish social work, the church has defended the welfare state and fairness in local networks.

LT parish social worker: "*The state has to take care of disadvantaged and unemployed people, but the church has to fulfill its own prophetic duty in its actions. Somehow it should be out in the trenches.*"

The local parish workers notice how the activating policy and the responsibility of people's welfare is in transfer. The public sector in Finland does not solely aim at comprehensive responsibility for people's welfare; but rather aims to motivate people to seek employment (Björklund 2008). This is a challenging situation for marginalized people and citizens with the fewest chances to find employment.

PARISHES BECOME VISIBLE ACTORS IN LOCAL NETWORKS

In the projects, parishes wanted to pay attention to groups whose needs are not identified or who are not noticed (see also Lehtinen 2007, 152). Parishes were motivated by, for example, highlighting social injustices such as the actual possibilities of ex-convicts or immigrants to find work.

LT church social worker: "*We point out the injustices, and then the state needs to do something about them after we have shown where they are and have helped people in those situations.*"

When working with the unemployed, parish staff understood in what kind of a vicious circle an unemployed person in Finland ends up in. Parish staff informed other agents that the state of people's lives situations needed closer and more individual observation.

In the projects, parishes have defended the rights of the unemployed to receive help. The projects were used as a vehicle to criticize, for example, the way job centers operated.

LT project manager: "*Our main aim is to work as watchdogs and try to find out how these people could be served differently than bureaucratic and traditional Finnish civil servants usually do.*"

Projects sought change and were utilized to find an alternative way to work in the public sector. The parish was looking for a combination of social work and helping the unemployed. Possibly the most important challenge in the projects was to direct people back to public services.

While working with the unemployed, parish social workers revealed that there were many obstacles for not finding work, such as economic problems and homelessness in the worst cases. These obstacles could also consist of a lack of education or language skills, mental health problems or a prison sentence. Parish staff aimed at enhancing communality, stressing that in addition to individual support, the unemployed need a community where they can find their way back to work.

LT parish social worker: "*The parish cannot solve the unemployment question. The state is responsible for creating employment. The task of the parish is to support people in their lives.*"

Problems leading to and arising from unemployment became familiar to the parish staff. While working in the projects, they could experience the situation of an unemployed. When knowledge and expertise in unemployment issues were accumulated, disseminating this knowledge became a new task of parish social workers. In the projects studied, the parishes were praised for their fieldwork and the knowledge of the people's needs by municipal officials. Municipal staff emphasized the role of the church in bringing social problems the projects focused to the fore.

Acting in projects showed that parishes are willing and able to actively take part in the decision-making process and the opening of new debates. With the help of projects parishes wanted to highlight people's concrete needs. For example, in projects for prisoners it was shown that when prisoners are released, they are entitled to certain forms of support, for example, accommodation and subsistence. However, ex-prisoners might have other needs that they want to conceal from the authorities, for example, debts accumulated by drugs. Parish social workers were not seen as authorities but as reliable persons bound by confidentiality. A parish social worker could give financial help or be present during debt mitigation. This way a person could really obtain a new chance in his or her life.

Instead of economic efficiency, parish social workers tried to find fulfillment in life both for those as well as for those unable to return to work. Parishes sought goals in projects that were different from the ones set by the EU. LT parish social worker: "*The parish has all the time had the objective of maintaining some kind of a Christian view of the person, that a person is important even though s/he cannot be productive.*"

The parish workers said that one of the main reasons they participated was that the work stemmed from their own values and the Christian view of personhood. Through acting in projects, parishes wanted to pass a message to the whole of society. They demonstrated a way of showing love for your neighbor in authority networks. However, at the same time they cleared a path themselves with the projects to secular authority networks.

Organizing activities has been an especially important part of the work of the parishes in project cooperation (Lehtinen 2008). Project activities often took place outside office hours (Lehtinen 2007, 156). The parishes' contribution to the projects was flexible due to the staff having no fixed hours. Meaningful activities were also offered with volunteering opportunities. The work performed by parishes with the unemployed was more flexible and adaptable compared to the rest of the public sector also because they are not bound by strict legislation.

LT parish social worker: "*We are not bound by any kind of detailed legislation, for example, about who we can give assistance to.*"

Parishes supported local authorities in the projects and contributed to welfare.

Organizing peer support is seen a typical work done by the third-sector actors. The parishes were involved in organizing different groups. Parish staff planned group activities, ran groups and evaluated group meetings. They took part in maintaining mental health groups and organized a group for people doing traineeships and for the long-term unemployed who had returned to work after a long break. The parishes took up the role of the caring agent in project cooperation. What may seem a fuzzy argument or situation, in fact reflects a dual face of the parishes in their local roles: on the one hand they are part of the public sector, meaning the parish as a public corporation. But in their behavior and the perception of their active members, as well as the EU, they behave like third-sector agents. Parish staff gave pastoral counseling and coached people on how to find work, and thus relieved the anxiety caused by unemployment. Discussions centered on dealing with bitterness arising from unemployment and giving support. The parishes wanted to give hope and a sense of meaning to the unemployed in the projects. By participating in ESF projects, they signaled their strong commitment to unemployment issues. Taking part in projects also gave parishes chances to take part in public debate, to bring about change, to reach out to those in need and to disseminate their values.

THE UNCLEAR ROLE OF THE PARISHES CHALLENGES THE COOPERATION

Mixed attitudes of project managers towards parishes revealed that the status of them was not clear in the local networks. The EU, the state, and the municipalities hoped that the third sector, as well as parishes, would take more part in activating labor policy through projects. A parish representative said in an interview that participation in projects has to be contemplated each time one is invited to take part; new invitations come in all the time. While parish social workers worked together with other professionals in project networks, project partners noticed that parishes have many useful resources in meeting social challenges. Parishes acted as specialists in project networks and offered practical and moral support to project partners as well. The parish social workers passed information in both directions, to the authorities and to the target groups of the projects. Because of the role of parish social workers as an informant, the role of the parish was essential for project participants.

Expectations for the results of the projects were high. In some projects, parish staff received criticism from the local authorities on the low numbers of people finding work although they had participated in the projects.

Local authorities also hoped that the parishes themselves would employ more of the unemployed. It seems that Finnish parishes were expected to both create employment and support unemployed people in the ESF projects studied.

Even though parishes are seen as public sector agents in Finland, municipal authorities do not count them as public and official actors in project cooperation. This is supported by the fact that parishes were often ignored in project reporting (Lehtinen 2007). Managers of parish-led projects had difficulties in receiving ESF funds from the Ministry for Social Affairs and Health, the authority in charge of distributing the funds. The money arrived late, and a local Member of Parliament had to intervene. There were also problems with local public administrators like the Kela (The Social Insurance Institution of Finland) when trying to help an unemployed person.

LT project manager: *"The Kela, for example, when you give a collegial call and ask for some general information, they were very uncooperative. Usually they wanted to know who we are asking about . . . We solved the problem by beginning to contact Kela offices in other towns when they would not give the information we needed."*

Even though the expertise and the equality of the third sector and the parishes as co-actors are emphasized in local project cooperation, in practice problems existed.

LT project manager: *"Even though my boss and employer are here, the responsible city official in charge, this labor force official, made me run around almost like a servant before I realized at some point that I don't need to jump through hoops every time this person calls me from the city hall."*

Cooperating with state labor officials posed challenges, too. The problems present in encounters between the efforts of the authorities and parishes came out in project cooperation. Parish social workers felt that they were seen as strange middle-ground agents who were not taken seriously by the authorities. In contrast, there were no problems with the social services, with which parishes had a long history of cooperation.

The task of the parish in these projects was to socialize and integrate target individuals back into society. Long-term unemployed people have difficulties with daily routines and with managing their lives. They need different forms of support and training in order to go back to work. Parish staff gave out information on practical matters and directed the unemployed to different courses. A prisoner has to get rid of intoxicants and to find a place to live, and an immigrant has to learn the language and cultural matters. Many immigrants received their first experience of working in Finland and Finnish work culture from the projects in traineeships and tryouts. Parish staff also told them about Finnish culture, history, traditions, and celebrations. The EU supports the integration of immigrants into Member States through ESF projects. In Finland, parishes have been given and also taken responsibility, together with municipalities in these projects, in the integration of new citizens into Finnish society and working life. In project cooperation, the parish is seen as part of the public service structure, offering social counseling, traineeships, and apprenticeships to people at risk of marginalization.

DISCUSSION

In the EU social partners, parishes included, occupy a central role in the dissemination of EU goals. This research has indicated that in ESF projects the goal of the EU to reach out to the unemployed and people at risk of marginalization through project actions has succeeded. The social problems of the people encountered in the ESF projects are complex and challenging. Unemployment and obstacles in finding work are not the direct cause of social problems, but rather a result of other causes. This raises the question about how much attention should be paid to a more holistic view of being human by the labor force administration.

In the ESF projects studied, the social work done by parishes is a part of the local secular social cooperation network. Project cooperation has both changed shared modes of action and developed them further. The parishes themselves have also reshaped their activities to fit better in local networks. The unclear role of parishes in relation to official agents in helping the unemployed is partly responsible for parish activities becoming part of labor policies aimed at activating people. It seems that it is difficult for parish staff to see their role and the status of the parish in general in relation to official labor force administration. In ESF projects both the project partners and the parish representatives see parishes as grass root level social actors with a broad spiritual framework. On the one hand they see altruistic speech and on the other concrete social activities as the most essential work done by the parishes.

In the context of project cooperation, compared to the municipalities, the activities of parishes are seen as more flexible. This is due to the specific characteristics of parishes, such as the lack of fixed working hours, a broad-based repertoire of activities and a wide operational framework. Especially the ability to react to acute problems in the ESF projects has been the special strengths of parish activities. Since the parish social workers have a lot of expertise they have a lot to give in decision-making by describing the reality in which unemployed live. They have expertise in the kinds of services the unemployed need and how these could be developed. In the projects studied networking and lobbying are emphasized in developing parish activities. In contrast to the public administration, which emphasizes motivating people to seek employment, parish staff may defend their unemployed clients, who are incapable to fight for their rights by taking a holistic approach to their situation. The analysis here has shown that parish staff possesses an expertise and perception of the social problems at hand which would qualify them as consultants in municipal decision-making.

The main task of parish social work, meant as temporary help when other help is out of reach, is not to maintain the services managed by the state and municipalities such as creating employment, offering services and taking responsibility for finding employment for the long-term unemployed. As quality criteria for public agents define the guidelines for the parish work, without adequate training, the possibilities for parishes to employ people are limited. Tightened economic resources also restrict the ability of the parishes to employ people. However, it is possible for the parish to create volunteering opportunities. One of the projects studied developed into a social enterprise. Hence, entrepreneurship is not a core activity of parish social work in Finland. Instead, motivating people towards entrepreneurship, training and independent activities can be included in the work done by parishes.

In the project cooperation, the parishes have taken a critical role together with the unemployed in project cooperation towards the state and the EU. Parishes have criticized both the labor force administration for an excessively one-sided approach to the unemployed and the EU for forgetting human dignity in the midst of demands for productivity. The results resonate with the arguments of Casanova (1994). According to him, the transformation of the churches from being state centered to defending people's rights, have opened them up for public debate. In the ESF projects, the third sector and parish social work as part of it look like subcontractors of the state and the municipalities. In these projects, parishes seem to have been authorized to carry out actions that the state or the municipalities do not execute, empowering the unemployed from passivity and inability to active and capable employees.

In the ESF projects, the status of the parishes in relation to other agents is unclear and full of tensions posing challenges to work together. In light of project cooperation, it seems that the role of local parishes is in transition in Finland. Making demands and transferring the responsibility of creating employment, to voluntary and non-profit actors, is a sign of this. What is curious is that it is done with the most challenging groups of people. In the ESF projects the local agents, parishes included, should consider their activities from their own starting points. Tying project funding to quantitative and economic goals has a restricting effect. This happens through legislation and reporting duties, when the funding body, here the EU, begins to dictate work. This is harmful to the communality, the innovativeness and the independency of the local actors.

Along with EU membership, the definitions of social policy and welfare are in transition in Finland. The importance of work in the accumulation and the level of social security have increased. The state central Nordic welfare model, influenced by Lutheranism, has encountered the political thinking of the EU largely shaped by Catholicism, where the responsibility for one's own well-being and of those in one's immediate circle rests largely on families and immediate communities (Vuorela 2008, Kari 1998, Tiilikainen 1998, Esping-Andersen 1990). In the Nordic countries the welfare responsibility of the state and the municipalities is still central and the role of churches or local parishes in producing welfare services is minimal (Yeung, Beckman, and Pettersson 2006). However, in ESF project cooperation there are growing expectations relating to parishes what comes to employment questions and welfare responsibility. In terms of welfare responsibility in Finland, the role of the local parishes is unclear and parish social workers are seeking their place in the society.

The social policy systems of Member States are converging gradually along with EU membership. It remains to be seen whether Nordic welfare states have to capitulate to economic demands or whether social questions will become more important in EU decision-making. Parishes as local agents are promoting the goals of the EU by joining its labor policy in the ESF projects. This is in contradiction with the Lutheran doctrine of two regiments, acknowledging the status of secular authorities and the responsibility for people's material well-being and fairness. However, religious agents can make a difference if they comply with political processes and public administration. They do not have a say in which social problems are funded and focused by the EU, but they can tailor their own activities according to this secular context (Beckford 1990) if they use non-religious language and do not appear as the spokesperson for or lobbyists for the church, but rather for the citizens.

The differentiation of society has assisted the separation of the church and state in European societies. In Finland, on the local level, questions relating to unemployment have brought state officials and parish representatives around the same table. Finnish parishes taking part in employment policy actions, in the ESF project work, have partly taken part in EU policies extensively based on economic demands. However, participation in the ESF project network in a secular society has promoted the values and aims of the parishes—supporting hope and human dignity without the obligations of productivity.

NOTES

1. In 2007 there were 1,462 parish social workers (Kääriäinen 2008, 269).
2. ESRA database November 20, 2008.
3. The data consists of 9 project descriptions, 72 project documents, and 10 interviews. The research method applied was qualitative content analysis.
4. In one project description the number of participants was not mentioned.
5. In a social enterprise at least 30% of staff is made up of long-term unemployed people or those who have physical or mental difficulties.
6. *Textari-helppi* became a permanent service of the parish after the project finished.

REFERENCES

Beckford, James A. 1990. The Sociology of Religion and Social Problems. *Sociological Analysis* 51(1): 1–14.

80 Sanna Lehtinen

Björklund, Liisa. 2008. *Kannustaminen ja moraali. Kannustamisen idea suomalaisessa yhteiskuntapolitiikassa 1990-luvulta alkaen.* Helsinki: Helsinki University.
Casanova, Jose. 1994. *Public Religions in the Modern World.* Chicago: University of Chicago Press.
Davie, Grace. 2000. *Religion in Modern Europe: A Memory Mutates.* Oxford: Oxford University Press.
Dobbelaere, Karel. 2000. Toward an Integrated Perspective of the Processes Related to the Descriptive Concept of Secularization. In *The Secularization Debate,* edited by William H. Swatos Jr. and Daniel V. A. Olson. 21–39. Lanham, MD: Rowan and Littlefield.
Esping-Andersen, Gösta. 1990. *The Three Worlds of Welfare Capitalism.* Cambridge: Polity.
ESR Suomessa. 2008. ESR Suomessa / ESR 2000–2006 / Tavoite 3 -ohjelma / Tasaarvo ja yhtäläiset mahdollisuudet.
http://www.esr.fi/esr/fi/esr_suomessa/ohjelmakausi_2000–2006/tavoite3/tlinja2/index.jsp. (Accessed December 12, 2008).
European Communities. 2007. European Social Fund 50 Years Investing in People. http://ec.europa.eu/employment_social/esf/docs/50th_anniversary_book_en.pdf Luxembourg: Office for Official Publications of the European Communities.
Friedner, Lars. 2005. State and Church in Sweden. In *State and Church in the European Union: In Conjunction with the European Consortium for State and Church Research,* edited by Gerhard Robbers. 537–551. Baden-Baden: Nomos.
Hadden, Jeffrey K. 1980. Religion and the Construction of Social Problems. *Sociological Analysis* 41(2): 99–108.
Heikkilä, Markku, Knuutila, Jyrki, and Scheinin, Martin. 2005. State and Church in Finland. In *State and Church in the European Union: In Conjunction with the European Consortium for State and Church Research,* edited by Gerhard Robbers, 519–536. Baden-Baden: Nomos.
Helander, Voitto. 2002. *Kolmas sektori.* Helsinki: Gaudeamus.
Julkunen, Raija. 2006. *Kuka vastaa? Hyvinvointivaltion rajat ja julkinen vastuu.* Helsinki: Stakes.
Kari, Matti. 1998. *Meeting with EU Social Policy: The Experience of a New Member State.* Antwerpen: Maklu.
Kirkkojärjestys. 2005. Kirkkojärjestys. In Kirkkolaki, kirkkojärjestys, kirkon vaalijärjestys, kirkon säädöskokoelma. Helsinki: Kirkkohallitus.
Kirkko numeroina. 2010. *Evl.fi / Evl.lut. kirkko / Kirkko numeroina.* http://evl.fi/EVLfi.nsf/Documents/BB22B8B72B6F6A06C22572E5003A8E9E?OpenDocument&lang=FI. (Accessed April 31, 2010).
Kääriäinen, Kimmo. 2008. *Monikasvoinen kirkko. Suomen evankelis-luterilainen kirkko vuosina 2004–2007.* Tampere: Church Research Institute.
Lehtinen, Sanna. 2007. Projektiyhteiskunnan verkostoissa. Seurakunnat Euroopan sosiaalirahaston projekteissa. *Diakonian tutkimus -aikakauskirja* 2/2007: 137–159.
Lehtinen, Sanna. 2008. Yhteisöllisyys tavoitteena seurakunnan ESR-projektiyhteistyössä. *Janus* 16(4): 311–327.
Minkenberg, Michael. 2003. The Policy Impact of Church–State Relations: Family Policy and Abortion in Britain, France and Germany. In *Church and State in Contemporary Europe. The Chimera of Neutrality,* edited by John Madeley and Zsolt Enyedi. 195–217. London: Frank Cass.
Möttönen, Sakari, and Niemelä, Jorma. 2005. *Kunta ja kolmas sektori—Yhteistyön uudet muodot.* Jyväskylä: PS-kustannus.

Niemelä, Kati. 2004. Jäsenet. In *Kirkko muutosten keskellä—Suomen evankelis-luterilainen kirkko vuosina 2000–2003*. 89–103. Tampere: Church Research Institute.

Pessi, Anne Birgitta. 2009. Religion and Social Problems—Individual and Institutional Responses. In *The Oxford Handbook of the Sociology of Religion*, edited by Peter B. Clarke. 942–961. Oxford: Oxford University Press.

Rönnberg, Leif. 2000. Diversity and New Communality in the Third Sector. In *The Third Sector in Finland*, edited by Martti Siisiäinen, Petri Kinnunen, and Elina Hietanen. 70–91. Helsinki: The Finnish Federation for Social Welfare and Health and University of Lapland.

Tiilikainen, Teija. 1998. *Europe and Finland. Defining the Political Identity of Finland in Western Europe*. Aldershot: Ashgate.

Vuorela, Mika. 2008. *Työtä haluaville uusia mahdollisuuksia työhön*. Työ- ja elinkeinoministeriön selvitys. http://www.tem.fi/files/18750/Vuorela_loppura-portti.pdf. (Accessed December 15, 2008).

Yeung, Anne Birgitta. 2003. The Re-emergence of the Church in Finnish Public Life? Christian Social Work as an Indicator of the Public Status of the Church. *Journal of Contemporary Religion* 18(2): 197–211.

Yeung, Anne Birgitta, Beckman, Ninna Edgardh, and Pettersson, Per. 2006. *The Changing European Landscape of Welfare and Religion. Churches in Europe as Agents of Welfare—Sweden, Norway and Finland*. Uppsala: Diakonvetens-kapliga institutet.

6 Religion as a Solution to Social Problems

A Christian Orthodox Approach to International Humanitarian Issues[1]

Lina Molokotos-Liederman

In this chapter I will explore the relationship between religion and social problems from the perspective of religion as a solution. The role of Christian social service in addressing human needs is thus particularly relevant. Religious Non Governmental Organizations (NGOs) focus on charity and philanthropy and are motivated by God and religious belief with a holistic focus on the spiritual, material, and physical well-being of individuals they wish to help (Berger 2003). In that sense they make material, community and spiritual claims in solving social problems (see Hjelm 2009). The focus of this chapter is on the Orthodox claim to solving social problems, namely on how Orthodox Christianity contributes to alleviating human need across the globe and on what the Christian Orthodox approach is in addressing social issues of poverty, injustice, and inequality through social action. After tracing the origins and historic development of Orthodox social theology and service, I will concentrate more specifically on how they have been translated into current action and implemented practically in the field.

The contribution of Religious NGOs (RNGOs) and Faith-Based Organizations (FBOs)[2] to the field of international social policy, development, and humanitarian assistance has grown to become a topic of increasing research and interest, as indicated by publications and conferences since the late 1990s, particularly on North American Protestant, Evangelical, and Catholic organizations, which seem to have dominated Christian humanitarian aid across the globe. Some examples include the 2005 international conference in Oslo on "Religious NGOs and the International Aid System: An International Research Conference,"[3] as well as the work of scholars from various disciplines, as indicated briefly by Berger (Berger 2003). But social service and social justice initiatives worldwide from the Christian

Orthodox tradition have not been examined much in previous scholarship and remain a relatively under-researched field.

THE SEEDS OF ORTHODOX SOCIAL SERVICE

Orthodox social service is based on social theology and more particularly on the Christian concept of *diakonia* (social service). Diakonia is social service based on solidarity, inspired by Christian values (God's love and compassion). It is expressed through charity and philanthropy towards those in need. The term diakonia was used in early Christianity to indicate philanthropy and love (love of the human person) which were used almost interchangeably in Christian theology. During the Byzantine Empire the Church was in charge of philanthropy, ranging from giving at an individual level to looking after the needs of all in a more organised and structured way by overseeing social welfare services, including hospitals, orphanages, homes for the elderly, and so on. In developing an institutionalized philanthropic platform the Church was able to promote its moral greatness and attract clergymen, bishops, believers, and members. Therefore, the philanthropic diakonia of the Byzantine Empire became a prototype and source of inspiration for the social consciousness of the western Church. Since then Christian theology has aimed to integrate social action into its spiritual life and theology by trying to address social welfare issues (Constantelos 2004).

In this context, Orthodox social service has been at the core of the social mission of the Orthodox Church with the aim of delivering mankind from poverty, oppression and injustice (Ferris 2005; Orthodox Academy of Crete 1978). As Orthodox Christianity is marked by diverse geographic and ethnic variations that affect many areas of church life, Orthodox social service has developed in a specific way through various historical periods and geographic areas: in Byzantium, during the Ottoman period, the nineteenth century, the Communist regimes for most of the twentieth century and, more recently, in the post-Communist period with the renewed social and political engagement of Orthodox Churches in the public sphere (Belopopsky 2003). Orthodox Churches have become an increasingly pan-European reality, first when Greece joined the European Community in 1981, and subsequently when the EU expanded by adding new member countries with predominantly Christian Orthodox populations, such as Romania and Bulgaria. Orthodox Christianity is also a global reality through historic and ongoing waves of migration, especially when taking into account the diversity of Orthodox Churches and communities worldwide that are spread across the Russian Federation, the former Soviet republics and South Eastern Europe, but also among the Orthodox Diaspora in North and South America, Africa, Western Europe, Asia and the Pacific, with affiliations to many ecclesiastical jurisdictions and Patriarchates. In this context the role of Orthodox Christianity in the United States, Canada, and Australia for example in the global reorientation of Orthodoxy through Orthodox immigrant communities in the nineteenth and twentieth centuries has to be noted.

The fall of Communism and the opening of Eastern and Central Europe and the Balkans witnessed the revitalization of national Churches in the public sphere and more specifically the re-activation of Orthodox Churches in the social arena as political, social and cultural actors (Roudometof, Agadjanian, and Pankhurst 2005). After two world wars and civil wars, many Eastern Orthodox Churches in the 1990s found themselves in a precarious socio-economic position. Along with opportunities came great need and high demand for humanitarian assistance, particularly after the break-up of Yugoslavia and the wars in the Balkans. National Churches in these areas, having come out of particularly challenging socio-economic and political circumstances, were faced with a double challenge of great need for social/humanitarian services *and* scarce resources to offer social welfare services in socially, economically politically fragile societies.

During times of necessity and moments of crisis Orthodox Churches and related organizations offered social assistance to local populations and communities using informal but also some formal channels. Various informal charitable initiatives by Orthodox Churches, dioceses, monasteries, and related associations, indicate the existence of diakonia at the local and national level. This is especially the case in regions with predominantly Orthodox populations, including the Russian Federation, the former Soviet Republics, and South East Europe. Humanitarian assistance is offered to individuals or small groups and communities through local Orthodox NGOs offering social and humanitarian assistance in a rather unstructured fashion through personal and informal networks and through contacts between dioceses, parishes, monasteries and Orthodox brotherhoods or sisterhoods. This form of Orthodox diakonia at a "micro" level, offering charitable assistance to individuals and small groups in need, is often referred to as *micro-diakonia*.[4]

Compared to the work of many international Catholic and mainline Protestant churches and organizations that have engaged in issues of social justice and international humanitarian work, Orthodox diakonia is distinctly different. As indicated above, Orthodox Churches have not always responded adequately, consistently and systematically to social problems and humanitarian concerns. This indicates the lack of a vibrant Christian Orthodox involvement in humanitarian relief prior to the 1990s. This in turn has not favored the development of an organized pan-Orthodox approach in the provision of humanitarian assistance worldwide. Most Orthodox churches and organizations, many of them having at their disposal limited financial resources, grant priority to the pressing requirements of populations in their respective countries. The bulk of Orthodox organizations are based primarily in South-East Europe, the Russian Federation and the former Soviet Republics, which have predominantly Orthodox populations. For this reason there are few Orthodox humanitarian NGOs that provide a truly international humanitarian aid. For many organizations, lack of resources means low public and international visibility. Furthermore, some Orthodox Churches consider that giving public and media visibility to their social action would be in contrast to the principles of authentic philanthropy and Orthodox ethos (Stathopoulos 1999). This is one reason for some ecclesiastical organizations involved in humanitarian work to usually act locally and informally, being more interested in offering social services than expecting any form of public recognition or visibility. Therefore, Christian Orthodox organizations seem to have a weaker international presence and public profile in the arena of humanitarian work, whereas many secular and other RNGOs and FBOs (many of them Christian) have contributed to the field of international social policy, development, and humanitarian assistance and have been visibly active particularly after World War II in response to urgent humanitarian needs.

Beyond the determining historical circumstances outlined above, there are characteristics specific to Orthodox Christianity that have shaped the current state of Orthodox social service across the globe. First, in the Orthodox Church there is no predominant centralized and hierarchical administrative structure, such as we find in the Catholic Church (Roudometof, Aqadsaurian and Panichurst 2005, 10). Orthodox churches are autocephalous entities headed by autonomous Patriarchates that have the right to elect bishops in each administrative jurisdiction. Local Churches are decentralized, but united in spirit through the Ecumenical Patriarchate and the other Orthodox Patriarchates. The absence of centralization and the important role of the diocese and the parish in Orthodoxy make Orthodox diakonia more prone to develop locally and often at an informal and unstructured level.

Second, national churches are often deeply connected to ethnic characteristics, thus blurring the dividing line between spirituality/religion and ethnic/national characteristics (Ashanin 2006). The propensity of Orthodox Churches towards identifying themselves with a specific nation also means that they can set themselves apart in favor of maintaining strong ties to the state and local or regional institutions (Meyendorff 1981). This can have implications on the ability of Orthodox social service organizations to implement a well coordinated social action on a trans-national pan-Orthodox scale.

Third, the Eastern Orthodox Church has often been criticized as being "other-worldly" and unresponsive to social issues (Ashanin 2006, 125). Georges Florovsky noted for the Russian case the absence of active or visible social involvement by the Orthodox Church at least until the collapse of Communism (Florovsky 1950–1951, 41–51). John Meyendorff underlined the detachment of the Christian East from historical and social realities and its dedication to mysticism and contemplation (Meyendorff 1979). Eastern Orthodox mystical spirituality has typically looked inwards and "above" the affairs of this world, placing more emphasis on salvation and the celebration of rites and sacraments and less on direct missionary action or social service, such as we find in the Western Churches. However, despite the absence of organized forms of social service, there is a great deal of activity "on the ground" as social problems are often addressed practically (Ashanin 2006).

Therefore, until the 1990s, historical circumstances, the decentralized structure of Orthodoxy, the prevalence of national/ethnic Churches and the mystical and often detached spirituality of Christian Orthodoxy have all collectively contributed to the current state of Orthodox diakonia. However, Orthodox micro-diakonia has grown into wider-reaching initiatives involving a broader commitment to solidarity and social justice (*macro-diakonia*). Recent developments indicate strong interest in a renewed and visible social involvement in worldwide Orthodox diakonia. Furthermore, there is an increasing degree of cooperation and partnership between Orthodox organizations and a variety of other actors, such as secular and faith-based NGOs, international organizations, government agencies, etc.

After 1961, when the majority of Orthodox Churches joined the World Council of Churches (WCC), the WCC developed a program to assist them in the development of Orthodox diakonia programs, including the requirement that bishops and priests be actively engaged in social problems and demonstrate public and practical acts of philanthropy (Belopopsky 2003). The 1978 international conference on "An Orthodox Approach to Diaconia" at the Orthodox Academy of Crete located in Greece, upon the initiative of the World Council of Churches Orthodox Task Force marked a change of direction in Orthodox social theology and service. The conference acknowledged the need for the Orthodox Church to engage more actively in social service. It also clearly indicated the need to further develop its social mission in order to articulate more clearly Orthodox social action and *diakonia* (locally, regionally, and internationally) to offer both preventive and therapeutic social services (Orthodox Academy of Crete, 1978).

Subsequently, after the fall of Communism, Eastern Orthodox Churches strengthened their commitment to social mission, as indicated by an Orthodox diaconal renewal in the Russian Federation, Romania, Serbia, Belarus, Albania, etc. (Belopopsky 2003). More recently, multiple public interventions by Orthodox leaders, notably Ecumenical Patriarch Bartholomew and Archbishop of Tirana, Durres and All Albania, Anastasios, on the environment, peace, globalization, and social justice using a more transnational vision are another example (Anastasios 2003). Finally, in 1992, the foundation of International Orthodox Christian Charities (IOCC) as the official international humanitarian organization of the Standing Conference of Canonical Orthodox Bishops in the Americas (SCOBA), was an important stepping stone in developing an integrated Orthodox humanitarian agency using a global perspective and responding to social and humanitarian concerns in a way that superseded territorially centered Orthodox diakonia initiatives, rooted to a specific nation-state.

In 2004 the WCC, the IOCC and Orthodox Church Aid from Finland (OrtAid) organized for the first time an international conference on Orthodox Social Witness and Diakonia in Finland. During the meetings leaders and practitioners of Orthodox social service organizations, theologians, academics, and church hierarchs exchanged reflections and practical experiences on Orthodox social service worldwide.

MAPPING ORTHODOX DIAKONIA ACROSS THE GLOBE

In 2007 the IOCC commissioned a piece of research to map Orthodox diakonia worldwide in order to provide a snap-shot of the state of Christian Orthodox social service and gain a global perspective on the range of organizations and their work in the field. The survey report constitutes an initial assessment of the development and current state of Orthodox diakonia across the globe, a relatively under-researched area in the field of religious NGOs. As such it can become a starting point for further research and analysis.

The mapping survey identified humanitarian and social service organizations whose mission is driven by a predominantly Christian Orthodox ethos, namely: Officially affiliated Orthodox organizations mandated by national Churches or Patriarchates (official social arms of national Churches); recognized Orthodox organizations, but not officially affiliated with a Church; and local small scale initiatives (Orthodox associations, etc.). Organizations that are not strictly Orthodox, but are located in a mostly Orthodox region or include a strong Orthodox presence were also of interest.

The absence of a centralized administrative structure in the Orthodox Church as a whole and the lack of a coordinating body of Orthodox social service organizations worldwide presented a challenge in the data collection process. Orthodox diakonia organizations are often local, working with limited resources and staying away from formal documentation and communication channels, which make them hard to identify and approach. A total of 51 organizations were identified using a variety of sources, including the list of conference participants in the 2004 Orthodox diakonia conference, organizations in the partner directory of the WCC Diakonia & Solidarity Europe Desk, web-based research, existing partners of the IOCC, and so on.

The survey was conducted in 2008 in the sending out of 51 questionnaires containing 16 brief questions on the structure, mission/objectives, funding sources, type of services offered, challenges, and future aspirations, etc. The response rate was 54.9%, thus 28 completed questionnaires. For organizations that did not respond to the survey, some basic data was obtained from their respective websites or publications, if available (for example in the case of Solidarity in Greece).

A TYPOLOGY OF ORTHODOX NGOS

Most surveyed Orthodox diakonia organizations are fairly young, and most are between 15 and 20 years old, having been formed in the 1990s after the collapse of many Communist regimes, but there are of a few older and well established organizations in Africa and the Middle East. They are small- to medium-size organizations with a staff of 5 to 20 people, with the exception of the historic large and well-established organizations in Africa and the Middle East and the IOCC. They operate and offer their services mostly in areas with predominantly Orthodox populations in South-Eastern Europe and in the former Soviet Republics; there are also a few regional and international organizations and others based in Africa, the Middle East, and Asia. Most of the surveyed organizations are affiliated with a national Orthodox Church or a Patriarchate. They are governed by a Board of Directors, including both religious and non-religious board members, or are under the authority of a Holy Synod.

Almost all Orthodox diakonia organizations are charity/philanthropic organizations offering emergency relief (food, clothing, medical supplies, and care, etc.), but many have ventured into the area of sustainable and community development. There are both advisory/coordinating/funding bodies and/or implementing organizations. Donor or umbrella organizations are solely responsible for funding, coordinating and/or advising on the provision of services and programs that are offered by other implementing bodies (associations, agencies, etc.). Implementing organizations have the added role of actually offering services and implementing programs themselves. This distinction has implications on their size and staffing, geographic location, funding, and existing partnerships. Most organizations work with, and are funded by, multiple sources with whom they have formed working partnerships; these include Church based, ecumenical, international organizations and alliances/networks and government structures and agencies.

While additional data on more Orthodox diakonia organizations is necessary, five types of organizations can be distinguished: (i) *historic organizations*: older, well-established and fairly large organizations in the Middle East and Africa. For example: BLESS (Egypt), DICAC (Ethiopia) and St. Georges Hospital (Lebanon); (ii) international organizations: they use a global approach to Orthodox diakonia, funding, coordinating or providing humanitarian assistance internationally (for example: IOCC, OrtAid and Solidarity); (iii) middle-sized organizations: the bulk of organizations offering humanitarian assistance and social services, some with an emphasis on sustainable development and capacity building. They work locally and nationally in countries with predominantly Orthodox populations (Central and Eastern Europe and in the former Soviet Republics). For example: Philanthropy, Diakonia Agapes, Armenia Inter-Church Charitable Round Table Foundation Office (ART), etc.; (iv) small organizations or associations: they offer assistance locally and nationally in a relatively informal or unstructured way. For example: the Pastoral and Philanthropic Foundation of the Diocese of Switzerland of the Ecumenical Patriarchate in Switzerland, the Alexandrian Lighthouse/Archbishopric of Johannesburg and Pretoria in South Africa; and (v) consortium organizations: secular and ecumenical organizations, including some (but not exclusive) Orthodox participation (for example: AidRom and the MCIC).

PROFILING CHRISTIAN ORTHODOX NGOS

Orthodox Affiliation, link to Church and Governance

There are only a few Orthodox Churches (in Korea and New Zealand, for example) that do not have a dedicated philanthropic or charitable organization. Although these Churches do not seem to offer services in a structured or institutionalized way, they regularly help people in need and/or when there is an urgent necessity. Some national Orthodox Churches that have been increasingly providing social assistance to local populations may have decided to institutionalize and structure their services by creating a social organization or arm of the national church in view of formalizing and expanding their commitment to providing social assistance to the local community. FPO (Switzerland) is indicative of a small Orthodox organization directly linked to an Orthodox Church in a Western European country offering assistance to groups or individuals for whom social services are no longer available or possible. There are similar small organizations, such as ACER-Russie in France and the St. Gregory's Foundation in the United Kingdom, and others in other countries, such as in Italy, Belgium, Germany, Finland, etc.

Most of the surveyed organizations are directly affiliated with a national Orthodox Church. They are official social arms of national Churches and Patriarchates or other Orthodox organizations that have received mandates to offer humanitarian and social assistance. However, there are organizations that are not directly linked to a national church or Patriarchate, namely the IOCC and MCIC. The IOCC is the humanitarian organization of the Standing Conference of the Canonical Orthodox Bishops in the Americas (SCOBA). The Macedonian Center for International Cooperation (MCIC) is a secular organization but its Council and Board includes three representatives of the Macedonian Orthodox Church (MOC).

Most organizations are governed by a Board of Directors and Trustees or by the Holy Synod of the Church with which the organization is affiliated. The Board is chaired by a President, typically a Patriarch, Archbishop or Metropolitan and includes usually four to seven Board members from different sectors society, including some clergy. The day-to-day management of organizations is usually undertaken by an executive director and an administrative team. Most organizations are structured according to program departments reflecting their activities and work on the ground, for example, HIV/AIDS, Water/Rural or Agricultural Development, Refugee and Returnee Affairs, Health, Children/Youth, Education/Culture, Nursing/Medical Departments (in the case of St. Georges Hospital).

Mission Statement, Mandate and Service Provision

In as much as most organizations that provide any form of organized humanitarian assistance inherently have some coordinating functions, there are some organizations, whose activity is almost exclusively that of an advisory or coordinating body without any direct implementing functions. The Charity Sisterhoods Union of the Belarus Orthodox Church (part of the Moscow Patriarchate), the Christian Interchurch Diaconal Council of St. Petersburg (CIDC) and the Social Philanthropic Department of the Romanian Patriarchate are representative examples. The Charity Sisterhoods Union of the Belarus Orthodox Church is involved in coordination and consulting of the social work of charity sisterhoods and church social services of the Belorussian Orthodox Church and in the distribution of funds for such projects. The CIDC is a Christian NGO supporting and coordinating the social diakonia initiatives and activities of its founding churches (Orthodox, Evangelical Lutheran and Roman Catholic) in the Northwestern region of the Russian Federation. The Social Philanthropic Department of the Romanian Patriarchate is the institutional body of the Romanian Orthodox Church (ROC) and a bureaucratic structure of the administrative body of the Romanian Patriarchate, strategizing and supporting the development and strengthening of the social work of the Church all over the country.

Orthodox diakonia organizations seem to follow Clarke's model of "faith-based charitable organizations," mobilizing support for disadvantaged social groups and funding and running programs that tackle poverty and social exclusion (Clarke 2006). An important question here is how Christian NGOs, and in this case Orthodox diakonia organizations, use faith in their humanitarian work, namely in a relatively passive or active way. Religious affiliation can play a primary and/or a secondary role for example in identifying which communities in need will be supported, in determining which social services to provide (or not), or even in deciding with beneficiaries and partners to work with (Clarke 2006). There is no clear (either/or) answer as Orthodox diakonia organizations can use faith in different ways depending on the situation and geographic area in which they work. They are inspired by Christian values of philanthropy and maintain that they offer assistance to people in need and vulnerable groups in precarious situations that have been left behind, regardless of religious affiliation. Disadvantaged groups that are served by these organizations include the elderly, poor, homeless and sick, people with disabilities, orphans, victims of human trafficking, and people displaced by war and conflict or natural disasters.

Smaller organizations with somewhat limited resources that focus on charity and humanitarian relief usually offer clothing, food, shelter, and medical and social care in emergency situations (disaster/emergency relief), thus catering to the immediate needs of people in suffering. Such material support is also offered on an ongoing basis to long-term disadvantaged people and communities, such as the elderly, disabled, orphans, etc. Some indicative examples are the services offered by the Alexandrian Lighthouse in South Africa, Milosrdie in the Republic of Macedonia, the PSOC in India, St. George's Hospital in Lebanon, the Social Centre Agapis in Moldova and the Union of Charity Sisterhoods in Belarus.

Most organizations originally started as structures providing charity, emergency relief, and social care to local and national populations, but they were eventually able to evolve in order to shift their focus towards more long-term capacity building and sustainable development work. Their aim has shifted, offering to assist and empower marginalized communities into becoming self-reliant. Poverty reduction, agricultural production and rehabilitation, health education and vocational training have become high priority areas for these organizations. Organizations that adopted this broader focus have ventured into *macro-diakonia*. It is usually larger organizations with sufficient resources that are able to work towards long-term goals and projects that are able to develop and implement this type of community development work. Their activities include a variety of programs that are aimed towards the development of financial, material, and human resources for long-term growth of communities such as rural and agricultural development, environmental and infrastructure rehabilitation, health education, HIV/AIDS prevention and control, social change through conflict resolution for the promotion of peace and social harmony, education and training, youth programs and vocational training, technical assistance, and capacity-building training for social welfare institutions. The work of the Serbian "Philanthropy," the Armenia Inter-Church Charitable Round Table Foundation, the IOCC, the MCIC (Republic of Macedonia), the All-Ukrainian Church Charity Fund "Faith- Hope-Love," DICAC (Ethiopia), OrtAid (Finland), BLESS (Egypt), and the Foundation "Spirit of Love"— Diakonia Agapes (Albania) are indicative examples.

There are some organizations, including Zarebi and Porkrov in Bulgaria, among others, that are also involved in the promotion of Orthodoxy through educational and cultural activities, such as religious education programs and religious publications and information services. In this case, if humanitarian assistance is the primary goal of most organizations, some seem to go beyond that and offer additional services that spread the Orthodox faith by supporting local Orthodox churches survive or grow stronger in their respective local communities. Therefore, when Orthodox diakonia organizations offer cultural or educational services with a religious focus, faith takes on a primary role in social service provision. This issue points to a major topic of discussion and debate on the role of RNGOs and FBOs and the uncomfortable and tense relationship between humanitarian assistance and promotion of religious message and agenda (or even proselytism). This is an important and topical issue that deserves extensive analysis and discussion, but which is not possible to cover in this chapter.

Location, Geographic Coverage, Foundation Date and Size

The majority of the surveyed organizations are based primarily in regions and countries with predominantly Orthodox populations (for example, in South East Europe and in the former Soviet Republics). However, there are also organizations operating in Africa and South East Asia where there is a great need for humanitarian aid. Looking at the geographic location and coverage of such organizations it is apparent that most typically offer their services in the country or region in which they are based. Thus, there is an overlap between the country/region where they operate from (where they are based in) and the country where they provide their services (where they work in). There are also some organizations with a regional focus. The Georgian organization Zarebi and the Serbian Philanthropy offer services in Georgia and in Serbia, but also in neighboring countries, such as Iran, Turkey, Bosnia-Herzegovina, Montenegro, and Croatia, respectively. Finally, there are organizations such as the IOCC, OrtAid, and Solidarity that have adopted a global scope and international outreach. They fund, coordinate, and/or provide humanitarian assistance worldwide in diverse regions and continents that are not usually served by most other Orthodox diakonia organizations, such as Africa and Asia, but that are covered by many secular and other Christian or religious humanitarian organizations.

The majority of Orthodox diakonia organizations have been both established in, and work in, countries and regions where there is a great humanitarian need. Most surveyed organizations tend to be based in and offer services in areas where Orthodoxy is the historically dominant faith among the local populations (such as in South East Europe, the Russian Federation, and the former Soviet Republics), with the exception of some historic organizations operating in Africa and South East Asia. Furthermore, most of these organizations have limited financial/human resources and infrastructure, which restricts them to helping primarily populations in their own country of operation without extending their services to other countries or regions. The combination of limited financial and other resources (human, technical expertise, etc.) and the great need for humanitarian aid in the areas in which these organizations are based are key factors for the national and regional orientation of their work and the relative absence of humanitarian work on an international scale (with the exception of OrtAid, Solidarity and the IOCC). This issue points to the question of whether faith could also play a role in the decision-making process of selecting which populations and communities in need will be assisted. The IOCC and OrtAid seem to benefit, not only from material resources (financial and human), but also from technical expertise and an organizational infrastructure that gives them the capacity to fund, coordinate or provide services worldwide in many and diverse areas where there is a need.

When looking at the age of the organizations (when they were founded) there is a correlation between the geographic location of some organizations and the date when they were established. Many organizations in the Russian Federation, in the former Soviet Republics and in South East Europe were created in the 1990s after the collapse of many Communist regimes. These historic events gave more opportunities for a stronger public social involvement of national Orthodox Churches in their respective countries. The oldest organizations are St. Georges Hospital University Medical Centre in Lebanon, BLESS in Egypt, and DICAC in Ethiopia. These organizations have a long history and an established presence in the Middle East and in Africa as they were founded as early as 1878, 1962, and 1972 respectively. The newest organizations in the survey are the Alexandrian Lighthouse in South Africa (affiliated with the Orthodox Arch. of Johannesburg and Pretoria), the Social Centre Agapis (affiliated with the Orthodox Church in Moldova), and FILANTROPIA (the Federation of Romanian Orthodox Church Related NGOs) founded in 2005, 2004, and 2007 respectively.

More than half of the organizations are small to medium size in terms of number of employed staff, ranging between 5 and 20 paid staff, with an average of 7 paid employees. The largest organizations in the survey, which seem to employ a paid staff of approximately 400–500 people, are also the oldest and most established (being in the field for over 35 to 40 years or even for 100 years), notably the case of the 100 year old St. Georges Hospital (with a total staff of 1,050 people), followed by BLESS and DICAC. The IOCC and the Philanthropic Society of the Orthodox Church (PSOC) in India, follow with a worldwide staff of approximately 110–120 people. Of these five large organizations, only the IOCC (given its international work) has staff spread out worldwide, while the other four seem to use primarily local staff given their national focus.

Financial Support, Cooperation and Partnerships

Funding is critical for the survival and operation of a humanitarian organization and has a direct impact on the geographic coverage, service provision, and staffing capacity of an organization. It includes primarily funds in the form of grants from local, national, regional and/or international secular and/or faith-based bodies and governments, individual donations and corporate sponsorships. It also includes other forms of support, such as tax exemptions, gifts in kind, free equipment and materials and free technical support, training, and staffing, including volunteers. Many Orthodox organizations and Churches received financial support for their social work and various diakonia programs from ecumenical bodies, especially in the 1990s.

Most organizations depend on volunteers in different areas of their work. The PSOC, BLESS and the IOCC have an extensive network of volunteers: approximately 200, 600, and 800 people respectively. Other organizations provided figures for volunteers ranging between 1 to 10 people, with an average of approximately 5 unpaid staff. Volunteers usually offer their support in various ways. For example, in the case of the IOCC, volunteers work on the actual programs and/or in fundraising and governance (as board members), etc.

Slightly over half of the surveyed organizations receive some form of international support, which means that some more than others have experience in working with funding bodies and partner organizations abroad on an ongoing or project basis. These include: (i) church based organizations such as national (Orthodox and non-Orthodox) churches (Finnish, Swedish, and Norwegian Church, Orthodox Archdioceses, Swiss Interchurch Aid, etc.), local parishes, Christian agencies (Caritas, Catholic Relief Services, etc.) and missionary societies (Church Mission Society UK, etc.); (ii) ecumenical organizations and consortiums: WCC, ACT (ACT Development and ACT International), APRODEV, Church World Service, etc; (iii) international organizations and alliances/networks: UN affiliated organizations (UNFPA, UNAIDS, etc.), IOM, etc; (iv) government structures and agencies: national (USAID, Hellenic Aid, national and foreign ministries, etc.) and international bodies (European Commission, World Bank); (v) individual donations: contributions from local populations and Diaspora communities (Armenian, Greek, Serbian diasporas, etc.), fundraising events.

There are very few small organizations that offer humanitarian assistance single-handedly without any assistance from, or partnership with, another national or international entity. Most organizations (regardless of their age) operate within a somewhat established network of cooperation and partnerships. This suggests the existence of a broad, but sometimes relatively unstructured network of Orthodox humanitarian organizations. As is the case of funding, the majority of surveyed organizations have formed collaboration schemes and partnerships and some are members of larger consortiums at various levels, including national, regional and/or international, with both secular and/or church-based organizations. International, regional and national development agencies, government agencies, NGOs, universities, and church organizations are mentioned as frequent cooperation partners on an ongoing or project basis. These different forms of cooperation have been put in place for funding, coordination, program implementation, and service provision purposes. For example, the Department of External Church Relations of the Moscow Patriarchate (DECR) is a leading organization in several partnerships and consortiums; it is a working/programmatic partner of the IOCC and a member of the Executive Committee of ACT International.

In some cases regional or other special interest networks of organizations, rather than specifically Orthodox partnerships/alliances, have been formed. For example, the BCSDN is a network of 12 civil society and ecumenical organizations from 8 South East European countries and territories with the aim of empowering civil society through the strengthening of civil society actors and sharing and developing local practices.

Challenges

Organizations face various levels of inter-related difficulties and obstacles during the course of their humanitarian work. The lack of adequate and sustainable funding at a time of an economic crisis and decreasing resources worldwide is by far the greatest difficulty that most organizations face today. Lack of funds usually means insufficient materials and equipment, but also in insufficient human resources or poorly qualified or trained staff, thus lack of expertise in the planning, management, and implementation of the humanitarian or social work offered. This has an impact on service provision for the short term and on the implementation of programs for the medium and long term. This difficulty seems to have implications, not only in the implementation of services and programs, but also in the ability to apply for and secure long-term funding (for ex. accessing funding available from the European Union or from international organizations), which can help the long-term sustainability of these organizations. In some cases, organizations also mention poor management and lack of planning and coordination among local diaconal organizations, social structures of churches, and church related NGOs in the implementation of humanitarian assistance and social services is. This issue relates back to funding as it is a criterion for securing sustainable funding from international agencies and governments.

Beyond the lack of financial, material and human resources, many Orthodox diakonia organizations have to deal with adverse economic, social, political, cultural and religious conditions in the regions where they work. Political instability, corruption, conflict and violence are severe obstacles to the work of any humanitarian NGO, as are inadequate legal frameworks and insufficient infrastructures (transportation networks, health and education systems, etc.). Additionally, extreme poverty, unemployment, illiteracy, the spread of HIV/AIDS epidemic and Islamic or other forms of religious extremism are additional challenges.

CONCLUDING REMARKS

Over the past 20 years Orthodox diakonia has gone through sweeping historic developments. The fall of Communism created new socio-economic opportunities and challenges. National Orthodox Churches in many Central and Eastern European and Balkan countries and in the former Soviet Republics were faced with the opportunity of revitalization and greater social engagement in the public domain. But along with this opportunity came a great challenge: how to alleviate poverty and other urgent socio-economic problems by offering social welfare and humanitarian relief with minimal financial, material and human resources.

Most of the Orthodox diakonia organizations were established in Central and Eastern Europe, the Balkans, and the former Soviet Republics in the 1990s. They started as charitable and philanthropic entities offering social services and emergency relief locally and nationally. During their course of work many organizations evolved into structures that provided a more sustainable form of aid, thus venturing into community development and capacity building programs, thus making material and community building claims in solving social problems. The IOCC was founded in order to do exactly that, thus responding to pressing human needs, but in an internationally coordinated effort that superseded territorially rooted Orthodox diakonia initiatives that are linked to a nation-state. The aspiration by increasingly more Orthodox Churches and organizations to shift their social action from local and national philanthropy towards sustainable community development alongside the ongoing work by governments and international NGOs (both religious and secular) is a noteworthy development in the Orthodox world. In this effort, most surveyed organizations indicated that they aspire to work more closely with partner organizations in order to coordinate initiatives and programs efficiently, especially during times of humanitarian crises, when time and resources are critical and a quick humanitarian response is vital.

There is a need for Orthodox diakonia organizations to be able to work together not only with one another, but also in partnership with other RNGOs in an ecumenical and inter-religious spirit and in cooperation with secular NGOs. If Orthodox NGOs responded positively to this challenge this would also indicate a will to adopt a vision of diakonia and solidarity that is less territorially rooted and more ecumenical in spirit. This would also be a factor in determining if and how, Orthodoxy, through social action, can become even more global, or a "de-territorialized" or transnational religion.

NOTES

1. This work is based on research commissioned by the International Orthodox Christian Charities (IOCC) that was conducted in 2008 and 2009. Parts of this chapter were reworked from the "Orthodox Diakonia Worldwide: An Initial Assessment" report (May 2009), used with permission of the IOCC.
2. Religious non-governmental organizations (RNGOs) and faith-based organizations (FBOs) are used interchangeably here to designate voluntary non-profit organizations that define themselves in religious/faith-based terms and which are dedicated to social activism and the public good at a national and international level (see Berger 2003). On the issue of terminology and definition of NGOs and FBOs see also Ferris 2005.

3. http://www.svf.uib.no/sfu/ngo.
4. The 1978 international conference on "An Orthodox Approach to Diaconia" at the Orthodox Academy of Crete that distinguished between "*micro-diakonia*" at the individual and community/local level (offering charitable assistance to individuals and small groups in need) and "*macro-diakonia*," involving a broader commitment to solidarity, social justice, liberation and salvation ("An Orthodox Approach to Diaconia" 1978: 24–25).

REFERENCES

Anastasios, Archbishop of Tirana, Durres and All Albania. 2003. *Facing the World: Orthodox Christian Essays on Global Concerns.* Crestwood, NY: St. Vladimir's Seminary Press.

Ashanin, Charles B. 2006. *Essays on Orthodox Christianity and Church History,* Rollinsford, NH: Orthodox Research Institute.

Belopopsky, Alexander. 2003. Orthodoxy and Social Witness. Unpublished text presented in the "Orthodoxy and Social Witness" conference organized by the Institute for Orthodox Christian Studies. Cambridge, United Kingdom.

Berger, Julia. 2003. Religious Non-governmental Organizations: An Exploratory Analysis. *Voluntas: International Journal of Voluntary and Non-Profit Organizations* 14(1):15–40.

Clarke, Gerard. 2006. Faith Matters: Faith-Based Organizations, Civil Society and International Development. *Journal of International Development* 18(6): 835–848.

Constantelos, Demetrios. 2004. *Origins of Christian Orthodox Diakonia: Christian Orthodox Philanthropy in Church History.* Paper presented at the conference on the Social Witness and Service of Orthodox Churches, April 30–May 5, 2004, The Lay Academy in the New Valamo monastery in Finland.

Ferris, Elizabeth. 2005. Faith-Based and Secular Humanitarian Organizations. *International Review of the Red Cross* 87(858): 311–325.

Florovsky, George. 1950–1951. The Social Problem in Eastern Orthodox Church. *Journal of Religious Thought* VIII (1) (Autumn/Winter): 41–51.

Hjelm, Titus. 2009. Religion and Social Problems: A New Theoretical Perspective. In *The Oxford Handbook of the Sociology of Religion*, edited by Peter Clarke. 924–941. Oxford: Oxford University Press.

Meyendorff, John. 1979. The Christian Gospel and Social Responsibility: The Eastern Orthodox Tradition in History. In *Continuity and Discontinuity in Church History: Studies in the History of Christian Thought*, vol. 9, edited by Forrester Church and Timothy George. Leiden: E. J. Brill.

Orthodox Academy of Crete. 1978. *An Orthodox Approach to Diaconia.* Consultation Report. November 20–25. Crete, Greece.

Roudometof, Victor, Agadjanian, Alexander, and Pankhurst, Jerry (eds). 2005. *Eastern Orthodoxy in a Global Age.* Walnut Creek, CA: Altamira Press.

Stathopoulos, Petros. 1996. *Koinoniki Pronoia. Mia Geniki Theorisi* [Social Welfare. A General Overview]. Athens, Greece: Ekdoseis Ellin.

7 Religion and Social Capital Research in South Africa

Mapping an Agenda in Progress

Ignatius Swart

At the end of 2003 the National Research Foundation (NRF) of South Africa awarded a grant of more than a half million rand to researchers in the Unit for Religion and Development Research (URDR) at the University of Stellenbosch to conduct a research project under the working title, "Developing a Praxis for Mobilizing Faith-Based Organizations for Social Capital and Development in the Western Cape" (short title: "FBOs, Social Capital and Development").[1] Awarded in the NRF focus area of "Sustainable Livelihoods: The Eradication of Poverty," this project opted from the conception stages for the concept of "social capital" to build a perspective on the social development role of faith-based organizations (FBOs)—the Christian churches but also broader and more generic expressions of religiously inspired non-governmental organization and practice[2]—in post-apartheid South African society.

The research project chose to apply the concept of social capital alongside the concept of social development in theorizing and question formulation. Focusing on the "the extent to which existing and new networks of trust, cooperation and care (in short the social capital) within and between communities can be mobilized for strategic action" (Swart 2004, 6), the project formulated the following hypothesis:

> In South Africa a number of indicators . . . suggest that FBOs may be regarded as one of the most important bearers of social capital at the community level . . . Potentially, therefore, they could also play a significant role in the social development challenge in South Africa . . . [T]his theoretical exploration will in an all-important sense be utilised by project participants to inform existing FBO social praxis and build and strengthen the sector's strategic capacity for mediating meaningful social development. (Swart 2004, 6)

This chapter marks an attempt to map the most important elements of the thematic and conceptual progress that has been achieved through the project on "FBOs, Social Capital and Development," to the extent that it has spurred on an ongoing research agenda in the thematic field of religion and social capital on the part of researchers from the initial URDR circle (Wepener et al. 2010). In particular, the following discussion identifies distinctive thematic elements that highlight the conceptual progress and reflect the topical and policy relevance of the research focus within both the general and specific social contexts in which it has been undertaken: South Africa and its province of the Western Cape.[3]

TOPICAL AND POLICY RELEVANCE OF THE RESEARCH FOCUS

Four angles from which the topic of social capital has been approached in the project reflections are discussed below. These highlight the topical and policy relevance of the research focus and develop a contextually relevant argumentation.

Firstly, national surveys seem to indicate (HSRC 2000; IJR 2008) that in present-day South African society churches and other religious institutions were not only very well represented in terms of membership and demographic spread (Hendriks 2006; Hendriks et al. 2004; Hendriks and Erasmus 2003) but they were also by far outscoring institutions from government, civil society, and business in terms of public confidence and credibility. Taken together these facts or claims could well be used to promote an argument about the strength of churches and the religious sector in general in South African society, to the extent that they could be regarded as most strategic in contributing to the challenge of moral regeneration and reaching the South African population at large (Erasmus and Mans 2005, 141–142; Hendriks et al. 2004: 382; URDR 2003, 7–8; 2004a, 4–5; 2004b, 4–5).

Secondly, the research has paid attention to the public claims of prominent actors in the post-apartheid religious scene, such as the National Religious Association for Social Development (NRASD), the Ecumenical Foundation of Southern Africa (EFSA) and the National Religious Leaders' Forum (NRLF). The analysis has involved a critical deliberation of two lines of argumentation promoted by these actors. On the one hand, there is dicussion about the extensiveness of religious social welfare networks in the country, their capacity to reach out and serve the people most in need, and the value-laden nature of their social programs. On the other hand, there is reflection on the various positive responses that this insight has evoked from representatives of government and the state, who have affirmed the importance of churches and other religious organizations as strategic partners in the field of social development (Hendriks et al. 2004, 382; Swart

2005a, b; URDR 2003, 7–8; 2004a, 4–5; b, 4–5; c, 4–5; cf. Koegelenberg 2001; Louw and Koegelenberg 2003).

Thirdly, the research has identified a new rise to prominence of a strategy of social capital formation in social development policy discourse in post-apartheid South Africa (Eigelaar-Meets et al. 2010; Swart 2006). The research project was initiated at a time during which the Western Cape Provincial Government formally adopted a strategy of social capital formation as part of its eightfold development vision known as "iKapa Elihlumayo" or "Growing Cape" (Eigelaar-Meets et al. 2010; PGWC 2005). Researchers in the project have been in the advantaged position to particularly draw on two sources from this province's social capital formation initiative to develop a contextually and conceptually relevant perspective: the draft document known as the "Social Capital Formation Document" (Department 2005) and "The Western Cape Social Capital Formation Strategy with Emphasis on Youth" (PGWC 2005). In essence, an exploration of these documents made it clear that a strategy of social capital formation was newly promoted by this provincial government as an important tool for public sector intervention to meet the challenge of social exclusion and provide disadvantaged communities with access to networks of information, resources and opportunities (Department 2005, 12, 22; PGWC 2005, 8–12). What attracted special attention in the initial reflections on the significance of this documentation was their use of a kind of language that, at least in the South African context, has been associated with the distinctive interests and strengths of religious actors such as the churches. In this regard, more specifically, the aforementioned documentation identified a kind of strategic action that would revive the traditional values of "ubuntu" and "neighborly love." In other words, values (or norms) that in turn could be seen as foundational to meeting the social capital goals of social cohesion, relationships of care and support, social trust and inclusion (Department 2005; Eigelaar-Meets et al. 2010; PGWC 2005; Swart 2006, 357, 349–352).

Finally, the project has identified an increasing interest shown in the role of churches and other religiously inspired organizations in the international academic debate about the relationship between social capital and development. Accordingly a proliferating corpus of literature has been identified on the subject matter (Swart 2006, 348, 370–372; Burger and Van der Watt 2010) with strong empirically-founded arguments about the strategic role that faith traditions and their associated organizations—such as churches—are playing in mobilizing the kinds of social capital that lead to communal actions of collective social outreach and caring. In a nutshell, it has been concluded that in this corpus of literature these traditions and their organizations not only represent a necessary source of the social capital values of co-operation, social connectedness, and trust that are required, but in some instances could also constitute the single most important factor of social capital formation and activity in certain communities (Swart 2006, 347–348).

A DERIVED PERSPECTIVE ON THE
CONTRIBUTION OF RELIGIOUS AGENCIES

The discussion so far suggests a valuable framework for a deeper, contextual scholarly engagement with the notion of social capital and its relation to the phenomenon of organized religion in South African society. As such, however, an important critical angle that has been taken in the project towards especially appreciating the aforementioned Western Cape Provincial Government's "Social Capital Formation Document," is the recognition of this document's limited perspective of the actors depended on to execute the social capital formation strategy. By appearing in essence to be a strategy firstly for a specific governmental actor, and secondly one for social workers and social development workers (Department of Social Services and Poverty Alleviation 2005, 23–35; Swart 2006, 351–353), the critical question asked was what possible role there could be for other actors in the envisaged social capital formation strategy. Most specifically, it has been argued that this question could be seen as particularly relevant when one considers the strategic challenge captured by the social capital formation notions of "relationships" and "values" in the document.

> Whilst one can fully concur with the document that there is a fundamental enabling role for government to play in the social capital formation process, one in which social workers and social development workers also have a very important facilitating role to play, it at the same time also seems very doubtful that these actors could be primarily responsible for mediating the deeper processes of relational and value formation that are asked for. (Swart 2006, 353)

This argument about "relations" and "values" has become an important ground to criticize the social capital formation documentation's lack of any explicit reference to actors from the religious sector in its perspective on agency. It could be argued that churches and other religiously inspired actors have a rightful place in a strategy of social capital formation, which should on the basis of perceived strengths naturally entail a consideration of their contribution or potential contribution to the relational and value foundations of the kind of social capital formation strategy asked for in this particular case. A perspective should be developed where the focus is on connections that are fostered through activities of local churches, and the levels of trust towards which they might be contributing to as a basis for meaningful social capital formation and development activity (Swart 2006, 353–354).

Steps have also been made towards integrating religious actors into the social capital-building framework. As pointed out most pertinently in a contribution by a team of three authors who were (somewhat ironically) directly involved in the initiation of the Western Cape government's social capital formation strategy, relations and values could (together with a third key element in the social capital framework, namely "social trust") be considered as belonging to the special features of organizations in the religious sector (Eigelaar-Meets et al. 2010, 53–56). For them this constituted an established given, as evident not only from what they saw to be a common perception in South African society, but also from the social survey and other research results already referred to in this chapter. In South African society, they hold:

> Given the standing that the religious sector has in society and the high levels of trust that society has in the religious sector, the sector is clearly an indispensable partner in social capital formation. Communities associate the religious sector with that which is morally good and wholesome, as torchbearers for the common good of society, especially for the vulnerable. It is also this association that leaves the religious sector with an opportunity to promulgate values supporting social capital formation. (Eigelaar-Meets et al. 2010, 54)

The preceding statement led the above-mentioned authors to formulate a thesis about the opportunity and challenge that the Western Cape's social capital formation strategy presents to the religious sector. Based on their inherent features, religiously inspired organizations in this province have the potential, through their leadership, to make a significant contribution to social transformation. To this extent their possible contribution could be directly associated with the possibility to foster "bridging" and "linking" social capital across ethnic, cultural and socio-economic divides. This implies that through the anticipated interaction between religiously inspired organizations from different communities, barriers to inclusion (such as social prejudice) could be broken down and, in turn, create opportunities for inclusive participation in newly founded networks (Eigelaar-Meets et al. 2010, 53–55).

DEMOGRAPHIC AND SOCIO-EMPIRICAL RESEARCH ON CHURCHES

A prominent feature of the research project has been the undertaking of demographic and socio-empirical research that, in the context of the

Western Cape province's social capital formation strategic outline, has contributed much towards the development of a more sophisticated and empirically founded perspective particular on churches as a stock of social capital in this province. The project used various social research methods— including GPS (Global Positioning System) and GIS (Geographical Information System) analysis, questionnaire surveys, structured interviews, and needs analyses (see Hendriks et al. 2004, 384–393; Swart 2005b; 2006, 354–367), and found that churches in particular represent a considerable resource for a social capital formation strategy in Western Cape communities (Swart 2005b, 328–329; 2006, 346–378). Figures 7.1 and 7.2a are examples of how the results provided significant visual evidence of the churches' comparative advantage over other institutions in the researched communities. Having presented itself as a consistent feature of the research results, the dense and widespread location of churches shown by the GPS and GIS work strongly supported the thesis about churches' potential and actual reach at the local community level.[4]

In more overt social capital language, the dense and widespread location of churches (shown in Figures 7.1 and 7.2a) in an important way suggests that this institution could be a significant constituting source of social capital networks through which the poor and deprived in particular could be reached and the collective problems in the communities be addressed by the local citizens themselves.[5] To this extent, for example as illustrated by a comparison of Figures 7.2a and 7.2b, the results have shown how churches are especially well represented in those areas of the communities where people were suffering most under particular social problems (Swart 2005b, 328–329; 2006, 355–357, 367–368; cf. Erasmus and Mans 2005; URDR 2003, 2004a; b; c).

Furthermore, it is to the notion of social trust, more than any other notion of social capital, that various aspects of the results from the above-mentioned forms of social research have been related explicitly. For example, by using the collective sample of mapped results from the survey and interview data in Figures 7.1, 7.2a and 7.2b, 7.3, 7.4, 7.5a and 7.5b as one concrete illustration, it has been argued that the churches command the respect and appreciation of many people in local communities. For those people churches constitute an indispensable social actor that should be involved in the social problems of their community and intervene in those areas where services are needed most crucially. Accordingly, those people also do not bear out the view that the churches do not care for the poor and, in fact, on the basis of the visual[6] and other research results, present the churches in their communities with a strong mandate to engage in strategic activities of social capital formation, to build relationships of cooperation between themselves as well as with government and the NGO sector (Swart 2006, 368; cf. 357–365; Erasmus and Mans 2005, 153–154).

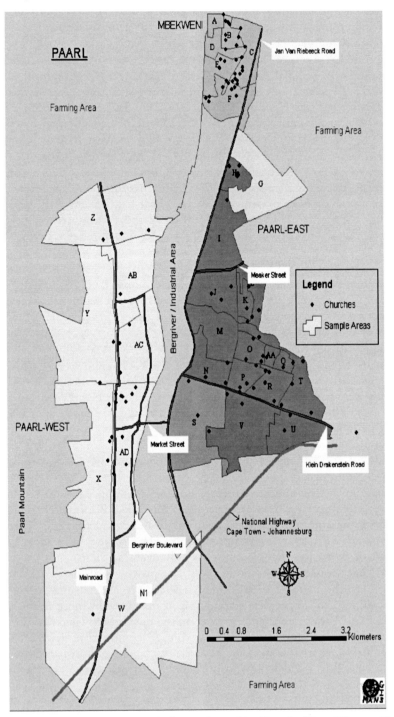

Figure 7.1 Orientation map and places of worship (churches) in a Western Cape community: the town of Paarl.

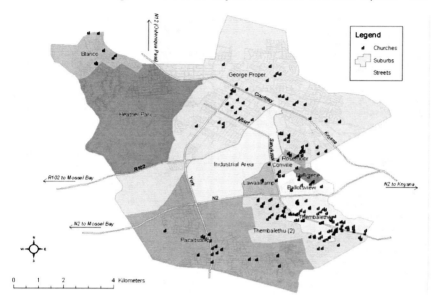

Figure 7.2a Orientation map and places of worship (churches) in a Western Cape community: the city of George.

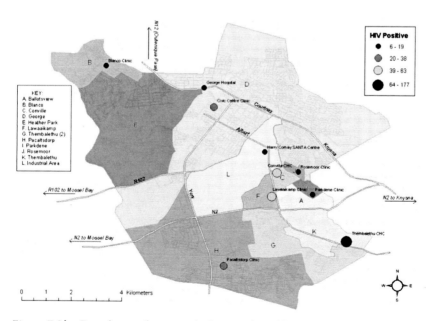

Figure 7.2b Prevalence of one particular social problem in a Western Cape community: HIV and Aids in the city of George.

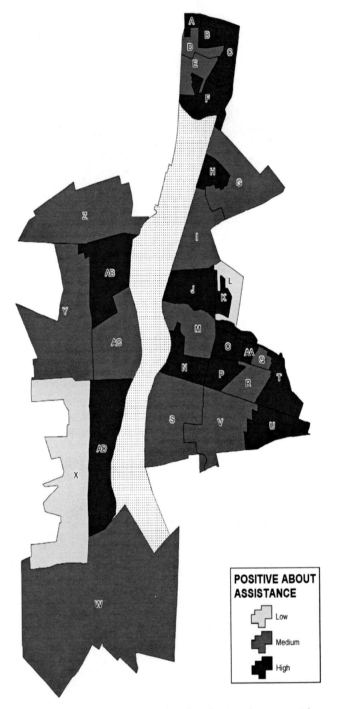

Figure 7.3 People's perceptions about the church's involvement with a particular social problem in a Western Cape community: sexual and violent crime in the town of Paarl.

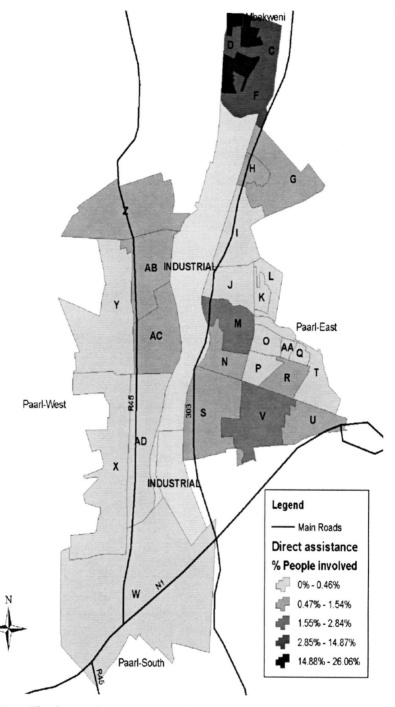

Figure 7.4 The degree of assistance to victims of a particular social problem in a Western Cape community through direct involvement: sexual violence and crime in the town of Paarl.

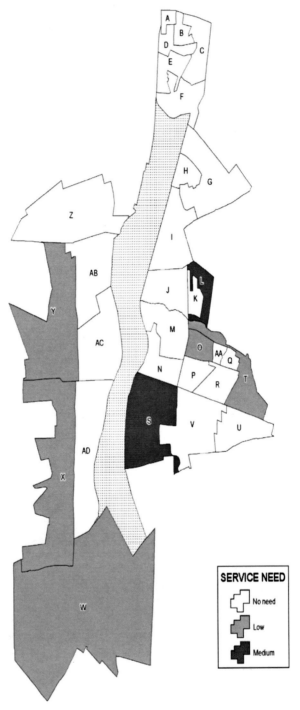

Figure 7.5a   Areas of high service need concerning a particular social problem in a Western Cape community: sexual and violent crime in the town of Paarl.

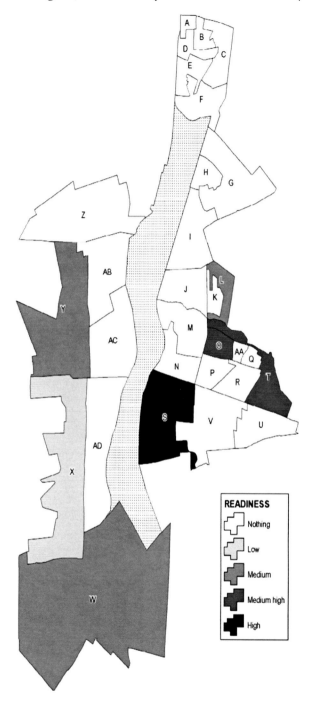

Figure 7.5b   Areas ready for church intervention with regard to a particular social problem in a Western Cape community: sexual and violent crime in the town of Paarl.

As an important further component of the empirical work and manifestation of the notion of social trust, Figures 7.6a, 7.6b, and 7.6c are examples of how the outstanding profile of the church sector can be illustrated by the results of the needs analyses that were undertaken. Because the research was conducted in communities characterized by extreme poverty and deprivation, this aspect of the research results has made it apparent that the religious sector far outscores those sectors that can be associated with the other plotted needs. In this sense therefore, the three profiles below (similar to numerous others that were drawn up) illustrate the extent to which the churches in the particular areas or communities present a significant channel of opportunity for policy-makers and other strategists to enter the respective communities and reach the local people (Swart 2006, 366–367, 369; cf. Erasmus et al. 2005; URDR 2004a; b; c).

Finally, in terms of an interpretation that also sought to move beyond the notion of social trust to more tangible manifestations of social capital formation and community action, the research results suggested that churches in the researched communities were acting as generators of voluntary outreach, caring initiatives and different modes of social service across a spectrum of social needs. In particular, the results suggested that such concrete actions were more extensive and successful in areas where people

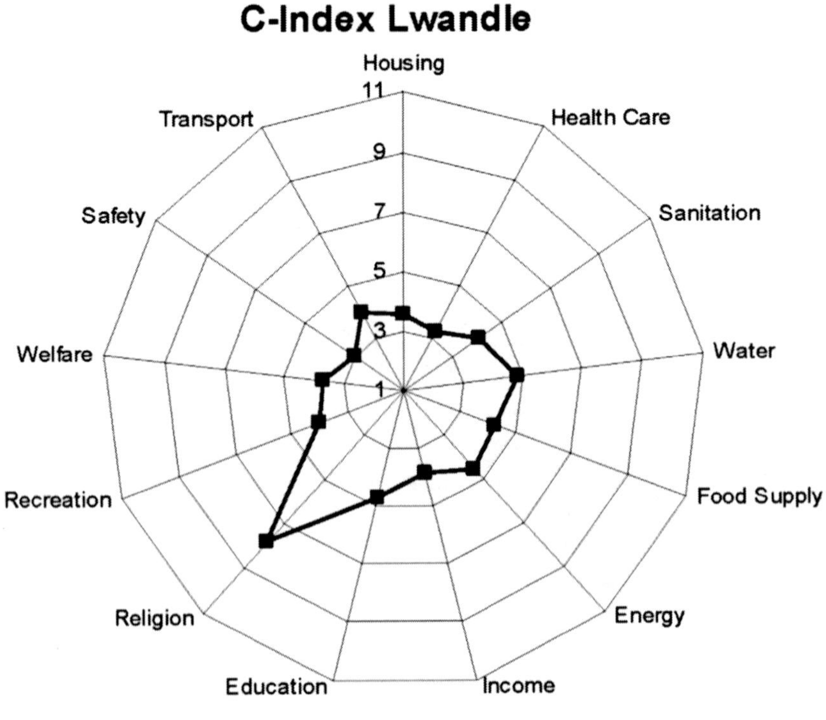

Figure 7.6a Community profile (C-Index) of needs satisfaction in a Western Cape community: Lwandle in the Helderberg Basin.

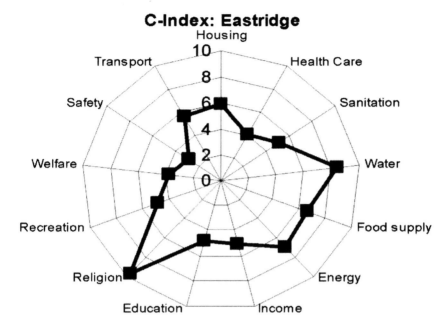

Figure 7.6b   Community profile (C-Index) of needs satisfaction in a Western Cape community: Lwandle in the Helderberg Basin.

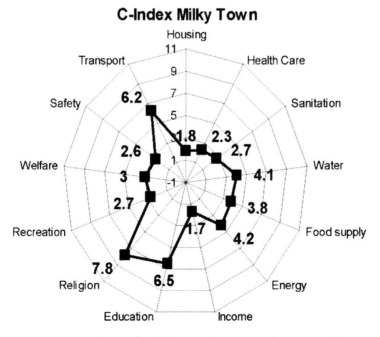

Figure 7.6c   Community profile (C-Index) of needs satisfaction in a Western Cape community: Milky Town in Paarl.

are more exposed to the various social problems, than in areas where the problems are less prevalent[7] (Swart 2006, 368–369; cf. 357–367; Hendriks et al. 2004, 388–393; URDR 2003, 14, 53–54).

A MORE AMBIVALENT AND CRITICAL PERSPECTIVE

Despite the considerable appreciation that could be expressed for the potential and actual role of the religious sector in a strategy of social capital formation, the results and conceptual insights that emanated from the overall research have by no means led to a mere celebration of this role. Thus, as an extension of both the aforementioned derived perspective and the demographic and socio-empirical research, a strong statement has been made about the political implications of the church and religious sector at large playing a more critical role according to the demands for so-called "bridging" and "linking" social capital identified in the Western Cape social capital formation strategy but also in the general South African context.

An important argument promoted in the research was that the religious sector was still to a large degree faced by the challenge to scale up their focus and activities to the sphere of the political in order for them to play their anticipated meaningful role in making a real difference to the lives of poor people and communities in South African society. Thus, while not per se making a statement against the concern with networks and partnerships that stands so central in the discussions about social capital, one of the earlier studies in the project strongly questioned the theoretical and ethical depth of a religious social development debate preoccupied with the notions of networks and partnership. In this case analysing and reflecting on a public religious social development debate that has come into existence in the post-apartheid dispensation by and large due to the efforts of those actors already mentioned in this chapter (the NRASD, EFSA, and NRLF), the argument was put forward as follows:

> [T]he crucial matter is what precedes the debate about, or concern with, partnerships. Is such a debate or concern part of a broader critical discussion that challenges the very practice of social partnerships and networks on the level of ideological orientation, ethics and politics? Does such a debate or concern emanate from deeper contextual analysis, from critical enquiry about the nature and causes of poverty, first of all and, therefore, from more profound theoretical consideration about the paradigmatic changes that are required in terms of thinking and action in order to address the causes of poverty sufficiently? Not least in as far as the discussion would be motivated by and informed by religious considerations, what are the ethical demands put before the various actors that are envisaged for or are already engaged in the partnership networks? Or to go one step further, what notions of an alternative

society inform the concern with partnerships and networks? (Swart 2005a, 32)

Along similar lines of argumentation, Eigelaar-Meets, Gomulia, and Almo (2010) have suggested that the religious sector needs to engage in public policy processes, actively take part in the debate about development and mobilize action on the ground. Yet, at the same time they stress the fact that a partnership relation with the state held the real danger of disenabling the religious sector to play its critical role in speaking out against social injustice and influence policies affecting the poor and vulnerable (cf. Swart 2005a). This furthermore implies that the religious sector would find its role reduced to the familiar one of being a mere provider of social services at grassroots level with little scope beyond this function (Eigelaar-Meets et al. 2010, 55).

What is implied in the critical argument so far was to a large extent confirmed by the socio-empirical results touched upon in the previous section. While these results made it clear that a relatively large number of churches in the various communities have their own social service ministries that often constitute part of networks and cooperative endeavors with other religiously inspired organizations, contributors to the project also emphasized that the results showed little evidence that those networks and partnerships of collective action have proceeded beyond conventional activities of providing charity and immediate relief (Swart 2006, 364–365, 369; cf. Hendriks et al. 2004, 392–393; URDR 2003, 22). From the point of view of the Western Cape "Social Capital Formation Document," it became clear that the churches' current mode of involvement in the researched areas still seemed to be a far cry from the development approach and outcomes that this document set out as a fundamental characteristic of the social capital networks within its framework of understanding (Swart 2006, 369).

In addition, it also became clear on the basis of the socio-empirical results that a significant "grey area" remained with regard to the actual participation of the churches in addressing the identified problems. Thus the results suggested that no clear correlation exists between the different sets of results on local people's involvement and that of the churches themselves. This inconsistency suggested that while the local churches might in many instances function as the source that inspires some kind of voluntary action, they function to a lesser degree as an actual source of voluntary outreach and social service, which could rather involve NGOs and other religiously inspired organizations, the family, and persons in their personal capacity with friends in the neighborhood (Erasmus and Mans 2005, 153–154; Swart 2006, 365–369; cf. Erasmus et al. 2006, 306–307).

It follows from the above results that no evidence could therefore be found that the churches in the researched communities could be associated with the more radical politicized strategic agenda set out in the "Social Capital Formation Document". Particularly in those communities where historic inequalities have by and large been maintained, there was no evidence that the churches were in any way involved in strategic activities of social capital formation aimed at the building of relationships across the divides and the kinds of active redress spelled out in the document. At best, where churches might actually be involved, their activities of charity and relief assumed some kind of superficial social capital formation (Swart 2006, 370).

REINFORCING A POSITIVE STATEMENT THROUGH ADDITIONAL CASE STUDY RESULTS

Other participants in the research, although not directly discussing the Western Cape province's social capital formation initiative, have analyzed the religious sector's potential to contribute to a kind of social capital—that is, "bridging social capital"—that could assist in overcoming current racial and class divides and promote social inclusion (Burger and Van der Watt 2010).

These scholars similarly relied upon sources that have been used by other participants in the project to promote their argument. This entailed using the mentioned survey results on social trust in South African society and empirically based international studies in the field of religion and social capital to present an argument on churches and other religiously inspired organizations' potential and actual contribution to bridging social capital formation (Burger and Van der Watt 2010, 394–396). In what could be understood as a positive background statement to both the South African and international findings, the two authors made use of a particular corpus of sociological material to write that:

> Bridging ties are critical for providing the poor with access to a larger and more complex social network, which could give individuals more opportunities, and better assistance and advice.
>
> Social theorists such as Comte, Durkheim and Sorokin have recognised that religion has the potential to fulfil and important role in communities plagued by fragmentation and strife. Comte and Durkheim both emphasise the unifying effect of religion. According to Comte, religion can enable individuals to overcome their selfish tendencies and transcend themselves. Similarly, Durkheim sees religion as "an eminently collective thing" that "binds men (sic) together." More recently, in Sorokin"s studies of social stratification and mobility, the church is depicted as an institution that can enable vertical social movement towards different strata and positions. (Burger and Van der Watt 2010, 394)

In order to provide empirical backing for these theoretical arguments, the authors considered five cases where non-governmental organizations

(NGOs) from different Christian interdenominational groups in various parts of the country (including the Western Cape) have in a formal, organized and structured way started to use their respective networks to act as brokers for and channel resources to poor and unemployed people (Burger and Van der Watt 2010, 395–396).

In conclusion, the authors emphasize that the evidence provided by the five examples by no means fulfilled the need for more extensive empirical research on the utilization and effectiveness of religiously inspired social capital in the South African context, since those examples predominantly involved the endeavors of middle-class religious groups to expand their resource networks to include people in need. Yet the evidence at the same time provided sufficient proof that existing faith-based social capital was in fact making a meaningful if not indispensable contribution towards economic inclusion in South African society, insofar as poor and unemployed people were benefiting in tangible ways from the new-found opportunities that such capital was creating. They concluded that:

> While there may be no systematic large-scale studies surveying the efforts of religious groups in channelling resources to the poor and promoting social integration, the above cases suggest that many religious groups are becoming involved in such initiatives. However, with enduring high levels of poverty, unemployment and social polarisation, the need for such efforts remains vast.
>
> More empirical research is needed in this area. Specifically, it would be useful to know to what extent these religious groups, who are often from the middle-class, are effective in expanding their resource network to include the indigent. It is also critical to understand how successful these groups are in avoiding exclusion based on faith. In cases where there is exclusion based on faith—whether intentionally or due to informal word-of-mouth targeting mechanisms—these efforts to promote social cohesion may perversely increase social polarisation along another dimension. (Burger and Van der Watt 2010, 396)

RELIGIOUS RITUAL AND SOCIAL CAPITAL FORMATION

In terms of the overall focus on the social capital theme, and especially also in the light of what is indicated in the conclusion below, special mention should finally be made of a contribution in which the role of religious ritual in the generation of social capital has been more purposefully explored (Cilliers and Wepener 2007). Concentrating on the liturgical practices of local Christian congregations, the authors argue that religious ritual could be regarded as an area in which religious actors such as churches could make, and were in actual fact making, an authentic contribution to social capital formation.

On the conceptual level, besides using the familiar notions of "bonding," "bridging" and "linking" social capital to make sense of the notion of social capital formation (Cilliers and Wepener 2007, 40), an innovative addition to the conceptual framework in the project has been the authors' application of Nancy Ammerman's identification of three expressions of social capital formation. This, however, also included their definition of poverty as entailing the absence of Ammerman's identified expressions (Cilliers and Wepener 2007, 40–44), namely:

- Social capital of association, which involves the creation of a sense of belonging and relationships of trust amongst groups and in the wider society;
- Civil capital of communication and organizational skills that, in turn, is facilitated by the first expression; and
- Material infrastructure and sources, such as spaces for gatherings that, in turn, may mobilize participants to take concrete actions to address poverty, etc. (Cilliers and Wepener 2007, 41; cf. Ammerman 1999, 362–367).

While space does not allow further discussion on the authors' creative articulations of the meaning of poverty in terms of the abovementioned three understandings (Cilliers and Wepener 2007, 43–44), it is worthwhile to elaborate somewhat on the empirical component of their article. On the basis of a limited ethnographic study undertaken for the purpose of their article of two Reformed congregations from diverse socio-demographic backgrounds in a particular local setting, the authors have shown how the two congregations were both contributing in a favorable manner to all three forms of Ammerman's social capital identification. [8] This, amongst other things but to different degrees, included contribution to: spaces of hospitality to strangers; identity and group formation/cohesion; provision and sharing of meals (especially also in a context of poverty and deprivation); renewed mechanisms of collective and individual coping as well as bonding and bridging interactions within the respective local faith communities, especially through intercessory praying activities; the development of performance, participatory and oratory skills through different liturgical practices; and spaces of information sharing and symbolic action that inspire broader actions directed towards poverty alleviation in the immediate communities (Cilliers and Wepener 2007, 44–53).

It is important to finally note how the authors concluded, on the basis of their own empirical results, with a rather critical statement. According to them, the results showed that expressions of linking social capital—something which they view as a crucial fourth dimension of social capital formation in addition to, but also cross-cutting, Ammerman's identified three dimensions—were still by and large absent from the two congregations' ritual activity. For them this would relate to an ethos and mode of action that confront structures and constellations of power, and work "in collaboration with other relevant agencies towards a real transformation of society in terms of equity and justice" (Cilliers and Wepener 2007, 42). For them, as reflected in the following quote, it would be in this area that the need for ongoing research and strategic innovation could be considered the greatest:

> The discussion has made it clear that linking capital and its role regarding real transformation [is] still largely a missing dimension in the rituals. We have already made suggestions about the role that preaching can play in this respect, but the other elements of liturgy should also be enriched to attend to the linking dimensions of social capital . . . The ability to facilitate the participation and distribution of power is one of the most important skills that church leaders ministering in contexts of poverty should acquire. This kind of leadership will help to develop the liturgy as an open space, a space where silent voices are heard, where the truth in all its facets is spoken, where rich and poor are confronted by one another, and thus a space facilitating real transformation. (Cilliers and Wepener 2007, 53–54)

BUILDING ON THE EXISTING RESEARCH: AN ONGOING AGENDA

From the vantage point of the discussion in this chapter, one could confidently state that research on the subject matter of religion and social capital in the present-day South African context constitutes a worthwhile and necessary undertaking. Clearly, in terms of the conceptual and contextual exploration that has already been achieved through the completed project on "FBOs, Social Capital and Development," a strong, empirically supported argument could be put forward that religiously inspired actors, most notably churches and their associated organizations because of their demographic strength, constitute a noticeable stock of social capital in local communities that should be further researched and strengthened through participatory research initiatives.

Yet, it would also be appropriate and important to emphasize the way in which the research to date (that is, with reference to the above-mentioned project) has presented an appraisal that is at the same time critical and balanced in terms of churches and other religiously inspired organizations' limited contribution to sophisticated forms of social capital formation in the South African societal context. In terms of a perspective that could be related to the current South African policy context's demand for a development approach to the problems of poverty and social suffering, as well as interconnected but also separate debates and discourses on social capital formation, the discussion of results and findings in this chapter has highlighted to some extent the shortcomings of the researched churches and religious organizations, including their larger public constituencies.

It is these two sets of juxtaposed results and findings from the completed project that currently constitute the foundation for a newly initiated follow-up research project on the subject matter. Consisting of researchers from the completed project but also a noticeable number of new members, this project likewise falls within the NRF focus area on "Sustainable Livelihoods and the Eradication of Poverty" and can be closely associated with the focus on ritual discussed in the last section above.

Accordingly, in the newly initiated project the manner and extent to which religious rituals contribute to, or do not contribute to, social capital formation for the sake of poverty alleviation in South African communities have been chosen as the central research question[9] (Wepener et al. 2010). The aim of the research is to develop a perspective that in comparison to the previous project may still do greater justice to the actual strengths of religiously inspired actors in the area of poverty alleviation and social development[10] (Wepener et al. 2010). This appreciation certainly does not imply that the new project will not continue to be critical towards institutional religion's inability to create tangible transformative practices in order to build social capital. But it does mean that as a prolonged research endeavor that builds on the existing research output, a more informed, focused and dynamic perspective may be developed on the role of essential religious activities in social capital formation within the domain of particular local churches. And, added to this is also the promise that a more informed perspective may be developed on how elements of the inner essence of social capital formation—values and relationships of trust—are negotiated, formed and sustained within particular religious settings and activities.

ACKNOWLEDGMENTS

All maps presented as figures in this article are the intellectual property of the Unit for Religion and Development Research (URDR) at Stellenbosch University and are reprinted here with the full permission of the URDR. This material is based upon work supported by the National Research Foundation of South Africa under Grant number 65620. Any opinions, findings and conclusions or recommendations expressed in this material are those of the author and therefore the NRF does not accept any liability in regard thereto.

NOTES

1. The interdisciplinary nature of the project could indeed be regarded as one of its outstanding features, as it at various stages included scholars, students and notably also public professionals from a range of fields including

practical theology, missiology, religious studies, sociology, economics, youth work, social welfare and social work, community development and geography. Furthermore, although formally running and funded in the period 2004–2006, a number of masters and doctoral studies have continued after this formal duration as well as a book project on the project results and findings: Ignatius Swart et al. 2010. *Religion and Social Development in Post-Apartheid South Africa: Perspective for Critical Engagement.* Stellenbosch: SUN Press (Swart et al. 2010).

2. This focus on the churches, in terms of organized religious affiliation, could especially be motivated given the fact that different Christian faith groups (as determined by official census data) comprise close to 80% of the South African population (Hendriks 2005; Hendriks and Erasmus 2001). In addition, however, the project wanted to expand its horizons by also exploring a broader base of religiously inspired NGO activity affiliated to the Christian faith but also other religious traditions in South Africa.

3. This discussion constitutes a thoroughly revised version of a paper that was presented by the author at the Third International Conference of the The Social Capital Foundation (TSCF), "Perspectives on Social Capital and Social Inclusion," Malta, September 19–22, 2008.

4. In the context of the social service fields this technology has been described as a research instrument that "allows a social agency to produce meaningful, attention-grabbing maps that visually show important administrative, policy, and practice issues" (Queralt and Witte 1998, 456).

5. Through the participatory approach that was followed in the execution of the various forms of research the social problems that were prioritized by members of the communities as the areas of greatest concern were: HIV and Aids, unemployment, sexual and violent crime, and substance abuse.

6. Here the arguments could be more specifically illustrated by a comparison of the maps in Figures 7.1 and 7.3, 7.1 and 7.4, 7.2a and 7.2b, and 7.5a and 7.5b.

7. In terms of the mapped results, a comparison of Figures 7.1, 7.4, 7.5a and 7.5b here serves as an illustration.

8. The research was conducted in the local Western Cape town of Paarl and included an Afrikaans-speaking Dutch Reformed congregation and a Xhosa-speaking Uniting Reformed congregation.

9. The working title of the project has been formulated as: "Exploring the role of religious ritual in social capital formation for poverty alleviation and social development in poor South African communities" (Wepener et al. 2010, 1).

10. This specifically involves studies of congregations from the African Independent and Reformed traditions in rural parts of the Eastern Cape and the Western Cape town of Worcester (Wepener et al. 2010, 11–13; Wepener and Barnard 2010).

REFERENCES

Ammerman, Nancy. 1999. *Congregations and Community.* New Brunswick, NJ: Rutgers University Press.

Burger, Ronelle, and Van der Watt, Carina. 2010. Bridging South Africa's Deep Divides: Religious Networks as a Resource to Overcome Social and Economic Exclusion. In *Religion and Social Development in Post-Apartheid South Africa: Perspectives for Critical Engagement*, edited by Ignatius Swart et al. 391–400. Stellenbosch: SUN Press.

Cilliers, Johan, and Wepener, Cas. 2007. Ritual and the Generation of Social Capital in Contexts of Poverty: A South African Exploration. *International Journal of Practical Theology* 11(1): 39–55.

Department of Social Services and Poverty Alleviation. 2005. *Social Capital Formation Document*. Prepared for Cabinet Lekgotla, February 9–10, 2005.

Eigelaar-Meets, Ilse, Gomulia, Carolin, and Almo, Geldenhuys. 2010. An Emerging Strategy of Social Capital Formation: Opportunity and Challenge for the Religious Sector. In *Religion and Social Development in Post-Apartheid South Africa: Perspectives for Critical Engagement*, edited by I. Swart et al. 45–59. Stellenbosch: SUN Press.

Erasmus, Johannes and Mans, Gerbrand. 2005. Churches as Service Providers for Victims of Sexual and/or Violent Crimes: A Case Study from the Paarl Community. *Acta Criminologica* 18(1): 140–163.

Erasmus, Johannes, Mans, Gerbrand and Jacobs, Cindy. 2005. Transformation Africa: Pray and Work—the Role of Research. In *South African Christian Handbook 2005–2006*, edited by J. Symington. 147–165. Wellington: Tydskriftemaatskappy van die NG Kerk.

Erasmus, Johannes, Hendriks, Jurgens, and Mans, Gerbrand. 2006. Religious Research as Kingpin in the Fight against Poverty and AIDS in the Western Cape, South Africa. *Hervormde Teologiese Studies* 62(1): 293–311.

Hendriks, Jurgens, and Erasmus, Johannes. 2001. Interpreting the New Religious Landscape in Post-Apartheid South Africa. *Journal of Theology for Southern Africa* 109(March): 41–65.

Hendriks, Jurgens, and Erasmus, Johannes. 2003. Religious Affiliation in South Africa Early in the New Millennium: Markinor's World Values Survey. *Journal of Theology for Southern Africa* 117(November): 80–96.

Hendriks, Jurgens, Erasmus, Johannes, and Mans, Gerbrand. 2004. Congregations as Providers of Social Service and HIV/AIDS Care. *Dutch Reformed Theological Journal* 45(2) Supplementum: 380–402.

Hendriks, Jurgens. 2005. Religion in South Africa with Denominational Trends 1911–2001. In *South African Christian Handbook 2005–2006*, edited by J. Symington. 27–85. Wellington: Tydskriftemaatskappy van die NG Kerk.

Human Sciences Research Council (HSRC). 2000. Broken Trust, a Wake-up Call for Major Institutions. http://www.hsrc.ac.za/Media_Release-140.phtml. (Accessed February 18, 2008).

Institute for Justice and Reconciliation (IJR). 2008. South Africa: Trust in Institutions Takes a Dive, *Business Day*, January 22, 2008. http://allafrica.com/stories/200801220202.html. (Accessed February 18, 2008).

Koegelenberg, Renier. 2001. Social Development Partnerships between Religious Communities and the State: Perspectives from the National Religious Association for Social Development (NRASD). *Journal of Theology for Southern Africa* 110(July): 97–109.

Louw, Lionel and Koegelenberg, Renier. 2003. Building a New South Africa: The Building of a Caring, Democratic and Equitable Society through Partnerships between the State and the National Religious Leader's Forum (NRLF). Position paper prepared for the NRLF meeting with President Thabo Mbeki, April 29–30, 2003. A perspective from the National Religious Association for Social Development (NRASD). http://sarpn.org.za/documents/d0000557/index.php. (Accessed February 20, 2008).

Provincial Government of the Western Cape (PGWC). 2005. *The Western Cape Social Capital Formation Strategy with Emphasis on Youth*. Cape Town: PGWC.

Queralt, Magaly and Witte, Ann. 1998. A Map for You? Geographical Information Systems in the Social Services. *Social Work* 43(5): 455–469.

Swart, Ignatius. 2004. Developing a Praxis for Mobilising Faith-Based Organisations (FBOs) for Social Capital and Development in the Western Cape. National Research Foundation Grant Application 2004, Project No. NRF8467, March 13, 2003.

Swart, Ignatius. 2005a. Networks and Partnerships for Social Justice? The Pragmatic Turn in the Religious Social Development Debate in South Africa. *Religion and Theology* 12(1): 20–47.

Swart, Ignatius. 2005b. Mobilising Faith-based Organisations for Social Development through a Participatory Action Research (PAR) Process. *Maatskaplike Werk/Social Work* 41(4): 323–336.

Swart, Ignatius. 2006. Churches as a Stock of Social Capital for Promoting Social Development in Western Cape Communities. *Journal of Religion in Africa* 36 (3/4): 346–378.

Swart, Ignatius, Rocher, Hermann, Green, Sulina, and Erasmus, Johannes. 2010. Introduction. In *Religion and Social Development in Post-Apartheid South Africa: Perspectives for Critical Engagement*, edited by Ignatius Swart et al. 1–12. Stellenbosch: Sun Press.

Unit for Religion and Development Research (URDR). 2003. *George Aids Forum Research Report*. Stellenbosch: URDR.

Unit for Religion and Development Research (URDR). 2004a. *Transformation Research Project: Paarl/Wellington*. Stellenbosch: URDR.

———. 2004b. *Transformation Research Report: Helderberg Basin*. Stellenbosch: URDR.

———. 2004c. *Transformation Research Report: Mitchell's Plain*. Stellenbosch: URDR.

Wepener, Cas, Swart, Ignatius, Ter Haar Gerrie, and Barnard, Marcel. 2010. The Role of Religious Ritual in Social Capital Formation for Poverty Alleviation and Social Development: Theoretical and Methodological Points of Departure of a South African Exploration. *Religion and Theology*, 17 (2010): 61–82.

Wepener, Cas and Barnard, Marcel. 2010. Initiating Liturgical Research in an AIC. *Acta Theologica* 30(2).

8 Campaigning for Justice

Religious and Legal Activism in Challenging Illegal Immigration as a Social Problem in the U.S.

Gastón Espinosa

Very little has been published on Latino religions and social problems in the United States. This is ironic given the fact that Latino popular Catholicism, Pentecostalism, and other metaphysical traditions and social practices have often been quite literally demonized and characterized as a social problem by American society in general and Euro-American denominational or religious leaders in particular (Dolan and Hinojosa 1994, 57–58, 135, 179, 282, 306; Sandoval 1991, 32–50; 118–127). The most recent manifestation of arguing that Latinos are a social problem is the movement to criminalize and punish undocumented immigrants by defining them as "illegal aliens" and lawbreakers. This transforms the Latin American immigrants into a socially and politically subversive element in American society.

After briefly exploring key social problem theories, this chapter will examine how and why progressive Euro-American and Latino Evangelical and Catholic leaders used the Bible and Catholic social teaching to reframe the notion that undocumented immigrants were a social problem and instead argued that immigrants are children of God and fellow sojourners that Americans were commanded to welcome and care after. As a result of these views, progressive religious leaders put pressure on President George W. Bush and Congress to promote comprehensive immigration reform legislation that would have transformed the status of Latino undocumented immigrants from illegal aliens and criminals into people with legally protected civil rights and a path to U.S. citizenship. Although beyond the scope of this study, President Obama has picked up this agenda and is now promoting comprehensive immigration reform.

THEORIZING SOCIAL PROBLEMS

There are several major interpretations of what constitutes a social problem. These different interpretations and definitions are themselves socially constructed based on the values and framework of the person and community constructing them. Richard Fuller and Richard Myers argue that a "social problem is a condition which is defined by a considerable number of persons as a deviation from some social norm which they cherish" (Fuller and Myers 1941, 320). This "deviation" from a cherished social norm may help explain why some white Americans criticize Latino immigrants and other U.S. Latinos in the Southwest. Their cultural practices and perceived unwillingness to assimilate has led some to see them as a social problem that is invading and undermining Euro-American society (Schlafly 2001). This claim is based on the fear that the American society in the Southwest is in danger of losing its cherished Euro-American cultural, political, and religious ideals and values.

In his seminal work, *Outsiders*, Howard Becker challenges earlier definitions by arguing that a social problem cannot be objectively measured by impartial and trained observers. Instead,

> [S]*ocial groups create deviance by making the rules whose infraction constitutes deviance,* and by applying those rules to particular people and labeling them as outsiders. From this point of view, deviance is *not* a quality of the act the person commits, but rather a consequence of the application of others of rules and sanctions to an "offender". (Becker 1991 [1963]: 9; emphasis in original)

This definition of a social problem unmasks and deconstructs how the power elites and grassroots that follow them delegitimize social groups, cultural practices, and people in society that threaten their cherished American norms. Applied to the U.S. Latino context, undocumented immigrants and even the larger U.S. Latino community itself are defined by some Americans as a cultural, social, and political threat because they refuse to fully assimilate into Euro-American society on its own terms. This view is articulated in books by scholars such as Harvard University Professor Samuel P. Huntington (*Who Are We: Challenges to America's National Identity*), syndicated talk show host Patrick J. Buchanan (*State of Emergency: Third World Invasion and Conquest of America*), and popular grassroots activists like Paulette Poole (*Wake Up, Congress! America or Amexico?*).

Malcolm Spector and John I. Kitsuse argue that labeling is not necessarily based on objective reality or criteria but rather on a very subjective perception of what the labeling group has deemed unacceptable (Spector and Kitsuse 2001, 75–76). Similarly, Blumer argues that a "social problem does not exist unless it is recognized by the society to exist" (1971, 302). The result, as Mauss (1975) points out, is that claims about social problems, the claims-makers and their claims-making activities form a social movement in itself. This is where religious groups and actors can step into the conflict to contribute to the construction or (and I would add) deconstruction of the social problem and provide solutions that may either benefit or contribute to the continuing delegitimation of the deviant group (Hjelm 2009, 931).

This was most clearly the case for the abolitionist movement, the suffrage movement, the civil rights struggle against segregation, the 2006 debate over comprehensive immigration reform, and the conflict over Arizona Governor Jan Brewer's April 23, 2010 decision to sign an immigration law SB 1070, which seeks to identify, prosecute, and deport illegal immigrants. In many of these cases, religion and/or law were used to both suppress and liberate African Americans, women, and Latin American immigrants by challenging and in some cases transforming the religious, social, and legal underpinnings that supported the superstructure of their social and political marginalization.

Religious clergy, lay leaders, and faith-based groups and organizations have often been the primary claim makers in these types of social and political justice movements and struggles. These social reform movements (often on behalf of groups deemed socially deviant) are often "driven by religious motivations" (Hjelm 2009, 931). Many of these religious groups point out the problem, seek legislative changes, and often "aim to change perceived problematic conditions by more direct action, constructing solutions themselves" (Hjelm 2009, 931). This process was also true for comprehensive immigration reform movement.

The Latino contribution to social problems theory lies in its emphasis on law and religion as a vehicle for creating and defining social problems. In the case of Latinos, undocumented immigrants are socially marginalized, exploited, and then conveniently cast aside when they have finished providing their inexpensive labor for American society in general and small businesses in particular, because the businessmen do not have to provide for their material and social well-being by providing a healthy work environment, health care, workman's compensation, life insurance, and other social benefits that they would have to provide—due to existing laws—to U.S. citizens. Their low incomes force undocumented immigrants to pool their resources and live in overcrowded housing and communities, which only further contributes to their social marginalization and the rise of barrios and ghettos that become an eyesore to the larger Euro-American community. Poverty, unemployment, underserved schools, and peer pressure to engage in gang life, drugs and alcohol abuse, and other harmful practices put young people at risk and can in fact lead to unhealthy social behaviors and practices. Because their children often turn to gangs for protection in harsh urban contexts they are in some cases socially constructed as a criminal-prone population and social problem. This leads many Euro-Americans to use their social and political capital to construct these Spanish-speaking and underserved populations as "illegal" and "alien," even if many of their children were born in the U.S. and/or have work permits. When these attitudes are given the force of law and reinforced by scholarly books and law enforcement, it creates a hostile and unfriendly environment that only reinforces their social marginalization and status as a social problem.

Given the strong social stigma attached to racial prejudice, many people are reluctant to say what they actually believe in public about undocumented Latin American immigrants and U.S. Latinos. As a result, they often hide behind the law by calling undocumented immigrants "lawbreakers," "illegal," and "aliens." This social marginalization and criminalization enables them to hide the deeper ideological, cultural, racial, and social attitudes and biases that drive their desire to label them a social problem, all the while exploiting their services as inexpensive laborers. The racial and cultural dimension of this legal and social othering is evident in the fact that Latin American immigrants are often singled out for particular derision.

This process allows nativist and vigilante groups like the Minute Men to draw on law enforcement, the Federal government, and scholarly books to promote and enforce their political and social views. It provides a vehicle by which they can justify the policing of the border and their own communities. It also indirectly helps to justify their own actions by "protecting the border" and nation from lawbreakers, with a line of reasoning that argues that if they break one law they may break more. Although this may be true in some cases, it is hardly true in all cases. However, the result is that the entire U.S. Latino community is tarnished and socially marginalized in American society as people use phenotypical and cultural racial stereotypes and English-language skills to determine if a person is an undocumented immigrant and potential social problem. This contributes to an atmosphere of fear among Latin American immigrants and Euro-Americans. Fear is one of the driving forces that helps to perpetuate the social structures that define undocumented immigrants as a social problem.

Together, the aforementioned factors contribute to the criminalization of undocumented immigrants and transforms people trying to seek a new life in order to provide for their families into a dangerous and subversive social problem and fifth column in American society. The only way to counter the construction of Latinos as a social problem in the United States is by reframing the community, their contributions, and their value to society. Many secular civil rights organizations like the National Council for La Raza, the League of United Latin American Citizens, and the Mexican American Legal Defense Fund have defended and reframed the undocumented Latin American immigrants and U.S. Latinos. They have provided important services on behalf of immigrants.

However, the one dimension they often lack is moral and spiritual authority, which would enable them to speak to the heart and conscience of the American people, which according to every major poll is one of the most religious in the Western world. Latino secular organizations are seen as strictly partisan Democrat and having few loyalties to the larger Euro-American society. Clergy, on the other hand, are often part of larger denominations that serve Euro-Americans and Latinos, thus forcing them to examine both sides of issues and concerns. As a result, they are seen as more fair-minded mediators and powerbrokers with a sense of grassroots activities, as they have access, through their pulpits and radio shows, to hundreds if not thousands of people on a weekly basis. These facts combined with the reality that many younger clergy were shaped by the African American and Mexican American civil rights movements of the 1960s and 1970s, have created a new generation of Protestant and Catholic clergy and lay leaders that are willing to take their faith to the streets to fight on behalf of the undocumented immigrants because they believe that the Gospel of Jesus Christ compels them to do so. As we shall see in this chapter, many of them like Cardinal Roger Mahony and Rev. Samuel Rodriguez drew a direct link between the role of religion in the civil rights struggle and their current push for comprehensive immigration reform. They also recognized—like Martin Luther King, Jr. and César Chávez before them—that religion and law were intimately connected and crucial in bringing about real social change in an American society that was not yet fully prepared to treat blacks and Mexicans as equals. By so doing, they could reframe undocumented immigrants as children of God that should have the same inalienable rights as any other guest in American society. Although not new, this public trend in religious lay and ordained leaders seeking to use faith-based activism to shape legislation and laws appears to becoming more pronounced. This is most definitely true in the recent 2006 and 2010 struggles over immigration reform.

CONTEMPORARY LATINO STRUGGLES FOR INCLUSION IN U.S. CIVIL SOCIETY

"Today We Act, Tomorrow We Vote" read thousands of posters plastered across Los Angeles liquor stores, telephone poles, and Catholic and Protestant church bulletin boards in April 2006. A rainbow coalition of religious, secular, and faith-based organizations joined forces in opposition to the U.S. House of Representative's immigration reform bill HR 4437 *Border Protection, Anti-Terrorism, and Illegal Immigration Protection Act*, because it, shaped by the specter of 9/11, criminalized undocumented immigrants, churches, and/or organizations that assisted them. Cardinal Roger Mahony and other organizers, intentionally drawing upon religious symbols and rhetoric that resonated with the masses, called for a "Candlelight Vigil and Procession" from the La Placita Church to Fletcher Brown Square in downtown Los Angeles. The final location was as strategic as it was symbolic. At the bottom of the poster, the organizers cited the Bible to invoke moral authority for their cause: "And you are to love the stranger, for you yourselves were strangers . . . Deuteronomy 10:19." The goal of their faith-based protest was to support President George W. Bush's moderate immigration reform policies and to pressure the Senate to reject the House bill, which earlier passed by a margin of 239 to 182. On April

10, 2006, the struggle came to a flash point as a broad-based coalition of people from over twenty nationalities and many churches, synagogues, mosques, and secular organizations marched, protested, and prayed for a more humane outcome.

Although many racial-ethnic groups and nationalities participated, the vast majority of more than two million protestors who took part in the 102 marches across the nation were of Mexican, Caribbean, and Latin American ancestry. The Latino community has not only attracted national attention because of the large protests but also because the population has blossomed from 22.4 million in 1990 to 42.7 million in 2005. It is projected to climb to 103 million by 2050 or 25% of the U.S. population. The critical role of Latinos in the 2004 election, with 40 to 44% voting for Bush, has also prompted many Democratic and Republican politicians to pay close attention to the immigration reform debate (U.S. Census Bureau Facts for Features 2006, 1). Obama was able to reverse this trend by taking 67% of the Latino vote to McCain's 31% , a major drop in support for an otherwise popular Republican candidate (Espinosa 2010, 255–265, 277–285).

However, Latino faith-informed struggles for political, civic, and social empowerment and acceptance in the United States are neither new nor unique. In fact, there is a long tradition of Latino faith-based political, civic, and social activism in the United States (Espinosa, Elizondo, and Miranda 2005; Espinosa, 2010, 234–237). The immediate role-model for the contemporary struggle has been César Chávez (1927–1993), who in 1965 organized the United Farm Worker's (UFW) union and became a symbol of the Mexican American civil rights movement (Acuña 1972, 231–232; Sandoval 1983, 380; Rosales 1997, 283). Inspired by the social teachings of Jesus Christ, Catholic encyclical *Rerum Novarum* on the rights of unions and labor, books on St. Francis of Assisi, Martin Luther King Jr., and Gandhi, Chávez framed his struggle as a faith-based non-violent struggle for farm workers via pilgrimages, fasts, prayer vigils, and old-fashioned picketing (Sandoval 1983, 384; León 2005, 53–62). Chavez's struggle and reframing of the Mexican American and U.S. Latino experience served as a major turning point in the history of Latino political, civic, and social activism in the United States. He and others like him signaled a new paradigm in Latino activism and in many respects revived the indigenous pattern of faith-based activism carried out earlier in the Southwest, and by other social revolutionaries like Emilio Zapata in Mexico (Rosales 2000, 159–160, 194–204; Stevens-Arroyo 1980, 120).

Cardinal Roger Mahony and the Catholic Campaign for Justice

Cardinal Roger Mahony intentionally patterned some of his public strategies for immigration reform after Chávez, including nonviolent protest, citing Catholic social teaching, and sponsoring pilgrimages and candlelight prayer vigils. He and other Euro-Catholic leaders and laity created their

Justice for Immigrants Campaign (JIC) to reframe how lawmakers, religious leaders, and American society viewed the social problem of "illegal immigration." They used the JIC to platform their proactive national opposition to the House of Representatives congressional bill HR 4437 of 2005 because they said it criminalized undocumented workers and any churches and faith-based organizations that ministered to them. On December 30, 2005, Mahony sent a letter to President George W. Bush urging him to reject HR 4437 and any legislation that would make it a crime to help or provide sanctuary for undocumented immigrants. In this letter he stated that although he supported the government's action to protect the borders, he vigorously rejected the proviso in the bill that would require churches to check the immigration status of the people they served in their parochial schools, hospitals, and charities because this would make them, and every other priest, minister, rabbi, and clergy official, "quasi-immigration enforcement officials," he said. He particularly lamented as unchristian the punitive penalties for undocumented immigrants—up to five years in prison and the seizure of assets. Clearly frustrated and concerned about the ramifications of the bill he wrote, "Are we to stop every person coming to Holy Communion and first ask them to produce proof of legal residence before we can offer them the Body and Blood of Christ?" He said that such restrictions were impossible to comply with. Furthermore, he stated that they were compelled to follow Christ's example, words, and actions in Matthew 25:31–46. He went on to end his letter by stating:

> It is staggering for the federal government to stifle our spiritual and pastoral outreach to the poor, and to impose penalties for doing what our faith demands of us. Throughout your Presidency, you have encouraged Faith Based Organizations to be strong partners in meeting the needs of those in our communities. Yet, this Bill will produce the opposite effect. You must speak out clearly and forcefully in opposition to these repressive—and impossible—aspects of any immigration reform efforts. Your personal leadership is needed to counter such ill-advised efforts. (Mahony 2005)

In order to counter the growing hatred and hostility towards immigrants inside and outside of the Church, Mahony followed up by helping to create the Justice for Immigrants Campaign in January 2006. He asked all Catholics to devote forty days to prayer and fasting for humane immigration reform and just laws beginning on March 1. This enabled him to transform the issue from a strictly legal issue into a religious and moral campaign. The goals of the multiyear campaign was fourfold: (1) to educate Catholics about the benefits of immigration, (2) to strengthen public opinion about the positive contributions of immigrants, (3) to advocate for just immigration laws that promote legal status and legal pathways for migrant workers and their families, and (4) to organize Catholic legal service networks to assist immigrants to access the benefits of reform. The final goal was to try to change the laws so that immigrants can support their families in "dignity" (a concept also used by Chávez), so families can remain united, and so that their human and civil rights are respected. Over twenty Catholic organizations with national networks came together to form and support the organization (Justice for Immigrants Campaign 2006).

On March 22, 2006, Mahony sought to take his case to the American people by writing an op-ed piece for *The New York Times*. In it he—like Chávez before him—invoked the Bible and Catholic social teaching when he stated that he stood by his recent decision that instructed priests to engage in civil disobedience by disobeying HR 4437. He did it not to support undocumented immigration, he claimed, but rather because not providing humanitarian assistance to those in need "violates a law with higher authority than Congress—the Law of God." He further charged that HR 4437 would not only criminalize undocumented workers but also "drive them further into the shadows." Pushing the prophetic envelope further and again echoing Chávez and Catholic social teaching on exploitation and the rights of labor, he sought to reframe the issue in a different way from the Minute Men and other nativist groups when he wrote, "The unspoken truth of the immigration debate is that at the same time our nation benefits economically from the presence of undocumented workers, we turn a blind eye when they are exploited by employers. . . . While we gladly accept their taxes and sweat, we do not acknowledge or uphold their basic labor rights . . . we scapegoat them for our social ills and label them as security threats and criminals to justify the passage of an anti-immigrant bill." He concluded by stating that because the "dignity" (a word explicitly used by Chávez and in Catholic social teachings) of millions of our fellow human beings is at risk, immigration is ultimately a moral and ethical issue and that was why he and the Catholic Church were "compelled" to "take a stand against harmful legislation and to work toward positive change." This approach enabled Mahony to help transform an ostensibly secular debate about undocumented immigrants into a religious one that rather than weaken the Catholic Church's influence in American society actually strengthened it (Mahony 2006a; Dalton 2003, 62–90).Mahony and other Anglo and Latino cardinals and bishops like Cardinal Theodore McCarrick (Washington, D.C.), Bishop Gerald Kickans (Tucson, Ariz.), Bishop Jaime Soto (Orange County, Calif.), Bishop Nicholas DiMarzio (Brooklyn, N.Y.), and Bishop Gerald Barnes (San Bernardino), chairman of the U.S. Conference of Catholic Bishops Committee on Migration, proactively worked to reframe and defeat HR 4437. They supported the McCain-Kennedy S 1033 / HR 2330 *Secure America and Orderly Immigration Act* because it did not criminalize immigrants or churches that assisted them, provided a guest worker program, and provided a path toward earned citizenship. Their critics charged that these alternatives were little more than amnesty. They responded by stating that "earned legalization" required the undocumented to learn English, pay fines, wait at the end of the line in applying for a green card, wait for a criminal background check, and earn permanent status over a six-year period before qualifying for citizenship (USCCB—Comprehensive Immigration Reform Statement 2006).

Echoing Chávez, Mahony, and other social justice advocates, Bishop Barnes and the USCCB Committee on Migration sought to reframe how society viewed "illegal aliens" by citing Jesus' parable of the Good Samaritan (Luke 10:29), Matthew 19:19 about loving their neighbor as themselves, Matthew 25:35 about feeding the hungry, and Pope John Paul II's teaching on how society should treat undocumented immigrants. In a complete reversal of the social problem of "illegal aliens," Barnes and the USCCB declared: "Jesus made the Samaritan—who was looked upon as an unholy outcast and foreigner—the model because he came to the aid of the injured man who was a stranger to him. Now is our chance to come to the aid of those among us who come from a foreign land. Now is our chance to care about the *strangers* whom Jesus called our neighbor!" They also attempted to shift the focus away from the rule of law by focusing on the biblical theme of hospitality and welcoming the stranger. The theme of welcoming the stranger in a foreign land was a notion later picked up by politicians like President Bush, Ted Kennedy, and many others. The USCCB also circulated a pastoral letter authored by a joint statement of U.S.-Mexico bishops entitled, "Strangers No Longer: Together on the Journey of Hope," which called for people on both sides of the border to respect the "human dignity" and rights of migrant laborers (USCCB 2003). They concluded by citing John Paul II's 1996 *Annual Message for World Migration Day*: "Today the illegal migrant comes before us like that 'stranger' in whom Jesus asks to be recognized. To welcome him and to show him solidarity is a duty of hospitality and fidelity to Christian identity itself." By reframing the struggle in terms of "Who is my neighbor" (Good Samaritan) and "welcoming the stranger" (Matthew 25:35–40), they sought to use the moral authority of Jesus and the Bible to persuade politicians and the American public to take a more humane approach to how they treated the social problem of "illegal aliens" and ultimately immigration reform legislation (Justice for Immigrants Campaign 2006).

As the date for the Senate vote on HR 4437 approached, Cardinal Mahony designated April 5, 2006, a "day of Prayer and Fasting for Just and Humane Immigration Reform." On April 10, like Chávez 40 years before, he used a "Candlelight Vigil and Procession" in downtown Los Angeles to attract national attention to the struggle, where they had a rally that included prayer, music, speeches, and testimonials. Despite the prominent Catholic presence, Mahony, like Chávez before him, linked up with other faith traditions. The speakers included Cardinal Roger Mahony, Father Mike Gutiérrez of St. Anne's Catholic Church, who led the interfaith procession and rally, Pastor Lewis Logan of Bethel AME Church, Rabbi Mark Diamond, Imam Ali Siddiqui, Abdullah Muhammad of ACORN, Maria

Durazo of the LA County AFL-CIO, Joon Kim, the popular Latino DJ El Cucuy, and several others. The decision to include other racial-ethnic minority and social groups was another strategic attempt to reframe the movement as a much larger struggle for civil rights and social justice that transcended the Latin American immigrant experience.

These activities were followed up by Mahony taking part in a march to MacArthur Park on May 1 and by encouraging his parishioners to send postcards (downloadable on his diocese Web site) to senators Bill Frist and Harry Reid advocating just immigration reform. The card asked Congress to enact realistic and humane comprehensive immigration reform that included a path to citizenship, provided an effective visa program, kept families together, protected immigrant civil rights and liberties, and did not criminalize immigrants or their allies. Finally, on September 21, 2006, Mahony sent a letter to Congress asking them to view the issue in terms of human dignity and resist passage of enforcement-only immigration bills. His letter specifically criticized the construction of a seven hundred-mile border fence and called on them to create a comprehensive immigration reform bill that provided an opportunity for the permanent legal status of "12 million" undocumented immigrants already in the United States and for their families to enter in a safe and legal manner (Watanabe 2006; Mahony 2006b).

Rev. Samuel Rodríguez and the National Hispanic Christian Leadership Conference (NHCLC)

At the same time as Mahony, Barnes, and others were reframing the debate over undocumented immigrants and comprehensive immigration reform in Los Angeles, Reverend Samuel Rodríguez and the National Hispanic Christian Leadership Conference (NHCLC) were doing the same on Capitol Hill. Although the two never spoke personally over the telephone, their representatives did coordinate their faith-based activities. They both shared a common commitment to comprehensive immigration reform and support for the McCain-Kennedy bill. Patterned after the African American Southern Christian Leadership Conference and its goal to fight for civil rights through nonviolent faith-based strategies, the NHCLC claims its committed to serving the "16 million Evangelical and born-again Christian community" and its 25,434 Latino-serving churches in the United States on key issues such as family, immigration, economic mobility, education, political empowerment, and social transformation. Rodriguez and the NHCLC is part of a new generation of Pentecostal and Evangelical leaders like Jesse Miranda (AMEN), Raymond Rivera (LPAC), Luis Cortes (Nueva Esperanza), Juan Hernandez, Mark Gonzalez, Noel Castellanos (CCDA), Lisa Treviño-Cummins, Wilfredo de Jesus, Miguel Rivera (CONLAMIC), and many other clergy, lay leaders, and organizations fighting for Latino political, civil, and social rights on the streets and on Capitol Hill (Thompson 2010).

The stated purpose and function of the NHCLC, is to: (1) provide leadership to exert a collective Latino voice before legislative, economic, and ecclesiastical authorities in Washington, D.C., and in state capitals, (2) host annual conferences throughout the nation where Latinos can come together for revival, renewal, and restoration, (3) provide networking opportunities for empowerment and service, (4) create apostolic partnerships with Hispanic churches in America with the purpose of creating Faith Based Community Programs, (5) engage in political and social advocacy and seek to empower Latinos via "spiritual progressive leadership" through voter registration drives, Latino-African American alliances, and other initiatives that directly affect Latinos, and (6) to serve as a prophetic voice on behalf of the voiceless undocumented and on other key political, social, and cultural issues. According to their promotional literature, they also seek to lead the Hispanic Evangelical Church in America in transforming the culture, preserving the Judeo-Christian value system, and building spiritual, intellectual, and social/political capital within the Hispanic American community (National Hispanic Christian Leadership Conference 2006).

Rodríguez and the NHCLC used a number of strategies to help reframe the comprehensive immigration reform debate and put pressure on President Bush and Congress to pass a comprehensive immigration reform bill. In April 2006 they used the mass media as a faith-based strategy to push for immigration reform. Rodríguez stated in an interview with the *Washington Post* that the immigration reform debate was a "watershed" moment between Euro-American and Latino Evangelicals. He said that if they joined in their efforts, they would forge a positive relationship that would last for "decades." However, he also warned that if they didn't "there is a possibility of a definitive schism" and that there would be serious "ramifications" in the church and in American politics—an allusion to Latino Evangelicals defecting in large numbers to the Democrats. He stated that Latino Evangelicals wanted to know why white Evangelicals did not support comprehensive immigration reform, why they only supported law enforcement against undocumented immigrants—without any mention of compassion or any Christian moral imperative to help immigrants (Cooperman 2006).

The NHCLC next engaged in bipartisan meetings, seminars, and colloquia with key Democratic and Republican political leaders and sought to promote a "middle path" between the extremes of HR 4437 and general amnesty. In this respect, they were very successful as they gained access to many of the most important leaders in both the Democratic and Republican parties eager to court the Latino vote such as the former Ted Kennedy and Nancy Pelosi, Hillary Clinton, Sam Brownback, Harry Reid, and John McCain.

Rodríguez and the NHCLC then sought to work on persuading Latino churches and clergy to become involved in the immigration reform debate. The NHCLC also encouraged them to flex their growing numerical muscle, influence, and moral authority on the issue of undocumented immigrants within their denominations and communities. They did this by holding conferences and workshops aimed at political mobilization before, during, and after the April 10 and May 1 rallies across the United States. They also sought to use these conferences to raise awareness in the United States via media coverage on "Hispanic-related" issues.

Rodríguez and the NHCLC further sought to reframe "illegal immigration" and comprehensive immigration reform by engaging in dialogue with the National Association of Evangelicals (NAE), Focus on the Family, and the Family Research Council, with the specific goal of either gaining their support or keeping them from becoming an outspoken critic of their goals. They were largely successful in this endeavor as the NAE supported their cause while Focus on the Family and the Family Research Council decided to not take a position for or against comprehensive immigration reform. They also sought to persuade these national evangelical organizations to adopt more moderate views on immigration. In an effort to move the evangelical community to support their views, Rodríguez wrote an open letter to Evangelicals in April 2006 on immigration reform. In it, he said that Evangelicals had a moral obligation to speak out on behalf of a comprehensive immigration reform. He cited findings from the Pew Forum, which found that many white Evangelicals were fearful of Hispanic immigrants. He challenged them to follow the example of World Relief, the development arm of the NAE, in calling for comprehensive immigration reform. He made it abundantly clear that, like Mahony's Campaign for Justice, the NHCLC was not calling for amnesty but rather a policy that protected the border, stopped undocumented immigration, and applied the rule of law in a matter that is "consistent with a biblical worldview." He ended by stating that he believed that Latino Evangelicals presented a "viable bridge" between both sides of the issue and he hoped they could partner together to preserve their shared values (Rodríguez 2006).

Rodríguez and the NHCLC then sent letters to President George W. Bush and Congress in an endeavor to reframe undocumented immigration and apply pressure to support immigration reform. In the first letter on March 1, 2006, Rodríguez encouraged them to move beyond mere enforcement measures in HR 4437 to create a comprehensive immigration reform bill based on biblical mandates, the Christian faith and values, and a commitment to "civil and human rights," and justified this approach by invoking the Bible. He stated that God requires that people show love and compassion to aliens. He then cited Deuteronomy 10:18–19, which stated, "You are to love those who are aliens, for you yourselves were aliens in Egypt." He then cited Leviticus 19:33–34, stating that God's people are not to mistreat the aliens and that they are in fact to be treated as one of your native-born sons. He called on Bush and Congress to promote laws and values that "treat all individuals with respect." (Rodríguez, Neff, Sider, Buwalda, Wallis, Calver 2006).

On September 1, 2006, Rodríguez and the NHCLC sent a second follow-up letter to President Bush and Congress that seemed to go beyond the more diplomatic language of Mahony and the USCCB's statements. Rodríguez and the NHCLC stated that the lack of passage of a comprehensive immigration reform bill resulted in many Latinos facing the kind of "racial profiling, discrimination, and hostile ethnic" polarization that they had not faced since the days of the civil rights movement. They pointed out that cities across America were passing ordinances that "in essence legalize racial profiling" and "place the Latino community in an unnecessary posture." Pushing the envelope even further, they stated, "Americans have the intellectual wherewithal, the political acumen and the spiritual fortitude to reconcile the principles of law and order with a pathway to citizenship for those [Latinos] that seek to live the American Dream." They ended by calling on Congress to pass a bill and the president to sign into law legislation that protects the border, ends undocumented immigration, and creates a "market driven guest worker program that facilitate avenues by which the millions of families already in America that lack the legal status can earn such status in a matter that reflects the Judeo-Christian value system this nation was founded upon." In addition to their own signatures, they were able to receive endorsements from other prominent Latino clergy, professors, seminary presidents, and organizations (Rodríguez and Gonzáles, 2006).

These efforts by Rodríguez, the NHCLC, and their supporters did not fall on deaf ears as Democrats such as Nancy Pelosi, Ted Kennedy, Harry Reid, Ken Salazar, and Republicans like Bill Frist, John McCain, Lindsey Graham, Tom Tancredo, Sam Brownback, and others met with them to listen to their concerns and find alternative strategies to address immigration reform. In addition to meeting throughout 2006 with various members of Congress, President Bush also responded to these calls at the National Hispanic Prayer Breakfast on June 8, 2006, when he stated that the United States had to find a "common-sense" "reasonable middle-ground" on immigration reform that treats Latinos with "dignity" and "respect." He stated, "If you've paid your taxes, you've been here for a while, you can prove that you've been working, you've got a clean background; if you want to become a citizen you pay a fine, you learn English, you learn the values and ideals of America that have made us one nation under God" then you should be able to live and work in the United States. For this reason he called on Congress to support a guest worker program (Bush 2006c).

In addition to these formal letters and meeting with members of Congress, in 2006 Rodríguez and the NHCLC board had three meetings at the White House on the topic of immigration reform, including one meeting with President Bush. This kind of influence led Sydney Blumenthal to argue in the *Guardian* that the NHCLC "stymied" the Family Research Council and the religious right from getting Senate Republicans to pass HR 4437. Alan Cooperman of the *Washington Post* wrote that the NHCLC also prompted the Republicans and Evangelicals to soften their tone on immigration reform. Despite these efforts, other evangelical groups like the Christian Coalition and Phyllis Schally's Eagle Forum have strongly opposed the McCain-Kennedy bill and the position of Rodríguez and the NHCLC because they see it as an "amnesty" package (Blumenthal 2006; Cooperman 2006).

Contemporary Debate over the Arizona Governor's Immigration Law SB 1070

In order to fight what they believe is the criminalization of Latin American immigrants in particular and Latinos in general, Mahony and Rodríguez have taken to the streets again to protest the Arizona Governor Jan Brewer's SB 1070, which was signed into law April 23, 2010. The new law, one of the strictest in the U.S., would enable law enforcement officials and the courts to identify, prosecute, and deport illegal immigrants. The Governor and her supporters stated that the law was put into effect because President Obama and Secretary of the Department of Homeland Security Janet Napolitano did nothing to secure the border with Mexico and protect Americans from violent drug-cartel related crime, the murder of Arizona ranchers and the kidnapping and rape of young women by undocumented immigrants, and because nothing was being done to curtail the flow of the estimated 460,000 undocumented immigrants in Arizona. Brewer stated that the new law "represents another tool for our state to . . . solve a crisis we did not create and the federal government has refused to fix." She went on to state the new law "protects all of us." The new law requires state and local police officers to detain and arrest immigrants unable to provide legal documentation and it also makes it a crime to transport and hire undocumented and day laborers. This does not mean they would stop every Latino, just those with "reasonable suspicion." This law is part of a much larger and quieter wave of immigration reform sweeping across the U.S. wherein since 2007 hundreds of laws or bills have been proposed and/ or passed. In 2009 alone, over 222 immigration laws were enacted and 131 resolutions have been passed in 48 states, most of them conservative in nature (Schwartz 2010: 1–2; Archibold 2010: 1–4).

The struggle over immigration reform and the criminalization of Latin American immigrants as law breakers and a group that engages in other criminal activity disproportionately per their percentage of the U.S. population may also have distinct racial undertones and implications, which if not properly addressed may in turn lead to greater racial tensions in the future. The distinction between a tiny criminal element (which can be found in any large population) and the larger population of largely law-abiding immigrants is often overlooked. While the larger goal of stopping drug cartels, kidnappers, and organized crime is laudable, by not always making careful distinctions, it nonetheless also results in a kind of de facto criminalization of an entire population and class of people, creating a perennial "Other" and a subpopulation thereafter classified as a social problem.

This is no doubt part of the reason why the political and public outcry to the Arizona law was immediate. President Obama called the new law "misguided" and strategically sought to capitalize on the event by arguing that this law proved that what was really needed was comprehensive immigration reform, which detractors have called general amnesty. Latino civil rights activists like President Janet Murguia of the National Council for La Raza said the law would legitimize and legalize racial profiling of Latino immigrants and The Mexican American Legal Defense and Educational Fund said the new law would create a "spiral of pervasive fear, community distrust, increased crime and costly litigation, with nationwide repercussions" (Schwartz 2010, 1–2; Archibold 2010, 1–4). All of this would contribute to the criminalization of Latinos and to a new "Latino" social problem. The growing role of activists challenging legal issues is one of the reasons why Latino Catholics, Evangelicals, and Pentecostals supported the nomination of Supreme Court Justice Sonja Sotomayor, someone they believe will better understand both sides of the immigration debate.

Some of the sharpest criticisms of this new law and the othering and criminalizing of the Latino community came from Mahony and Rodriguez. Cardinal Mahony wrote on his Archdiocese of Los Angeles blog: "The Arizona legislature just passed the country's most retrogressive, mean-spirited, and useless anti-immigrant law." "The tragedy of the law," he continued, "is its totally false reasoning: that immigrants come to our country to rob, plunder, and consume public resources. That is not only false, the premise is nonsense." He lashed out and attacked the new law, stating: "Arizonans [are] now reverting to German Nazi and Russian Communist techniques whereby people are required to turn one another in to the authorities on any suspicion of documentation." He continued, "Are children supposed to call 911 because one parent does not have proper papers? Are family members and neighbors now supposed to spy on one another, create total distrust across neighborhoods and communities, and report people because of suspicions based upon appearance?" (Watanabe 2010,1–3; Schwartz 2010, 1–2; Archibold 2010, 1–4).

Mahony called on his followers to promote comprehensive immigration reform. He sought to do so by writing letters against what he calls the criminalization of undocumented immigrants. On his Los Angeles Archdiocese website, he further called for masses and rallies in support of immigrants. As in 2006, he drew on Catholic social teaching and the Bible to justify humane treatment of migrating people based on the dignity and sanctity of the human person. He called on his Justice for Immigrants Campaign to participate in the "Pray for Immigrants Weekend" by calling on all 19,000 Catholic parishes n the U.S. to include prayer for immigration reform on May 1 and 2, 2010 (Archdiocese of Los Angeles 2010).

Arizona Senator Russell Pearce, the sponsor of SB 1070, lashed out in return, stating that Cardinal Mahony had no credibility on the topic given that he's a leader "who's been protecting child molesters and predators all of his life. He's the last guy that out to be speaking out." In a radio interview on FKWB-AM 980, he continued, "This guy has a history of protecting and moving predators around in order to avoid detection by the law. He has no room to talk." He excoriated him not only for obfuscating the law when it suited him, but also for seeking cover for the child molestation scandal. He was particular incensed because Mahony completely ignored the plight of countless victims of criminal element in the illegal immigrant population, including police officers and ranchers "who have been killed and teenage girls who have been kidnapped and raped." "Where does he stand up for America and the rule of law? He ought to be embarrassed and he out to be drummed out as far as I'm concerned." Pierce said the law was only aimed at violent criminals and lawbreakers. He stated, "We love and admire immigrants who come here to assimilate to be Americans. This has nothing to do with immigration. It has to do with those who enter our country illegally." Still other critics accused Mahony of exaggerating the law when he stated that it requires regular citizens to report immigration violations, when in fact this is not the case (Watanabe 2010, 1–2).

In a similar vein, Rev. Samuel Rodriguez also criticized the Arizona bill. In a public press release, he called SB 1070 "Legislative Nativism" and declared a 40 day national fast for justice in Arizona. Both leaders took part and spoke at the massive comprehensive immigration reform rally in Washington, D.C., an event held on March 21and attended by tends of thousands of supporters and other speakers such as Rev. Jesse Jackson, Cornell West, and other leaders across the political and religious spectrum (NHCLC and Ramirez 2010, 1–2; Preston 2010,1–2).

On April 20, 2010, Rodriguez wrote: "Today, Arizona stands as the state with the most xenophobic and nativist supportive laws in the country. We need a multi-ethnic firewall against the extremists in our nation who desire to separate us rather than bring us together." After invoking select passages from the Bible (Isaiah 10:1–3, Proverb 31:8–9; Leviticus 19) on providing charity to immigrants and chastisement for unjustly treating immigrants, Rodriguez invoked Republican icons Abraham Lincoln and Ronald Reagan, who granted citizenship to over two million Latinos in 1986. He stated:

> The Arizona Law stands as evidence that in 21st Century America, we may no longer be in the Desert of Segregation or the Egypt of Slavery but we just discovered there are Giants to be slain in the land of Promise. The Arizona Law is without a doubt, anti-Latino, anti-family, anti-immigrant, anti-Christian and unconstitutional. In addition, the law is without a doubt, Anti-Conservative. It runs counter to the Republican vision of Abraham Lincoln and Ronald Reagan (NHCLC and Ramirez 2010: 1–2; Espinosa 2010, 237).

Rodriguez also chastised President Obama and the Democratic leadership in Congress for dragging their feet on comprehensive immigration reform and for not keeping his promise to pass comprehensive immigration reform in his first year in office. He also made it clear that he was not calling for general amnesty, but rather for a humane solution to the immigration problem. In order to bring about the desired change, Rodriguez called for a multi-pronged strategy centered on prayer vigils, 40 days of fasting, marches, boycotts, letter writing campaigns (1 million faxes, emails, texts and letters as a goal), and non-violent civil disobedience to "push back xenophobia, nativism and racial profiling."

Rodriguez sought a strategy that, "respects the God-given dignity of every person, Protects the unity of the immediate family, Respects the rule of law, Guarantees secure national borders, Ensures fairness to taxpayers, [and] establishes a path toward legal status and/or citizenship." He said his organization also supports what he calls a "just integration/assimilation strategy" that would require criminal background checks of all incoming immigrants, admonition of guilt if they crossed they broke U.S. laws, and learning English (NHCLC and Ramirez 2010: 1–2).

Rodriguez and his organization admitted the challenge was great: "But here lies the challenge: can we reconcile Leviticus 19 [human treatment of immigrants] and Romans 13 [obeying laws]? Can we repudiate xenophobic and nativist rhetoric, push back on the extremes from both the left and the right and converge around the nexus of the Center Cross where righteousness meets Justice, border security meets compassion and common sense meets common ground?" He ended by stating, "As Hispanic Christians, we stand committed to the message of the Cross. However, that cross is both vertical and horizontal. It is salvation and transformation . . . faith and public policy . . . righteousness and justice. . . . [W]e humbly encourage Congress to finally pass and sign into law legislation that will protect our borders, put an end to all illegal immigration . . . in a manner that reflects the Judeo Christian Value system" (NHCLC 2010: 1–2; NHCLC 2010).

CONCLUSION

The influence of the religious leaders and campaigns mentioned above is evident in the language and religious rhetoric both Democrats and Republicans used to promote some of their own comprehensive immigration reform bills. In a speech to an interfaith group of religious leaders in Boston, late Senator Edward Kennedy cited Matthew 25:35 about our society's responsibility "not only to feed the hungry and care for the sick" but also to welcome "the stranger." Drawing further from Mahony and the USCCB, Kennedy cited a passage from Leviticus 19: 33–34 that called on people to treat "the alien living with you . . . as one of your native-born. Love him as yourself, for you were aliens in Egypt." President Bush also drew on this language in defense of his own immigration reform program, which opposed HR 4437. In a speech given in celebration of Cinco de Mayo on May 4, 2006, President Bush stated that America needed to honor "human rights, help people out of the shadows of society, [and] treat people in a decent and humane way." At his press conference celebrating Hispanic heritage month on October 6, 2006, he likewise stated that Latin American immigrants must be treated "in a humane way" and "with respect and dignity" (Bush 2006b, 2006d). More recently President Obama has likened comprehensive immigration reform to the abolition of slavery.

The attention that Democrats and Republicans are giving to problem of immigration reform and the racial component associated with it is not entirely altruistic. In the past, Latinos have been a key Democratic voting constituency. Given the fact that Catholics make up 66% (30 million) of the nation's 48 million Latinos, their vote is significant, especially in swing states like Florida, Colorado, and New Mexico. There is also good reason for both parties to court the Latino Protestant vote (9.2 million). More than one million new Latino voters are added to the electorate every four years in the presidential election cycle. Furthermore, a very large percentage of the Latino community self-identifies as politically independent. Their relatively high birth and immigration rates and political volatility will continue to make them an attractive constituency for both political parties (Espinosa 2010, 277–280).

The growing political power of the Latino community is enabling them to successfully challenge stereotypes about the social problems associated with the community. Politicians in states with large and growing Latino populations are wary of losing their vote. What religious leaders do is provide politicians with a language, grassroots justification and support, strategy, and moral authority to stand up against other politicians who speak out against Latinos. For this reason, the religious discourse about reframing the debate about Latin American immigrants, the law, and immigration reform is important in American politics both now and in the future.

REFERENCES

Acuña, Rodolfo. 1972. *Occupied America*. San Francisco: Canfield.

Archibold, Randal C. 2010. "Arizona Enacts Stringent Law on Immigration," *The New York Times*, April 23.

Barnes, Gerald. 2006a. Comprehensive Immigration Reform Passed by the Senate: Statement by the Most Reverend Gerald Barnes, Bishop of San Bernardino, chairman, USCCB Committee on Migration, May 25.

———. 2006b. Statement of the Most Reverend Gerald Barnes on Presidential Address to the Nation on Immigration. May 15.

Becker, Howard S. 1991[1963]. *Outsiders: Studies in the Sociology of Deviance*. New York: The Free Press of Glencoe.

Blumenthal, Sidney. 2006. "An American Idea Shatters: The Reawakening of a Virulent Nationalism Is Tearing Apart Bush's Conservative Coalition." *Guardian/UK*, May 18.

Blumer, Herbert. 1971. Social Problems as Collective Behavior. *Social Problems*, 18 (Winter): 298–306.

Bush, George W. 2006a. "President Attends National Catholic Prayer Breakfast," April 7. http://www.whitehouse.gov/news/releases/2006/04/20060407.html.

———. 2006b. "President Bush Celebrates Cinco de Mayo at the White House," May 4. http://www.whitehouse.gov/news/releases/2006/05/20060504–9.html.

———. 2006c. "President Bush Attends National Hispanic Prayer Breakfast," June 8. http://www.whitehouse.gov/news/releases/2006/06/20060608–1.html.

————. 2006d. "President Bush Celebrates Hispanic Heritage Month at White House," October 6. http://www.whitehouse.gov/news/releases/2006/10/20061006–12.html.

California Catholic Conference. 2006. "California Catholic Conference of Bishops" Statement on Immigration Reform," March 21. http://www.cacatholic. org/h/bs/bs60322.html.

Campaign for Justice Website. http://www.archdiocese.la/. (Accessed May 11, 2010).

Cooperman, Alan. 2006. "Letter on Immigration Deepens Split Among Evangelicals." *Washington Post*, April 5.

Dalton, Frederick John. 2003. *The Moral Vision of César Chávez*. Maryknoll, NY: Orbis.

DiMarzio, Nicholas. 2006. Catholic Legal Immigration Network on The House Judiciary Subcommittee on Immigration, Border Security, and Claims, July 27.

Dolan, Jay P. and Hinojosa, Gilberto M. (eds). 1994. *Mexican Americans and the Catholic Church 1900–1965*. Notre Dame, IN: University of Notre Dame Press.

Espinosa, Gastón, Elizondo, Virgilio, and Miranda, Jesse (eds). 2003. *Hispanic Churches in American Public Life: Summary of Findings*. Notre Dame, IN: Institute for Latino Studies, University of Notre Dame.

————. 2005. *Latino Religions and Civic Activism in the United States*. New York: Oxford University Press.

Espinosa, Gastón. 2004. The Pentecostalization of Latin American and U.S. Latino Christianity. *Pneuma: The Journal of the Society for Pentecostal Studies* 26(2): 262–292.

————. 2010. *Religion, Race, and the American Presidency*. Lanham, MD: Rowman & Littlefield Publishers, Inc.

Fuller, Richard. C., and Myers, Richard. R. 1941. The Natural History of a Social Problem. *American Sociological Review*, 6 (3): 320–8.

Green, John C., Smidt, Corwin E., Guth, James L., and Kellstedt, Lyman A. 2005. The Religious Landscape and the 2004 Presidential Vote: Increased Polarization. Np.

Hjelm, Titus. 2009. Religion and Social Problems: A New Theoretical Perspective. In *The Oxford Handbook of the Sociology of Religion*, edited by P. Clarke. Oxford: Oxford University Press.

Justice for Immigrants Campaign. 2006. http://www.justiceforimmigrants.org/. (accessed May 28, 2006)

Kennedy, Edward M. n.d. "Statement of Senator Edward M. Kennedy to Interfaith Religious Leaders." http://www.tedkennedy.com/content/993/statement-of-senator-edward-m-kennedy-to-interfaith-religious-leaders.

León, Luís D. 2005. César Chávez and Mexican American Civil Religion. In *Latino Religions and Civic Activism in the United States*, edited by Gastón Espinosa, Virgilio Elizondo and Jesse Miranda. New York: Oxford University Press.

Mahony, Roger. 2005. Letter to President George W. Bush, December 30, 1–2.

————. 2006a. "Called by God to Help." *The New York Times*. March 22.

————. 2006b. "Cardinal Roger Mahony Issues Statement on Senate's Defeat of Immigration Reform," April 7.

Matovina, Timothy, and Poyo, Gerald E. (eds). 2000. *¡Presente! U.S. Latino Catholics from Colonial Origins to the Present*. Maryknoll, NY: Orbis.

Mauss, Armand L. 1975. *Social Problems as Social Movements*. Philadelphia: Lippincott.

Moffett, Stephen R. Lloyd. 2005."The Mysticism and Social Action of César Chávez. In *Latino Religions and Civic Activism in the United States*, edited by Gastón Espinosa, Virgilio Elizondo and Jesse Miranda. New York: Oxford University Press.

National Hispanic Christian Leadership Conference. 2006. http://www.nhclc.org/.

————. 2010. The Answer to America's Immigration Dilemma: A Just Integration Strategy. http://www.nhclc.org/news/answer-americas-immigration-dilemma-just-integration-strategy.

———— and Ramirez, Maritza. 2010. "Hispanic Evangelicals Call Arizona Bill SB1070 "Legislative Nativism, Declare a 40 Day National Fast for Justice in

Arizona." http://www.nhclc.org/news/hispanic-evangelicals-call-arizona-bill-sb1070-legislative-nativism-declare-40-day-national-fast.

Preston, Julia. 2010. "Latino Religious Leader Rodriguez Courts the Left, Right for Immigration Reform," *The Washington Post*, March 21.

Rodríguez, Samuel. 2006. "Open Letter to Evangelicals on Immigration Reform." April 1.

Rodríguez, Samuel, and Gonzáles, Mark V. 2006. "Letter to President George W. Bush and Congress," September 1.

Rodríguez, Samuel, Neff, David, Sider, Ron, Buwalda, Ann, Wallis, Jim, and Calver, Clive. 2006. "Open Letter to President Bush and Congress." March 1.

Rosales, Arturo F. 1997. *Chicano! The History of the Mexican American Civil Rights Movement*. Houston: Arte Público.

———. 2000. *Testimonio: A Documentary History of the Mexican American Struggle or Civil Rights*. Houston: Arte Público.

Sandoval, Moises. 1983. *Fronteras: A History of the Latin American Church in the USA Since 1513*. San Antonio: Mexican American Cultural Center.

———. 1991. *On the Move: A History of the Hispanic Church in the United States*. Maryknoll, NY: Orbis.

Schlafly, Phyllis. 2001. "Is it Assimilation or Invasion?" Eagle Forum. http://www.eagleforum.org/column/2001/nov01/01–11–28.shtml. (Accessed April 4, 2010).

Schwartz, David. 2010. "Arizona Governor Signs Toughest Immigration Law," *Reuters*, April 23.

Spector, M., and Kitsuse, J. I. 2001[1977]. *Constructing Social Problems*. New Brunswick, NJ: Transaction Publishers.

Stafford, Tim. 2006. "The Call of Samuel," *Christianity Today*, November 2.

Stevens-Arroyo, Anthony M., (ed) 1980. *Prophets Denied Honor*. Maryknoll, NY: Orbis.

Sue, Derek Wing. 2003. *Overcoming Our Racism: The Journey to Liberation*. San Francisco: Jossey-Bass.

USCCB—United States Conference of Catholic Bishops and the Mexican Bishops Conference. 2003. *Strangers No Longer: Together on the Journey of Hope*. New York: Migration and Refugee Services.

USCCB—United States Conference of Catholic Bishops. 2006. *United States Conference of Catholic Bishops Comprehensive Immigration Reform Statement*. New York: Migration and Refugee Services.

U.S. Census Bureau Facts for Features. 2006. http://www.census.gov/Press-Release/www/releases/archives/facts_for_features_special_editions/007643.htm.

U.S. House of Representatives. HR 4437. 2005. The Border Protection, Anti-Terrorism, and Illegal Immigration Control Act). http://www.govtrack.us/congress/bill.xpd?bill=h109–4437.

U.S. Senate. S. 1033 (HR 233). 2005. Secure America and Orderly Immigration Act. http://www.govtrack.us/congress/bill.xpd?bill=s109–1033. (Accessed April 4, 2010).

Watanabe, Teresa. 2006. "500,000 Pack Streets to Protest Immigration Bills," *Los Angeles Times*, March 26.

———. 2010. "Cardinal Mahony Criticizes Arizona Immigration Bill," *Los Angeles Times*, April 20.

———. 2010. "Arizona State Senator Fires Back at Cardinal Mahony Over Immigration Bill," *Los Angeles Times*, April 22.

Wuthnow, Robert, and Evans, John H. 2002. *The Quiet Hand of God: Faith-Based Activism and the Public Role of Mainline Protestantism*. Berkeley: University of California Press.

Zapor, Patricia. 2006. "Border Fence Bill Passes amid Opposition From Religious Leaders." *The Tidings Online*, October 6. http://www.the-tidings.com/2006/1006/immigration.htm.

9 Missionaries and Social Workers
Visions of Sexuality in Religious Discourse

Marian Burchardt

In present-day South Africa, with roughly 5.5 million people living with HIV and AIDS and an infection rate of 16.9% of the adult population, AIDS is arguably the greatest health risk not only for "risk groups" as defined in the laboratories of public health discourse but for the population at large.[1] With heterosexual intercourse—followed at a distance by mother-to-child-transmission—being the dominant mode of transmission AIDS has rendered intimate and sexual relationships problematic in novel ways; it attaches medical meanings to the sexual act that crosscut ideas of pleasure, romanticism, procreation, and marital union, inscribed into sexual practices in modern culture. While infection because of its terminal consequences is an utterly critical event in itself, its disastrous consequences go beyond the individual experience of illness and eventual death. At some stage AIDS incapacitates people and renders them unable to work and generate income. It is therefore linked to economic insecurity of individuals and families and threatens the capabilities of raising children. What is more, because of the stigma it carries, equally borne from close associations with illegitimate sexual practice and death, AIDS is likely to create depression and isolation, disrupt social ties and undermine the sense of biographical continuity (Burchardt 2010a). For all this, the HIV/AIDS epidemic might appear as one of the major social problems of contemporary South Africa.

From a sociological point of view, however, social problems only emerge inasmuch as social actors define some observable condition as such. For various reasons, churches, religious communities, and religious charity organizations had been expected to claim "ownership" (Gusfield 1981, 10–11) of AIDS as a social problem. Because of their long-standing involvement in charitable activities, their importance within the health sector, but also because of their supposedly privileged position in advertising sexual self-restraint as a prevention message, religious actors were assumed to take the lead in the struggle against HIV/AIDS. Historically, however, the relationship between religion and AIDS in Africa has been rather uneasy. The Papal ban on condoms evidently created confusion over public-health campaigns advocating condom-use. Within the Evangelical and Pentecostal camps, HIV-positive people were for a long time associated with sexual sin, receiving divine punishment in the form of disease. Whether religious discourse was actually pushing stigma or rather replicating moral judgments prevailing in wider public discourse is difficult to say. Yet, it was precisely sexual stigma that also imposed barriers against the provision of traditional forms of care for people sick with AIDS. Perceptions of "transmission through sin" and the fear that sexual education would rather raise young people's interest in sex instead of dispelling it, further discouraged religious actors to get involved in prevention work.

In recent years, this situation has changed dramatically. HIV/AIDS has become a much-debated issue in many religious communities; churches have set up initiatives, programs, and significantly even specialized NGOs that deal with AIDS. In this context, religious organizations are running countless support groups for HIV-positive people, offer counseling and have developed various theologies of hope and compassion. Eventually, they even made their way into public schools providing instruction in so-called life-skills education, which is essentially organized around issues such as AIDS, sexuality, love, and intimate relationships (Burchardt 2010b). Similar classes are offered to youth outside of public schools through church-based peer-education programs. This raises questions as to the mechanisms and processes whereby in the religious field AIDS is being "problematized" as well as to the complex of problems AIDS has come to symbolize as a consequence of this.

In this chapter, I will explore the practice of faith-based life-skills education to unpack the various ways in which the entire complex of love, intimate relationships, dating practices, and sexuality is being scrutinized and re-assembled in terms of ethical choice. In these processes, AIDS is construed as a problem of the *quality of social relationships*, specifically the relationships between women and men, for which religion provides a powerful, if heterogeneous, idiom. I begin by briefly discussing how social science research on the relationships between religion and AIDS in Africa can be conceptualized in terms of social problems theory. After that I outline the specific perspective of cultural sociology, arguing that the construction of social practices, such as sexual intercourse for instance, as a social problem should be seen as an ongoing accomplishment in which specific cultural competences come to bear. In the last section of this chapter, I discuss how in the context of urban South Africa HIV-positivity has given rise to heterogeneous discourses in which not only intimacy and sexuality but the management of everyday life as such have been rendered, and in fact *institutionalized*, as problematic.[2] The chapter is based on ethnographic field research in the city of Cape Town in 2006.

RELIGION AND AIDS IN AFRICA: THE
PERSPECTIVE OF SOCIAL PROBLEMS

Until now, social problems theory has had little impact on the way the links between religion and AIDS in Africa have been explored. I suggest, however, that this perspective is useful as a heuristic device for conceptualizing existing studies. The framework developed by Beckford (1990) seems particularly useful to this end. Broadly defining social problems as "(. . .) conditions that are widely believed to cause avoidable and remediable misery or frustration" (1, fn 1), he sets out to propose a dual problematic: on the one hand, "(R)eligious groups have often been at the forefront of efforts to identify, analyze, and remedy social problems."(ibid, 1). Reversely, we are confronted with the fact that religions can give rise to or aggravate social problems.

Most studies on the relationships between HIV/AIDS and Christianity in Africa are in one way or another situated within this framework of analysis. Regardless of whether they focus on the activities and impacts of organized religion in HIV/AIDS interventions or on the role of personal faith in dealing with disease and related biographical uncertainties, this research either highlights how religious discourse aggravates the epidemic and as such contributes to the social problem, or emphasizes the potential of religious organizations to provide support and care, and thus, a remedy to HIV/AIDS. The first line of investigation is primarily concerned with the negative discriminating effects of Christian teachings on sexual morality as a form of religious prevention campaigning, the related theological discourses blaming HIV-positive people as sinners and construing AIDS as a divine punishment (e.g. Dilger 2007; Agadjanian 2005; Pfeiffer 2004; Garner 2000). The second line of research explores the conditions and forms in which religious organizations give hope, care and support for sufferers in a traditional charitable fashion (Burchardt 2007; Dilger 2007. 59).

Both perspectives, however, also intersect. While Agadjanian (2005) points out that the cultural closure of the Pentecostal milieu keeps secular prevention messages effectively "outside," Garner claims that it is this very closure, which explains the much lower levels of pre- and extramarital sexual intercourse in Pentecostal groups compared to other denominations. Whereas Agadjanian sees religion as part of the problem, Garner views it as part of the solution. Sadgrove (2007) in her study on religion and sexuality among university students in Uganda manages to penetrate even deeper into the interstices between religious discourse and sexual practice. She shows how female students typically establish Christian facades as a way of "keeping up appearances." Moreover, she reveals how this façade mainly serves for rejecting unwanted male approaches while certainly not turning them into the kind of sexual abstainers that the façade suggests. In all this, AIDS was not a primary concern. What invariably seems to be at stake in these ethnographies is how precisely the problem of AIDS is perceived and by whom, and how such perceptions are acted out in social interaction. In the following section, I explore how these processes can be captured from the perspective of cultural sociology.

SOCIAL PROBLEMS: THE PERSPECTIVE
OF CULTURAL SOCIOLOGY

Since Durkheim's landmark study on the social origins of suicide (1979), research on social problems has fascinated sociologists, not least because of the practical relevance such studies appeared to convey. What is more, if sociology itself was an expression of the increasing reflexivity of modern society, then the sociology of social problems could be regarded as the epitome of such reflexive turn; it forged a notion of the social through studying the ways in which it was becoming problematic for itself. As Hjelm (2009) has recently shown, in addressing these ways the sociology of social problems gradually shifted from an emphasis on objective conditions, taken as problematic, and their subjective perception towards a more thorough appreciation of the putative character of such objective condition. Thus, it was recognized that social problems are, first and foremost, "(. . .) *the activities of individuals or groups making assertions of grievances and claims with respect to some putative conditions*" (Spector and Kitsuse 2001, 75; emphasis in original, cited in Hjelm 2009, 928). These shifts also reveal how the intellectual history of the field reflects the growing influence of social constructionism in social theory at large.

However, Hjelm also reminds us that despite these conceptual changes the sociology of social problems remained intimately tied to a relatively narrow theoretical framework of norms and deviance. Even if viewed as embodied in the process of *claims making*, social problems emerged in the form of deviance from norms "made public."[3] While this is not wrong altogether, it certainly fails to capture important aspects of contemporary public discourse such as social justice, financial crisis, or third world poverty for instance. These are unequivocally framed as social problems but have little to do with deviance. In this article, I want to propose and show that cultural sociology provides an alternative way of thinking about social problems, namely by focusing on the processes of *problematizing* proper. Combining insights from the neo-institutionalist take on culture and recent approaches of praxeology seems particularly helpful in this regard.

In an influential article, Ann Swidler (1986) has criticized the idea that culture shapes action by providing ultimate values towards which action is oriented. From this point of view, differences between individuals and groups in dominant patterns of action would have to be explained in terms of different values such groups adhere to. What is problematic here is that action is conceptualized as an atomized event in which choices among alternatives regarding means are made through selective links to values. This, Swidler argues, suggests a highly unrealistic view of both action and culture because it ignores time. Instead of an atomized event, action is embedded into enduring "lines of action," i.e. into strategies in the sense of more encompassing ways of organizing action (ibid. 277). She therefore proposes to understand culture as "toolkits" of symbols, stories, rituals, and worldviews; as an incorporated repertoire of competences, skills and habits people may use for persistently ordering action through time (ibid. 275).

If we depart from a concept of religion as a part of culture, this also suggests certain ways of thinking about religion and social problems, of which two stand out: Firstly, for people whose toolkits are deeply imbued with religion certain aspects of social change ("selfish individualism," "moral decay," etc.) may become problematic and articulated through religious symbols. What explains *claims making* here is not only that religion is the legitimate vocabulary; it is also the one "at hand," itself a component of their cultural competence. Secondly, religious symbols may also be deployed to express social concerns by people who do not define themselves as religious. In certain situations, people may unite under a religious banner because it is most powerful for scandalizing injustice, violence or war. Again, culture is in action not by defining what people want, but by providing repertoires of symbolic vehicles of meaning through which to articulate concern.

If the *cultural turn* in the social sciences was important in reminding us of the invariably symbolic and interpretive constitution of social life, it was the *practice turn* that even more radically transformed culture from an abstract system into something that takes place only in and through social practices. This practice turn is evident in the revival of ethnomethodology but also in Bourdieu's notion of praxeology and Butler's theory of performativity. What all of these approaches have in common is an idea of *culture as practice*. Praxeological perspectives draw attention to the fact that culture only exists inasmuch as it is practically performed, "acted out" and incorporated. However, instead of merely referring to processes of enacting *pre*-existing and *pre*-manufactured scripts embodied in available cultural repertoires, praxeology emphasizes how these are created, sustained or modified in and through social practice itself. More than the neo-institutionalist parlance of "drawing on" or "enacting" scripts or rules, praxeology points to contingencies, and thus the ways tensions between reproduction and creativity are constitutively inscribed into the practice of culture as a generative grammar. Generalizing the ethnomethodological notion of "doing gender" as the practical and interactive *accomplishment* of gender differences, these ideas can be summed up in the concept of *doing culture* (Hörning and Reuter 2004).

What are the implications of this concept for the study of social problems? First of all, it provides a social-constructionist approach that is liberated from the concerns with prevailing societal normativities. Instead of linking social problems to deviance, it sees them as products of an ongoing process in which the transformation of social issues into social problems is interactively accomplished. While it is very close to the notion of claims making, it places greater emphasis on the repertoires of competences, skills, and habits that are both enabling and limiting possible practices. Simultaneously, they are preconditions of how claims are made and at once its effects. However, what distinguishes the practice of social problems from, let's say doing gender or doing science, is its reflexive nature. The practice of social problems can be linked to many other cultural practices, for example in terms of cultural critique, by disrupting its taken-for-granted character. It is then, for instance, a *certain way* of doing gender, in other words: of performing gender arrangements through the deployment of skills and resources in the context of power relations, which becomes subject of claims making. This process, I suggest we may simply and tautologically refer to as *problematization*. Exploring problematizations from this point of view involves studying the processes and mechanisms whereby a part of culture is rendered problematic as well as examining which aspects of practice are being problematized. As a consequence, culture emerges at once as a subject of contestations and as a repertoire of symbolic tools for articulating them.

HIV/AIDS AS A SOCIAL PROBLEM

What effectively limits the volatility of cultural practice is the fact that much of it is enshrined in institutions. The same applies to social problems: Much of the social construction of social problems is hierarchically concentrated in institutions, which in a self-referential manner provide for the reproduction of both the solution and the problem itself. With regard to HIV/AIDS as a disease one of the primary institutions is the apparatus of biomedicine. Yet again, from the perspective of cultural sociology HIV-infection would be less an attribute of an individual than something inherent in the practice of scientific and medical interaction. We would then rather speak of HIV-positivity as an accomplishment of medical and other kinds of social interactions. Does that mean that HIV has no independent and prior materiality outside of cultural discourse?

One of the perennial points of debate in the study of social problems was precisely whether objective conditions "really exist" or at all matter to the sociological gaze. It seems that with regard to disease this problem imposes itself in a particularly significant way. There is an undeniable material, i.e. objective dimension to HIV-infection, which despite all efforts to laying open the contingencies of medical discourse in a genealogical fashion makes itself felt in the lives of HIV-positive people. Latour (1998) has suggested conceptualizing the ways non-human entities such as viruses are involved in social practices, and the way agency is practically assembled, through the notion of the "actant." Whenever interaction involving non-human entities or artefacts occurs, Latour argues, agency can neither be reduced to human beings nor to the non-human entity. Instead it is assembled and distributed, and therefore has to be viewed as the capability of the entire ensemble of actants. I contend that this perspective safeguards against some unrealistic implications of over-sociologizing social constructionism. It also prepares us for understanding how sudden changes, such as the inadvertent multiplication of HIV-positive blood cells and resulting disease or the "discovery" of a vaccine, may undermine all prior and carefully calibrated social arrangements of dealing with HIV/AIDS.

The reason the social constructionist perspective is nevertheless defensible is that the very same objective medical condition, in this case HIV-positivity, is being experienced in highly different ways. An infected person who has been abandoned because of stigma may receive very little material and emotional support, as a consequence of which she or he stops leaving the house and visiting doctors altogether and experiences a rapidly deteriorating health status. Another person finding herself in the same stage of the disease may receive full emotional support from relatives, and hence have a very different idea about HIV-positivity. Moreover, the virus may motivate infected and uninfected people alike to change their sexual practices. The actant here is the assemblage of virus and subject. It is precisely this contingency that sheds light on the social dimensions of disease, and that draws attention to the practice of HIV/AIDS as a social problem.

In the following analysis I will draw attention to the ways AIDS is being posited as a problem of intimate relationships in faith-based prevention discourse, and to how this problematization has morphed into a much broader discourse on ethical selfhood. Methodologically, this account is based on an interpretive analysis of participant observations in life-skills courses and narrative interviews with church employees and educators from various churches and faith-based organizations and participating youth.

"RELIGION IN ACTION:" TEACHING SKILLS FOR LIFE

In January 2006 the Anglican Church-affiliated AIDS initiative "Fikelela" established a peer-education program called "agents of change". Within this program, the church youth of any parish that participates is divided into groups of five young people, each of which elects its own leader. Peer-educators are between the ages of 15 and 18, and meet twice a week with the (adult) youth leader of the parish for regular feedback and evaluation sessions. Before the program starts, group leaders are taken to a training course, which is organized as a summer camp and in which they learn about their responsibilities and the contents of the program. Being elected as a group leader is itself viewed as bestowing a certain degree of pride, fame, and coolness on them. Moreover, group leaders are also expected to act as role models for their groups in their private lives. The program itself lasts for a about a year and covers themes such as "values, self-worth and vision", "love, sex and reasons", "HIV/AIDS and me" etc, all of which are put down in a manual.[4] During the pilot phase 11 out of the 132 parishes belonging to the diocese of Cape Town participated. Far from naturally emerging from the church agenda, however, the establishment of the program was the result of a long process of mobilization within the church hierarchies. As Cindy, director of the program and priest in the Anglican church explained to me, many moral barriers had to be overcome before sexual talk could finally emerge on the surface of religious discourse: "It is easy to say 'care for the sick, care for the orphans' but when it comes to prevention, you know, we've had people saying to us "you are promoting fornication."[5] Obviously, the cultural work of gradually overcoming these resistances and thereby establishing AIDS as a social problem not only in terms of "caring for the sick" but also in terms of sexuality began well before the program's inception. The program rather demarcated the historical moment in which—through embracing AIDS as a social problem—sexuality and the multiple forms and manifestations of sexual desires have been drawn into the spotlight of religious attention and rendered a legitimate subject of religious concern.

At the same time, other faith-based organizations were already involved in prevention work by offering so-called life-skills courses at public schools that are part of the compulsory high-school curriculum. Originating from the USA and the UK, the pedagogical concept of like skills education has been channeled to South Africa through the work of the WHO. Whereas in general life skills education is understood as assisting people to become socially and psychologically competent and is closely related to adolescent risk behavior, its introduction in South Africa has spawned the merging of life skills with health education as a result of the promotion of HIV-prevention in schools.[6] But what precisely are the techniques through which HIV and sexuality are addressed?

PROBLEM EXPANSION: SEXUALITY AS ETHICAL CHOICE

The educators frequently complained about the difficulties of speaking about HIV-prevention because the learners were "sick and tired of it." Partly as a result of this over-saturation effect, sexuality is placed upfront at the centre of group discourse, namely with regard to two dimensions: Firstly, in relation to the functioning of the human body, reproductive roles, and sexually transmitted diseases. Sexuality is thus understood through a medico-biological framework. Secondly, sexuality is depicted as a field of experience, shaped by cultural norms, understood through socially constructed categories, and manufactured in individual practice. Yet, regardless of whether they advocate condom-use or premarital abstinence for manufacturing "safe sex" or "no sex," the educators promote ideas whose enactment they can hardly monitor. What emerges as a substitute for sanctions is a model of moral education that strongly focuses *individual moral responsibility* whereby people are constantly reminded that sex needs rational management and that every sexual choice is an investment into a healthy future. The educators thus recognize that the message has to be communicated in terms of people's own *best interests*. In the courses, negative consequences of sex such as unwanted (teenage) pregnancy, sexually transmitted diseases, AIDS, and loss of self-worth are explained so as to profile the good reasons for not engaging in sex altogether. Yet achieving "healthy sex" or abstinence, people are told, is related to the quality of intimate relationships, which in turn is an outcome of the moral development and self-esteem of the "whole person." The practical accomplishment of HIV-prevention as a social problem thus unfolds as a series of progressive problematizations in which every aspect of everyday life is ethically scrutinized.

However, there are differences in the ways sexual discourse and religious ideology are intertwined according to the place of organizations in the religious field, and the educators' religious identity. These differences crystallize around the ideal-typical figures of *missionaries* and *social workers*. Missionaries are mostly found in the field of Evangelical and Pentecostal Christianity, social workers in the context of mainline Christianity.

COMPETING STRATEGIES, COMPETING COMPETENCES: MISSIONARIES AND SOCIAL WORKERS

The defining feature of the missionaries is that the concern with social issues such as AIDS is subordinated to, and part of, a much broader religious project. Thus, Daniel, who works for the Evangelical "Living Hope Community Centre" (LHCC), blatantly stated: "AIDS is not my main concern. To be honest, my main concern is to get them to know Jesus Christ and what the church says about lifestyles, about being abstinent, faithful and stick to one partner." While he self-consciously identified himself as a missionary, this mission project is about advertising a distinctly modern idea, as the talk of church-sponsored "lifestyles" palpably suggests. In this approach, health is essentially rendered a secondary, albeit not quite negligible, benefit of faith. In much the same vein, Steven, one of LHCC's senior managers, proclaimed that as a remedy against the "problems that arise from being free and loose, we *preach* the message of abstinence and be faithful." For the missionaries, prevention work is quite literally a newly acquired aspect of preaching the gospel, something that provides additional plausibility to a pre-existing concern. Indeed, within their educational efforts, concerns with health promotion and proselytizing thoroughly coalesce into an admonishing reminder of the connections between obedience to God's will and living a healthy life. Health emerges as a powerful, this-worldly sign for salvation. Whenever possible, missionaries gratefully seize the opportunity of pointing to the inherent health-promoting consequences of the

Christian "lifestyle" while at the same time carefully avoiding a purely instrumental understanding of faith.

The priority of evangelizing and the conviction that charitable work is eventually identical to preaching also explain the emphasis the missionaries lay on the role of the scriptures for their work. "Throughout," one of LHCC's educator insisted, "it is biblical values. (. . .) And biblical means everything we do must be according to what the Bible says." Similarly, another educator asserted: "I always use principles from the Bible and then they understand that no-one can go against what God says." The missionaries insist on a literal understanding of the scriptures, suggesting that the Bible provides direct prescriptions for moral action.

Missionaries thus lay primary emphasis on the principle of monogamous sexuality, reminding people, as Daniel does, that "just as much as God loves us he hates sin. All bad things in the Bible are related to sin, and wherever there is sin, destruction follows." It is important to note that the missionaries mostly avoid the over-simplifying condemnation of *all* HIV-positive people as sinners. Their discourse, nevertheless, reveals a strong tendency towards interpreting worldly crisis in terms of collective deviance from divine law, as an articulation of chaos and darkness spawned by the deviation from the God-given order. What underlies this interpretive figure is the Manichean dualism between the evil and the good characteristic of Evangelical and Pentecostal Christianity.

In the eyes of the missionaries, sinful sexuality is strongly associated with the negative effects of the freedoms that consumer culture provides to modern individuals, especially the televised license to deviate from "God's plan." Daniel explained:

> Life skills education gives me a platform to talk about pornography also, about the fact that society thinks it's normal and cool but it is not a wise thing to do because it starts infiltrating your mind and you start becoming addicted and tomorrow you start raping etc. (. . .) At the back of their mind they know it, sex and all those things, it's wrong but they are waiting for someone to tell them it is wrong.

The way pornography and everything that from the missionaries' point of view appears as sexual deviance is linked to crime, demonstrates how sexual activity is seen as bringing about all sorts of negative consequences. The freedoms of modernity—and thus, the moral possibilities to make use of them—peculiarly crystallize around an idea of sexual danger, perceived as the beguiling chimera of modern society that corrupts the positive potentials of individuals. In this context, it is the role of the missionaries *qua* critics of modern society to speak the moral truth, to tell the people what is wrong and what is right. Sexually "right" is to follow God's plan, to restrict sexual activity to monogamous marriage, for only in the context of marriage the destructive forces of sex can be neutralized; only within marriage the "uses of pleasure" conform to God's plan and may thus be reconciled with biblical faith. In other words: For the missionaries, the possibility of making legitimate use of sexual pleasure only *opens* inasmuch and as long as it is *locked up* within the walls of monogamous marriage.

The emphasis on "God's plan" for human sexuality, part of evangelically oriented Christianity, also explains the clear-cut *hierarchy of prevention messages*. As mentioned previously, missionaries lay exclusive stress on pre-marital abstinence and faithfulness in marriage. Interestingly, they suggest these concepts not only as religiously sanctioned but also as the only effective solutions for the AIDS epidemic at large. One of the educators dismissed the propagation of condom use since, in her view, the persistence of high levels of HIV-infection clearly proved the ineffectiveness of much state-sponsored condom promotion over the past decade. Moreover, Daniel questioned the technical effectiveness of condoms for HIV-infection by referring to supposed scientific evidence: "(. . .) what is cool is that there is now information that condoms aren't safe, the virus can go through the rubber, there's a 3% chance. So we don't say this only because we are an FBO but because it is the actual truth." Within this statement, the truth claims of science and religion are coalesced; the apparently selective take on "scientific evidence" serves to underpin the religious rejection of condoms, which are—as Pentecostals long suspected—not only conducive to sexual permissiveness but also lull people in a false sense of safety against AIDS. Similarly, in trying to elucidate the inherent difficulties of condom use missionaries often refer to the possibility that the condom breaks during the intercourse. Against this backdrop, missionaries promote abstinence for unmarried youth and faithfulness to one partner in a monogamous marriage, given that both are HIV-negative, as the only option, which is "100% safe." Moral sexual practice is seamlessly linked both to the possibility of salvation and to the promise of health.

What distinguishes the "social workers" from the "missionaries" within the field of faith-based HIV-prevention are not so much the objectives of their work than the priorities they attach to them. Indeed, they all agree on the value of monogamous marriage, the importance to de-stigmatize AIDS, and that personal faith can be an empowering asset for individuals to value their sexuality. What is particular about the social workers is how religious background either supports, or is severed from, a different notion of professionalism, which precipitates an essentially *liberal* approach to HIV-prevention and sexuality.

For the social workers, concerns with social justice, health and wellbeing clearly override efforts to mission. While being motivated by Christian faith they do place primary emphasis on separating their personal religious commitments from their professional engagement. With regard to the Anglican Church, Thapelo, Anglican AIDS' senior fieldworker, explicates this approach in the following way:

> (. . .) Coming from the Anglican background and with the ethics of hospitality the church has always wanted to be with (. . .) people that

are suffering, and are discriminated. So it is about the church being churchy. But then about the church also realizing we are not evangelizing. Hopefully once people encounter the church in that way, hopefully they will then begin to sort of believe or get a better understanding of their faith but in essence the church is not a self-sustaining body, it is not a body that seeks to maintain itself, it is one institution that is about doing good outside of its boundaries, (. . .) and to get involved with social activism. (. . .) Because the whole purpose is not about evangelizing *but it is about doing what the church is called to do anyway.*

Thapelo's perspective should be construed as the maximum contrast to the missionary. The passage unfolds as a reflection about the role and the responsibilities of the church in society, as a theological engagement with the relationship between the church and the people beyond its boundaries. For Thapelo, the role of the church in society is defined in terms of charitable activity. While this activity is religious by motivation, it is based on secular terms; for prioritizing the imposition of one's own religious conviction on the other diverts attention from what, in Thapelo's eyes, the church is "called upon to do anyway," i.e. to serve the needy through social work. Here, evangelizing appears cynical when the "real problems" are suffering and discrimination. In this perspective, the first duty of the church is to engage with suffering while conversion is understood as a possible secondary outcome. The role of the church, as his emphasis on dissociating AIDS and sin later in the interview forcefully vindicates, is not to judge but to help.

The strictly *private* nature of religious faith social workers subscribe to is similarly reflected in the approach of HOPE WORLDWIDE, an ecumenical organization working in schools in the township of Khayelitsha. Regarding the question of what kinds of paramount values the organization pursues, James, the directing manager, remarks:

Our focus is not necessarily what the Bible says. So I think that's personal convictions. (. . .) I think we don't go into schools and churches to teach them what the Bible says. I think we are very clear on that. But our education is values-based. So it is not just a call on, you know it is good for you health. We are trying to teach values that help them to make informed decisions about their lives for themselves. (. . .) I think there's that self-respect, you know protecting myself against abuse, you know protecting other people, taking responsibility for them. So its values that would help the person to not just you know sort of go for you know just do whatever according to the wind I guess. So it's values that are focused on their courage.

Although working for a faith-based organization, James rejects a biblical approach to his engagement, and similar to Thapelo he thereby dismisses the evangelizing mission as ideological framework of sexual education on the basis of the liberal credo. The missionaries' concept of "health through faith" and their emphasis on sharing the gospel is replaced by an ethical discourse on personal responsibility, self-improvement, and self-care.

Around this set of ideas, views and practices—privatized religious belief, a critical approach to the use of sacred scriptures, religious motivation but secular professional practice—crystallizes the figure of the religious educator qua *"social worker."* Social workers are driven by a holistically conceived humanism, trying to shape ethically accountable and autonomous subjects by focusing, as they invariably argue, on "the whole person" without, however, connecting this, as missionaries tend to do, to conversion. Social workers are inspired by an idea of collective progress through individual change and moral transformation for which the construction of ethical selfhood by propagating values of self-respect, self-esteem etc., is of great significance. Whereas missionaries insist that the actualization of individual potentials, impeded by the corrupting influences of modernity, rests with the individual submission to biblical faith and the corresponding moral code they propagate, social workers tend to construe individual empowerment as an effect of self-care that might or might not be underpinned by Christian faith. Because of their rather secular understanding of HIV prevention, they also show little inclination towards tendencies to demonizing condoms as giving license to "HIV-safe adultery" or fuelling the sexual permissiveness of youth that missionaries partly support.[7]

Another characteristic feature of the social workers is the interpretation of their engagement in terms of an ethically warranted social activism, in which religious groups are becoming actors in the struggle for social justice; the notion of "doing good beyond the church's boundaries" is essentially linked to a concept of a "good society." In this sense, both, missionaries and social workers entertain a *transformative* relationship to their social environments: Missionaries seek, by virtue of a cross-fertilizing effort of propagating Christian sexual morality and evangelization, to expand religious spaces within society by means of conversion. For the social workers, the transformative aspect is educational and *political* in that as a result of the emphasis on social activism they are much more inclined to address political issues such as gender-based violence, gender inequality, and human rights. All this puts social workers at great proximity to secular civil society actors from whom, thanks to the shared adherence to humanistic values, they are sometimes hardly distinguishable.

CONCLUSION: RELIGIOUS COMPETENCES OF PROBLEMATIZING SEX

The construction of AIDS as a social problem is an ongoing process involving myriad institutions such as the apparatuses of biomedical research, international development regimes, trans-national NGOs, welfare state apparatuses but also faith-based organizations and churches. Each of these embody specific discourses, which change over time and contribute to the fact that especially for young South Africans intimate relationships and sexuality have been rendered problematic in day-to-day interaction. Inherited ways whereby sexual life is organized have been questioned.

In this article I have argued that faith-based life-skills education is one of the most important ways in which this questioning has been institutionalized. Moreover, from the perspective of cultural sociology such institutionalizations are always interactive accomplishments in which stocks of knowledge embodied in competences and habits come to bear. For answering questions about the construction of social problems it is therefore mandatory to study how these competences are performed and relate to definitions as to what the problem "really" is. From this point of view, I have interpreted faith-based sexual education as a series of progressive problematizations in which through re-appropriated notions of "ethical life" and "good society" individuals are constantly invited to scrutinize and re-make their intimate relationships. I have also shown how differential interpretive and religious competences are grouped to form specific cultural styles of problematizing AIDS and sexuality, those of missionaries and social workers. While both can easily be accommodated with South Africa's entrenched religious pluralism, the question is which of them has the greater match with emerging South African consumer culture on the one hand, and urban poverty on the other. Whereas at first sight, the cultural liberalism characteristic of the social workers seems better suited to these circumstances, Pentecostalism often appears to forge much stronger religious identifications. For these reasons, it is difficult to predict whether one of the models is likely to prevail.

NOTES

1. The term "adult population" refers to those between the ages of 15 and 49.
2. The following account is limited to tracing the emergence of diverse languages in and through which religious actors define and construct sexual and intimate life as problematic. For an analysis on people's interpretations and responses to such constructions see Burchardt (2010b).
3. As I will show in the following analysis, especially religious groups may readily deploy frameworks of norms and deviance in claims making, for instance in terms of deviance "from God's plan." Nevertheless, we should avoid uncritically turning categories of popular discourse into concepts of analysis.
4. The manual was produced by the non-profit organization GOLD, which specializes on issues of development and AIDS education in South Africa and Botswana.
5. Resistances surfaced for instance, when in 2003 Fikelela members produced a T-shirt carrying the provocative slogan "Our church has AIDS." After receiving one of the T-shirts, one of the priests furiously commented: "I can't wear that T-shirt because if I wear it, it is like saying 'Our church has prostitutes'."
6. With regards to the educational activities of religious organizations in public schools, there was competing information as to whether this sets limits to religious expression. Some organizations reported having to stick to the

secular curricula and therefore having to clothe their messages in secular terms whereas others told me that no such limitations were applied to their work.
7. HOPE WORLDWIDE's directing manager reported having distributed one million condoms in Cape Town during 2005 (the year before the field research period) alone. Cindy from the Anglican church-affiliated FBO Fikelela explicitly criticized other religious leaders and educators (i.e. the ones I refer to as missionaries) for pointing to the supposed lack of safety of condoms and for thereby nourishing precisely the kind of cognitive confusion about HIV prevention, which Fikelela is trying to address.

REFERENCES

Agajanian, Victor. 2005. Gender, Religious Involvement, and HIV/AIDS Prevention in Mozambique. *Social Science & Medicine* 61: 1529–1539.
Beckford, James. 1990. The Sociology of Religion and Social Problems. *Sociological Analysis* 51(1):1–14.
Bourdieu, Pierre. 1977. *Outline of a Theory of Practice.* Cambridge; New York: Cambridge University Press.
Burchardt, Marian. 2007. Speaking to the Converted? Religion and the Politics of Gender in South African AIDS Discourse. *Comparativ. Zeitschrift für Globalgeschichte und vergleichende Gesellschaftsforschung* 17(5/6): 95–114.
Burchardt, Marian. 2010a. "Life in Brackets": Biographical Uncertainties of HIV-Positive Women in South Africa. *Forum Qualitative Sozialforschung / Forum: Qualitative Social Research* 11(1), Art. 3. http://nbn-resolving.de/urn:nbn:de:0114-fqs100135. (Accessed October 28, 2010).
Burchardt, Marian. 2010b. Ironies of Subordination: Ambivalences of Gender in Religious AIDS-Interventions in South Africa. *Oxford Development Studies* 38(1): 63–82.
Butler, Judith. 1990. *Gender Trouble: Feminism and the Subversion of Identity.* New York: Routledge.
Dilger, Hansjörg. 2007. Healing the Wounds of Modernity: Salvation, Community and Care in a Neo-Pentecostal Church in Dar Es Salaam, Tanzania. *Journal of Religion in Africa* 37(1): 59–83.
Durkheim, Emile. 1979. *Suicide.* New: The Free Press.
Garner, Robert C. 2000. Safe Sects? Dynamic Religion and AIDS in South Africa. *Journal of Modern African Studies* 38(1): 41–69.
Gusfield, Joseph. 1981. *The Culture of Public Problems: Drinking-Driving and the Symbolic Order.* Chicago: Chicago University Press.
Hjelm, Titus. 2009. Religion and Social Problems: A New Theoretical Perspective. In *The Oxford Handbook of the Sociology of Religion*, edited by Peter Clarke. 924–941. Oxford: Oxford University Press.
Hörning, Karl H. and Reuter, Julia (eds). 2004. *Doing Culture. Neue Positionen zum Verhältnis von Kultur und sozialer Praxis.* Bielefeld: Transcript.
Latour, Bruno. 1998. Über technische Vermittlung. Philosophie, Soziologie, Genealogie. In *Technik und Sozialtheorie*, edited by Werner Rammert. 29–81. Frankfurt a.M. and New York: Campus.
Pfeiffer, James. 2004. Condom Marketing, Pentecostalism, and Structural Adjustment in Mozambique. *Medical Anthropology Quarterly* 18(1): 77–103.
Sadgrove, Jo. 2007. "Keeping Up Appearances": Sex and Religion amongst University Students in Uganda. *Journal of Religion in Africa* 37(1): 116–144.
Swidler, Ann. 1986. Culture in Action: Symbols and Strategies. *American Sociological Review* 51(2): 273–286.

Part III
Religion as a Social Problem

10 Perception of Muslims and Islam in Australian Schools
A National Survey

Abe W. Ata

In Australia, attitudes towards Islam cannot be separated from the history of migration, the social and ethnic composition of Muslim communities, and the politics of global conflict. In this context, racism, particularly in the form of cultural racism, joins and is voiced as disapproval of morality. Such negative views are widespread in media, academic, and government texts (Goodall and Jakubowicz 1994; Human Rights and Equal Opportunity Commission 2004).

Internationally, negative stereotyping of Islam and Muslims has been linked to the first Gulf War, the war in Iraq, September 11, and other terrorist attacks. Poynting notes the increase in assaults on people of "Middle Eastern appearance," women wearing the hijab and men wearing "Islamic garb" after the outbreak of the first Gulf War (Poynting 2002). Women and girls emerged as the most frequent targets. At the same time there was an increase in arson, vandalism and threats of assault directed towards the newly discovered "enemy within." Poynting points to the role of tabloid media, in particular talk-back radio, in whipping up racist sentiments at this time, and in a similar way after September 11 (with a similar increase in racist incidents).

A discourse joining Arab-Muslim-Terrorist worked to join the terms Gang-Rapist-Arab-Muslim by the same means, particularly in Sydney, following a series of sexual assaults in Bankstown (Poynting 2002, 44). Concern about Middle Eastern asylum seekers, particularly in the course of the 2001 Federal election campaign contributed to distrust, fear, and the emergence of racist discourses. In these instances politicians joined with powerful talkback personalities and columnists to create a sense of moral panic. This process highlights the fact that the media is primary source of information on Islam (not the Koran or direct contact) and what it stands for (Brasted 2001). The economic, historical and religious diversity of some sixty Muslim countries are rarely represented in media accounts.

These patterns of representation and attack were felt in schools, with the emergence of SOB (straight off the boat) as a playground insult. The Australian Arabic Council's Racism Register records a school in South Eastern Melbourne being graffitied with "die Muslim scum" and threats being made at school to Muslim students (Australian Arabic Council 2001). At University level too students feel frustration at their teachers' lack of knowledge of Islam and reliance on media representations (Asmar 2001; Speck 1997).

By contrast, in an earlier period, Bullivant brushed off concerns about discrimination faced by migrant background students by postulating a migrant "success ethic" (Bullivant 1987; 1988). Cahill similarly concluded from a large scale study that "the general climate of Australian schools is healthy and positive for minority Australian students with cultural, religious and racial backgrounds different from those of mainstream Australian students" (Cahill and Gundert 1996, xv). This is despite a perception of hostility from peers and teachers expressed by some migrant background students (particularly girls), and teacher concerns about the participation of girls in activities and Ramadan (Cahill and Gundert 1996, 120, 156–159). Other reports have suggested school is the location for much discrimination on the basis of ethnicity (Human Rights and Equal Opportunity Commission 2004). A study of Victorian schools (Ata and Batrouney 1989) showed that the type of school attended correlated with the degree of stereotyping. Private school students were more likely to accept negative stereotypes of Muslims and Arabs. The study involved the application of words such as "rude," "rich," "intelligent," "aggressive," "lecherous," and "primitive."

This chapter reports some results from a large-scale study of attitudes towards Islam and Muslims among Australian secondary students. Widespread negative stereotypes and the relatively new presence of the Muslim community in Australia tend to suggest non-Muslim students may not be well informed about Islam, despite longstanding multicultural posture of educational policy suggesting otherwise. Variations in responses between boys and girls, and religious or non-religion affiliated students were apparent. The findings show Australian students are generally ignorant about Muslims and Islam, and few believe that schools are filling the gaps in their knowledge. While non-Muslim students agree that acceptance of Muslims does not come easily in Australia, school does not emerge as a site for change.

ISLAM IN THE AUSTRALIAN SCHOOL SYSTEM

Australian schools have not been the battleground for debates about Islam and Muslims in the way they have been in several Western countries where school is understood as supporting a universal national identity to the exclusion of all others. The Government adoption of multiculturalism after the Galbally report (Galbally 1978) in 1978 made the management of ethnic identity into a policy goal in Australian schools. That same year saw the establishment of the Committee on Multicultural Education by the Commonwealth followed by funding for the now defunct Commonwealth Multicultural Education Program (MEP).

More recently, equal opportunity legislation and the development of antiracism resources such as "Racism No Way" (Department of Education and Training 2000) has provided schools with further impetus to deal with discrimination. Teacher training and guidelines from education authorities provide advice on managing student diversity in schools through sensitive and inclusive approaches to pedagogy and curriculum. It is beyond the scope of this paper to review all curricula on managing cultural diversity or on Islam and Muslims; however I will draw on some Victorian examples to illustrate the general posture of Australian schools.

In the Victorian setting, the Department of Education provides no information or resources specific to Islam or Muslims. Under the rubric of cultural and linguistic diversity it provides a general set of guidelines with resources for teachers (Department of Education Employment and Training 2001) together with an overarching multicultural policy document (Department of Education 1997). Cultural diversity is operationalized primarily as linguistic diversity, with no reference to religion.

The Victorian documents seek to promote the valuing of diverse perspectives coming into the classroom and intercultural communication. Knowledge of particular backgrounds is mentioned as a goal, but does not form part of the approaches outlined (Department of Education 1997) and does not appear as something that schools can bring to students. This is in contrast to the emphasis on in depth understanding of cultural norms and practices (Donohoue Clyne 2000) and active critical interrogation (Kalantzis and Cope 1984) that is placed at the centre of intercultural communication by some. A reactive approach to dealing with perspectives and bias means that the content and extent of knowledge gained in the classroom will be dependent on the range of concerns, if any, students express on questions relating to religion, identity and their relationship to world events. This approach is illustrated in the advice provided by the Department of Education on dealing with international tensions:

Students bring with them into the classroom many preconceptions and assumptions which influence their views about how the world works. Classroom activities may therefore impact differently on individuals according to their cultural, religious and linguistic backgrounds. All schools need to strive to create learning environments that encourage the questioning of stereotypes, and the rejection of bias, bigotry and prejudice . . . Where controversial and worrying issues are involved, story telling, drama and creative arts activities have long been recognised as useful vehicles for allowing students to air their concerns in ways that provide opportunities for further discussion. For older students, the use of structured discussion techniques can also assist in opening up contentious issues without requiring a commitment to a particular point of view. (Department of Education 2003)

Many teachers do indeed take the opportunity to discuss Islam when it is raised by students, as an incidental and tangential part of teaching. Beyond multiculturalism as an approach, there appear to be few places in the curriculum where students are taught about Muslims and Islam. The main contexts in the secondary setting in Victoria are far removed from either the Muslim community in Australia or the wider world: the crusades, the Ottoman Empire, or classical Islamic architecture. Ata's study (Ata and Batrouney 1989) found that the absence of both comprehensive relevant curriculum material and teachers with complete insight into both cultures was a primary factor behind stereotyping.

The comparative lack of curriculum, and indeed Islamic studies in tertiary education, is all the more surprising given the mounting economic, professional and educational exchange between Australia and Muslim countries. In 2003 for instance Australia exported 7 billion worth of goods to the Gulf region and Middle East, Indonesia and Malaysia. A total of 20,000 Australian teachers, nurses, expatriates, and other professionals are estimated to be working in those regions. Likewise the number of full-fee paying Muslim students from overseas is at an all time high. Australia has about 400,000 foreign students. Malaysians, Sri Lankans, Bangladeshis, and Pakistanis either live in the dorms or in apartments.

There have been recent calls for schools to take an active role in managing a "Muslim problem" in Australia. The government sponsored National Muslim Youth Summit identified education and schools as central to resolving "the perceived conflict between Muslim and Australian identity" (Muslim Community Reference Group 2006, 36). However together with the Muslim Community Reference group, it worked on the basis that Muslims need to work to resolve problems with Muslims—included amongst which is the discrimination they face from broader society (Ata 2009; Ata, Bastian and Lusher 2009). The "victim" remains at the centre of resolution of the problem for which it bears the burden. In its response to the Reference Group's proposals, the Federal government adopted a similar perspective, aiming to support young Muslims to develop strategies for coping with their own discrimination and vilification (Muslim Community Reference Group 2006, 12).

Testing for the religious factor is of particular interest in the light of a recent national survey conducted at Catholic schools in Sydney. Patricia Malone of the Australian Catholic University in Sydney found in 1995 that Religious Education classes in those schools failed to improve secondary school students' tolerance to ethnic/religious groups such as Muslims.

They are also likely to refer to those who practice religion in negative terms (Malone 1995).

METHODS

The study used a structured questionnaire comprising 90 items as the primary instrument of data collection and analysis. Both open and close-ended questions were designed in a manner that elicited reactions and helped participants to focus on the following areas:

- Accommodation of a meaningful identity comprising religious affiliation and a core of national values.
- Basis and accuracy of facts and knowledge gathered at school as well as outside of school.
- Reasons behind certain societal beliefs, views, and notions.
- Level of antipathy and acceptance of realities, practices, and pluralistic values of the mainstream Australian society.
- Social distance and perception of stereotyping, discrimination, and inclusion in the wider society.

The participants were 1,000 students enrolled at 20 secondary schools from around Australia (excluding the Northern Territory and Western Australia[1]) who were administered a full-length survey examining general attitudes towards Muslims and Islam. Participating students were from Years 10–12. A Pilot Study was conducted at 9 schools with 552 students, and a Short Form survey was conducted at 13 schools with 682 students.

Secondary schools of Muslim or Jewish affiliation were not approached for this survey, nor were Muslim or Jewish students. Differences no doubt exist within these groups towards Muslims and Islam, and these groups will be examined in subsequent surveys. But, primarily, the responses of Muslim and Jewish students are likely to be unrepresentative of most Australians. The particular characteristics of our sample are presented in Table 10.1.

The sample consisted of 43% boys and 57% girls. Most respondents (42%) were at schools in New South Wales and the Australian Capital Territory; about a third (34%) were from Victoria, and the rest were from Queensland (5%), South Australia (8%), and Tasmania (11%). Almost half the sample came from Catholic schools (53%), and roughly one quarter each were from other Christian schools (26%) and nondenominational schools (21%). Most students (92%) were born in Australia, and 81% spoke only English at home. Few respondents (7%) had any Muslim neighbors. Over half of the respondents were at coeducational schools (58%), a minority at boys-only schools (14%), and about a quarter at girls-only schools (28%). In total, fourteen demographic attributes were recorded for each respondent, ten relating to the respondent and four to the respondent's school.

Table 10.1   Participant Characteristics by Gender (N=1000)

	Female (n=655)	Male (n=340)	TOTAL
Language			
English only	518	289	807
Other/English & Other	136	50	186
TOTAL			
Religion			
Christian	490	259	749
Non-religious	152	74	226
Personal social distance to other race	2.10 (0.9)	2.48 (1.0)**	2.23 (0.9)
Perceived parental social distance to other race	2.19 (1.0)	2.34 (0.9)**	2.25 (0.9)
Personal social distance to Muslims	2.86 (1.0)	3.20 (1.0)**	2.98 (0.9)
Perceived parental social distance to Muslims	2.82 (1.0)	2.94 (1.0)	2.86 (1.0)
Do you have Muslim friends?			
Yes	171	45	216
No	482	293	775
Do you have Muslim neighbours?			
Yes	43	11	54
No	612	329	941
Knowledge of Islam	2.88 (2.4)	3.34 (2.5)**	3.03 (2.4)
Attitude of school education about Muslims	3.51 (1.0)	3.49 (1.0)	3.51 (1.0)
Location			
Metropolitan (cities)	256	46	302
Non-metropolitan (townships)	399	294	693
School Type			
Private	569	311	880
State	86	29	115
School Type			
Coeducational	385	320	705
Girls only	270	0	270
Boys only	0	20	20
Year Level			
10	21	11	33
11	329	219	548
12	295	107	402
State			
NSW/ACT	292	181	473
VIC	119	82	201
QLD	31	0	31
SA	90	18	108
TAS	123	59	182

*$p<.05$ for gender comparison, **$p<.01$ for gender comparison

RESULTS

Under each heading I will first present results relating to the sample as a whole. Although the survey sample was not selected in a formally random way, it was large and was drawn from a wide geographic range of schools. Hence, we believe it is likely to be quite representative of secondary students in Australia. Three open-ended questions were put to respondents and the answers coded into a manageable number of categories as shown below. Naturally this entailed a degree of subjective judgment.

What are the first words that come into your mind when . . ."Muslim" is mentioned?

When asked for "the first words that come [to] mind when the word 'Muslim' is mentioned," respondents overwhelmingly (82%) offered either negative comments or comments that alluded to the differences between them and Muslims (Figure 10.1). Only 7% mentioned anything unequivocally positive. Of the 28% offering negative comments, 20% mentioned terrorism (half of them in combination with another comment) and the rest (8%) gave some other negative comment. Of the 54% alluding to differences, 13% stressed the appearance of Muslims. About one respondent in eight (12%) gave no response.

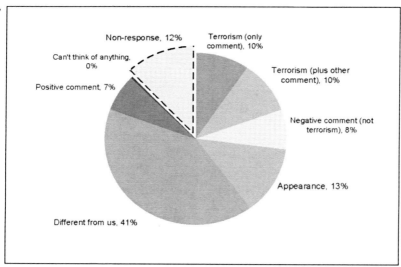

Note: Apparent errors in addition are due to rounding

N = 2023 (inc. non-response)

Figure 10.1 Response to "What are the first words that come into your mind when . . . 'Muslim' is mentioned?"

What do you like most about Muslims?

When asked what they liked most about Muslims, just under two-thirds offered a comment of some kind (Figure 10.2), and 44% gave positive comments: 4% alluded to courage, often with a mention of the difficult time Muslims have in Australia; 10% saw Muslims as benign just like other Australians; and 30% gave other positive comments. Seventeen percent of respondents gave superficial or facetious comments (7%), or explicitly stated that they could not think of anything they "liked most about Muslims" (not to be confused with no response, which might signify simply lack of motivation to respond). Just over a third of respondents (37%) gave no response.

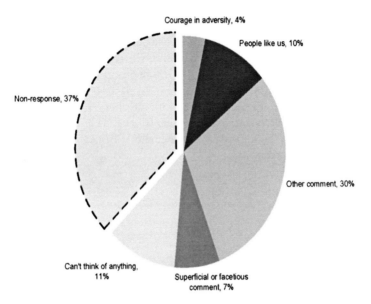

Figure 10.2   Response to "What do you like most about Muslims?"

What do you like least about Muslims?

When asked what they liked least about Muslims, just under two-thirds offered a comment of some kind (Figure 10.3). Twenty-seven percent mentioned terrorism, 8% alluded to the poor media image of Muslims, 5% alluded to threats to the Australian way of life, and 9% stressed the strangeness of Muslims. Ambivalent comments of some kind were given by 7% of the respondents, and 9% explicitly stated that they could not think of anything they "liked least about Muslims" (not to be confused with a no response, which might signify simply lack of motivation to respond). Just over a third of respondents (38%) gave no response.

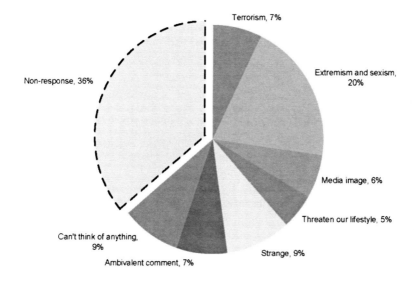

Figure 10.3 Response to "What do you like least about Muslims?"

Do Australians have good feelings about Muslims?

Goodwill towards the Muslim community resonates with more participants than otherwise. There are twice as many respondents (35% + 7% contrasted with 19% + 2%) who believe that most Australians have good feelings for Muslims (Figure 10.4). As a result it is correct to conclude that they are perceived as been accepted in the wider mainstream society. Those who expressed neutrality (38%) may want to seek firmer evidence of this reality.

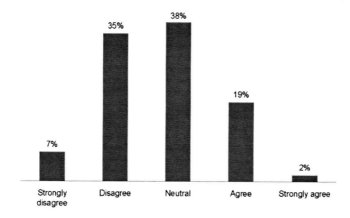

Figure 10.4 Proportion of respondents, by most Australians have good feelings for Muslims.

Having characterized the entire sample, I will next compare subgroups within the sample to address the question whether particular groups of respondents systematically differ in their attitudes towards Muslims, and, if so, how? This is of interest because it shows where and to whom policy measures might be directed.

HOW STUDENTS DIFFER IN THEIR ATTITUDES

Religion played a significant role in this area. There was a strong tendency for the two Christian groups (Catholics and Other Christians) to be less well-disposed towards Muslims and Islam than were the Nonreligious. On two statements, all three religious affiliations differed significantly from each other. With respect to the statement, "Muslims threaten the Australian way of life," all disagreed, but to different degrees: Nonreligious students disagreed most, followed by Catholics, and Other Christians disagreed least. All agreed with the statement, "most Muslims treat women with less respect than do other Australians," Other Christians agreed most, Catholics next, Nonreligious least. On one statement, "Australian TV and newspapers show Muslims in a fair way," all disagreed. Other Christians and Non-religious did not differ significantly, but did differ from Catholics who disagreed least.

Regarding gender differences, boys were less accepting of Muslims and Islam than were girls. Interestingly, boys agreed more than girls with the statement, "most Muslims treat women with less respect than do other Australians." Significant differences were found between the responses of boys and girls to a number of statements. These are listed in Table 10.2.

Table 10.2   Gender Differences towards Select Attitudinal Statements

Boys agreed more, or disagreed less, than girls	Girls agreed more, or disagreed less, than boys
• Most Muslims treat women with less respect than do other Australians. • Muslims threaten the Australian way of life. • Most religious fanatics these days are Muslims. • Most migrants are racist. • Most Australians are racist. • Australian TV and newspapers show Muslims in a fair way. • Muslims do not belong to Australia. • If I saw a Muslim student being abused in a public place I wouldn't care.	• Most Muslims have good feelings for Australia and Australians. • This school helps people of different cultures to get along better. • Learning about Muslims helps students to understand them better. • A person can be both a good Muslim and a loyal Australian. • Muslims have made a major contribution to Australia. • Most Australians have good feelings for Muslims. • The image of Muslims is as good as other migrant groups in Australia. • Australian schools should teach more about Muslims.

Does having Muslim friends make a difference? In a word, yes. Significant differences were found between the responses of those with Muslim friends and those without (Table 10.3). These findings suggest that those with Muslim friends tend to endorse positive attitudes towards Muslims, and although those who lack Muslim friends do not mostly endorse negative attitudes, they do tend to disagree less with them. In other words, positive attitudes are generally embraced by both groups, but more strongly by those with Muslim friends, and negative attitudes are generally opposed by both groups, but more strongly by those with Muslim friends. It should be noted that these findings say nothing about causation. Having Muslim friends might give rise to positive attitudes, or alternatively having positive attitudes might predispose one to seek or accept Muslim friends. Nevertheless, the two are strongly associated in a statistical sense, meaning that if one is present, the other is likely to be also.

State school students felt more positively (less negatively) about Muslims and Islam than private school students did. Of particular interest, State school students endorsed the statement, "Australian schools should teach more about Muslims," whereas private school students did not.

We cannot say that contact with Muslims reduces prejudice, merely that it is associated with reduced prejudice. It may be that people with reduced prejudice seek out Muslim friends. This issue would need to be disentangled with longitudinal analyses if we are to discover causality, although we suggest that the two may work in tandem. This supports a basic notion of the contact hypothesis that suggests that having some contact with others decreases prejudice.

Table 10.3 Having Muslim Friends by Attitudes

Those with Muslim friends agreed more, or disagreed less, than those without	*Those without Muslim friends agreed more, or disagreed less, than those with*
• Muslims have made a major contribution to Australia.	• Muslims find it hard to integrate into Australia.
• Muslims have made a major contribution to world civilisation.	• Muslims threaten the Australian way of life.
• Most Muslims have good feelings for Australia and Australians.	• Most migrants are racist.
• Most Muslims have stronger family ties than other Australians.	• Hollywood movies show Muslims in a fair way.
• Australian schools should teach more about Muslims.	• Muslims do not belong to Australia.
• This school helps people of different cultures to get along better.	• If I saw a Muslim student being abused in a public place I wouldn't care.
• Learning about Muslims helps students to understand them better.	
• A person can be both a good Muslim and a loyal Australian.	

DISCUSSION AND CONCLUSIONS

Agreement on the difficulties facing Muslims and some wide-spread misconceptions support a widespread perception of an all powerful media discourse, supported by political and economic interests The benefit of personal contact is supported by the distinctive views of students with Muslim friends, although having Muslim neighbors does not appear to make a significant difference to responses.

Changing patterns of work and communication mean that in the course of their lives young people are likely to meet and interact with people from many different communities, cultures, and backgrounds. What then is the role of schools in promoting intercultural understanding? Is there a role for school-based interfaith programs, intercultural studies, and student welfare programs? Does the school curriculum matter? If not, why not? How can it be made more effective?

Based on the attitude survey data, is appears that non-Muslim students do not perceive their own ignorance as the main difficulty facing Muslims in society, and further that the promotion of cultural harmony in schools does not necessarily work through increasing knowledge. The paradoxical disconnection of knowledge from the difficulties students see facing Muslims points to particular challenges for schools, where knowledge is after all the core business (Ata and Windle 2007).

Schools have an important role to play in increasing mutual understanding and respect and appreciation of cultural diversity. Eradicating racism and promoting racial equality must be an integral part of school life and should be explicit and implicit in all curriculum activities that take place within the school. National, regional, and local initiatives provide support, advice and guidance for schools to ensure all pupils are taught about equality. The National Curriculum guidelines for Citizenship and Personal, Social and Health Education (PSHE) identify what pupils should be taught in association with racial equality and antiracist behavior.

The degree to which students feel that their school is educative about Muslims and Islam is an important predictor of certain levels of tolerance. This suggests that it is the atmosphere created by the school that is supportive and educative of Muslims and Islam, rather than the level of knowledge that is important regarding prejudice. Therefore, it is not just a matter of knowing more facts about Muslims and Islam but perceiving that the school cares enough to educate students on these issues that is important (Ata and Windle 2007).

It is worth considering the contribution that outsiders to the education bureaucracy can make, particularly those from the Muslim community, to the development of policies, curriculum materials and pedagogical practices. Current multicultural policies and students alike appear to de-emphasize knowledge as a means to understanding and cultural harmony, and this appears to be a major problem as we head to the future.

NOTE

1. These locations were excluded because it would have been costly to survey them for logistical reasons; and in any case it was thought they would not contribute to the accuracy of the survey because there was no reason to suppose their responses would differ from those in other states.

ACKNOWLEDGMENTS

The author wishes to acknowledge the funding assistance from the Australian Commonwealth Department of Immigration without which this work would not have been possible to carry out. Parts of this chapter have been reproduced from Abe W. Ata's book *Us and Them: Muslim-Christian Relations and Cultural Harmony in Australia*. Brisbane, Australian Academic Press, 2009.

REFERENCES

Asmar, Christine. 2001. A Community on Campus: Muslim Students in Australian Universities. In *Muslim Communities in Australia*, edited by S. Akbarzadeh and A. Saeed. 138–160. Sydney: UNSW Press.

Ata, Abe. 2009. *Us and Them: Muslim-Christian Relations and Social Harmony in Australia*. Brisbane: Australian Academic Press.

Ata, Abe and Batrouney, Trevor. 1989. Attitudes and Stereotyping in Victorian Secondary Schools. *The Eastern Anthropologist*, 42(1): 35–50.

Ata, Abe, Bastian, Brock and Lusher, Dean. 2009. Intergroup Contact in Context: The Mediating Role of Social Norms and Group-Based Perceptions on the Contact-Prejudice. *The international Journal of Intercultural Relations* 33(6): 498–506

Ata Abe and Windle, Joel. 2007. The Role of Australian Schools in Educating Students about Islam and Muslims. *Australian Quarterly* 79(6): 19–27.

Australian Arabic Council. 2001. *Increase in Racial Vilification in Light of Terror Attacks: A Media Report*. Melbourne: Australian Arabic Council.

Bullivant, Brian. 1987. *The Ethnic Encounter in the Secondary School: Ethno-Cultural Reproduction and Resistance—Theory and Case Studies*. London: Falmer Press.

Bullivant, Brian. 1988. The Ethnic Success Ethic Challenges Conventional Wisdom about Immigrant Disadvantages in Australia. *Australian Journal of Education* 32(2): 223–243.

Brasted, Howard. 2001. Contested Representations in Historical Perspective: Images of Islam and the Australian Press 1950–2000. In *Muslim Communities in Australia*, edited by S. Akbarzadeh and A. Saeed. 206–227. Sydney: UNSW Press.

Cahill, D. and Gundert, A. 1996. *Immigration and Schooling in the 1990s*. Canberra: Australian Government Publishing Service.

Department of Education. 1997. *Multicultural Policy for Victorian Schools*. Melbourne: Author.

Department of Education. 2003. *Advice for Schools in Dealing with the International Situation*. (School Circular: 075/2003). Melbourne: Author.

Department of Education and Training. 2000. *Racism No Way: Anti-Racism Education for Australian Schools*. http://www.racismnoway.com.au/. (Accessed January 17, 2006).

Department of Education Employment and Training. 2009. *Guidelines for Managing Cultural and Linguistic Diversity in Schools*. Melbourne: Author.

Donohoue Clyne, Irene. 2000. *Seeking Education: The Struggle of Muslims to Educate their Children in Australia*. Unpublished PhD thesis. University of Melbourne.

Galbally, Fiona. 1978. *Migrant Services and Programs: Report of the Review of Post-Arrival Programs and Services for Migrants*. Canberra: Australian Government Printing Service.

Goodall, Heather, and Jakubowicz, Andrew. 1994. *Racism, Ethnicity and the Media*. St Leonards, New South Wales: Allen and Unwin.

Human Rights and Equal Opportunity Commission. 2004. Ismau Listen: National Consultations on Eliminating Prejudice against Arab and Muslim Australians. Sydney: Author.

Kalantzis, Mary and Cope, Bill. 1984. Multiculturalism and Education Policy. In *Ethnicity, Class and Gender in Australia*, edited by G. Bottomley and M.M. De Lepervanche. 82–97. Sydney: George Allen and Unwin.

Malone, Patricia. 1995. Attitudes Towards the Role of Religion and Religions of a Sample of Year 11 High School Students. *Religious Education Journal of Australia* 11(3): 2–10.

Muslim Community Reference Group. 2006. *Building on Social Cohesion, Harmony and Security*. Canberra: Author.

Poynting, Scott. 2002. Bin Laden in the Suburbs: Attacks on Arab and Muslim Australians before and after 11 September. *Current Issues in Criminal Justice* 14(1): 43–64.

———. 2009. Bin Laden in the Suburbs: Attacks on Arab and Muslim Australians before and after 11 September. *Current Issues in Criminal Justice* 14(1): 43–64.

Speck, Bruce. 1997. Respect for Religious Differences: The Case of Muslim Students. *New Directions for Teaching and Learning* 70(Summer): 39–46.

11 Religious Problems in Contemporary Japanese Society

Two Cases after the Aum Shinrikyo Affair

Michiaki Okuyama

This chapter deals with two Japanese cases that can be situated at the cross-roads of religion and social problems. Survey research of attitudes toward religion among the general public in contemporary Japan shows that religious groups receive little, if any, trust from the public. A substantial percentage of the population abhors forcible proselytizing and moneymaking that is supposedly attributed to religion in their minds. Religions in Japan are often seen as the cause or source of rather than a solution to social problems.[1]

With this basic understanding, how can we argue that some phenomena in Japan fall under the category of a "religion-related social problems," or rather, "religious problems," for short? Leaving aside attempts to contribute to theoretical or methodological considerations on the topic, this chapter will be essentially descriptive, with the purpose of explicating two contemporary Japanese cases, namely the "cult problem" and the Yasukuni shrine affair. Both have become a social problem in the eyes of the broader public and both cases have been challenged through the legal system. Therefore, the focus of this chapter will be on cases that relate to religious corporations under trial. Before moving on to detailed analysis, two clarifications should be made.

Firstly, the phenomena under consideration relate to religious juridical persons, or religious corporations. Naturally, religion cannot be simply reduced in legalistic terms to religious corporations, and in Japan there are numerous religious groups that have not acquired the juridical status but nevertheless are free to exist without registering for this status. Here I am focusing on religious corporations and insist that their existence and characteristics as religions are justifiable because they are recognized as religions. This approach will obviously avoid the crucial theoretical discussion regarding the definition of religion in the Japanese context, even though I do acknowledge its importance.

Secondly, the focus is on religious corporations that have been under trial under the Japanese legal system. These include court cases surrounding religious corporations and the so-called "cult problems." The "cult problems" are not the same as court cases related to other religions but they do overlap to some extent. This chapter will also discuss this overlapping area.[2]

1995 AS A BACKDROP FOR RELIGIOUS
PROBLEMS IN CONTEMPORARY JAPAN

The year 1995 has a special significance in the history of Japan. First, it memorialized the 50th anniversary of the defeat of the country's Asia and Pacific War, which still has left a number of unsettled problems (especially with regard to compensation for victims both in Japan and abroad). Secondly, Japan experienced the worst post-war natural disaster, the Great Hanshin-Awaji Earthquake, which claimed more than 6,400 lives. Thirdly, the nation was terrified by the religious violence of the Aum Shrinrikyo Affair, in which the sarin gas attack on the Tokyo subway system caused almost 6,300 injuries. Nearly 30 lives were lost in total due to Aum-related crimes, including the thirteen lost in the subway attack.

All of these cases have religious implications to some extent. The memory of the war has been significant not only to former soldiers and civilians with physical injury and/or mental trauma who survived a battle field, an air raid, or bombing, but also to a number of people who lost family members, friends, and loved ones. Their quest for the meaning of life, death, and survival has never ceased, and they feel the necessity, or obligation in some cases, to console the souls and spirits of the dead.

The 1995 earthquake has also stimulated the survivors to search existentially for the meaning of life and death, and to feel the need to console the dead. In addition, in this case of disastrous emergency, various religious groups dispatched rescue workers and sent relief funds and supplies. In terms of the material and spiritual recovery process, some of the support activities by religious groups are continuing. Here we see an example of religions' contributions to society by addressing a critical situation originally caused by a natural disaster. Thus these two cases, the first with commemorative acts 50 years after the end of war, and the second with social contributions of religions after a large-scale natural disaster, both clearly deserve scholarly attention, although this chapter will not deal with them further.

In regard to the third case, a couple of points need to be mentioned. In the Aum Affair the guilt of nearly 200 former followers has been confirmed among the almost 500 arrested. Shōkō Asahara,[3] and 18 former disciples (a few still continue to maintain devotion to Asahara) have been sentenced either to death or to life imprisonment, with three of the 13 sentenced to death appealing to the Supreme Court as of April 2010. Scholars and journalists have tried to trace the transformation of this group from people who were originally Yoga practitioners into an organization of anti-social terrorists.[4] Questions still remain, however, about the murders committed by a number of young, intellectual, and serious disciples, who may have led promising careers in society if they had not abandoned secular life by their own volition.

After Asahara and the other guilty members were arrested, some of the innocent disciples left Aum Shirikyo but others maintained their faith. The group has continued its religious activities—despite harsh criticism from journalists and society—under government surveillance that was legally introduced in 1999. In 2000, the group renovated its organization under a new group name, Aleph, with a new leader, Fumihiro Jōyū (b. 1962), who was discharged from prison in December 1999. Aleph officially started to pay compensation to the victims of the crimes committed by Asahara and his disciples, and continues to pay reparations. According to the Public Security Intelligence Agency, it is estimated that their membership in December 2008 numbers around 1,500 domestically, including 500 ascetics. Reportedly there are also 200 active members in Russia. Jōyū himself left Aleph in 2007 to organize a new group that tries to get rid of almost all influences of Asahara, and this new group, Hikari no Wa [The Circle of Rainbow Light] also shares the reparations on its own initiative. The Public Security Authority decided in January 2009 that the surveillance of both Aleph and Hikari no Wa will be extended for another three years until 2012 on the grounds that these two groups are still under Asahara's influence and maintain the dangerous aspects of Aum's doctrines to some extent.

As mentioned above, a number of former members left Aum or one of the succeeding groups, but some of them or their family members have suffered discrimination or social rejection. This was clearly evidenced in the case of one of Asahara's children whose admission to some private universities was cancelled in 2004, despite the fact that she passed the entrance examinations. She sued for admission and won the case in court.

CULT CONTROVERSIES IN THE JAPANESE CONTEXT

The Legal Situation Surrounding Cults

The Aum Affair was neither the first nor the last problem caused by religion in contemporary Japan, but it deserves special attention because it made the general public in Japan realize that religion can be the source of serious social problems. Some of the activists that began criticizing Aum

Shinrikyo from around the early 1990s continue their anti-cult activities today. Among them, several lawyers are known for supporting the families of cult converts, former cult members, and for taking legal action against religious groups they define as cults. Here I will summarize their understanding of cults in Japan.

According to Hiroshi Yamaguchi, a lawyer actively engaged in criticism of problematic religions, the following four points constitute the backdrop of the cult problem in Japan: Firstly, in an excessive reaction to the oppression of the freedom of religion until 1945, the post-war national and local governments in Japan were worried about involving themselves in religious matters, relegating them to the private sphere. Secondly, in the post-war Japanese society, a number of new religious movements (NRMs) have been actively proselytizing while traditional religions such as Buddhism and Shinto are not so active. In addition, public education has generally lacked any systematic teaching about religion. This situation has led to the lack of understanding about the religious situation in Japan among the general public. Thirdly, some of the larger NRMs have been influential in politics, which has prevented the Diet and local assemblies from discussing religious matters.[5] Fourthly, there is a widespread religious tradition among the Japanese wherein the living are supposed to pay due respect to ancestors lest negligence should cause suffering or vengeful spirits to curse the living (Yamaguchi et al. 2000, 10–11).

Based on these religious traditions, it may be natural for some Japanese to willingly engage themselves in activities to appease the unsatisfied spirits, especially in the form of donation to a religious authority. But a number of troubles have occurred in which a religious group appropriates or abuses this tradition by demanding monetary compensation for the appeasement of spirits. Formerly it was thought that these troubles were not suitable for a court to judge, but gradually the Japanese courts have started to pass judgment in cases of this kind. The promotion and enforcement of huge donations as a fictitious means of appeasing spirits are generally distinguished in two forms, "reikan shōhō" [goods and services that allegedly provide spiritual inspiration] and "reishi shōhō" [goods and services that allegedly provide spiritual vision], and these practices have been severely criticized by a number of lawyers and journalists. A group of lawyers was formed to deal with this problem in 1987. The number of lawyers in the group amounted to around 300 in the year 2000, and the number of counsels with the group counts around 1,000 every year. The object of the majority of these counsels are related to the Holy Spirit Association for the Unification of World Christianity (widely known as the Moonies but hereafter referred to as the Unification Church; ibid., 58). According to Yamaguchi, in the Myokakuji Case a district court found the group accused of selling goods and services that allegedly provided spiritual visions ("reishi shōhō") guilty for the first time in 1999, and ordered the compensation of 1.6 billion yen to approximately 580 victimized accusers. Nevertheless, in a number of other cases the court has not acknowledged the guilt of the accused religious groups (ibid., 16–18).

The Japan Federation of Bar Associations published a report entitled "Guidelines to Save Those Consumers Victimized by Anti-Social Religious Activities" in 1999, following their former reports in the same line in 1987, 1988, and 1995. This latest report delves into not only both forms of sales of spiritual goods and services but also other problems caused by religion-related activities. The report is intended to deal with particular problems when they emerge, and not intended to regulate religious activities nor judge the legality of any religious organization. In reaction to this report, however, the Japanese Association of Religious Organizations, an overarching federation of the five sub-associations of different religious traditions (roughly lumped together as Shinto, Sect Shinto, Buddhism, Christian, and New Religions), immediately made public their concern about "the Guidelines," and a working group related to this Association published a critical report entitled "Opinions about the Guidelines" in 2000. Not surprisingly, there are a number of disagreements between the lawyers and the religious organizations, and the arguments set forth in the above publications have set the tone for subsequent discussion.

Criticisms by a Journalist and a Sociologist

Shōichi Fujita, a journalist specializing in religious matters, published in 2008 a book that critically treats religion-related problems in Japan in the past 20 years or so. He traces a number of problems since the late 1980s, and according to his report, two categories are especially conspicuous in the religion-related problems in contemporary Japan. First are the cases in which religious groups are obsessed with prolonging life and rebirth after death, resulting in the inappropriate preservation of dead bodies in private facilities.[6] In Fujita's view, both the dead and the participants in the acts of preservation are victims of abuse of their spirituality and conscience.

The second category of religion-related problems that this group of lawyers has been tackling concerns the compulsory or enforced donations by religious groups or authorities. According to Fujita, from 1987, when the group of lawyers was formed to specialize in this problem, to 2007 the number of consultations they dealt with reached 28,996, and the amount of the claims in total was over one trillion yen. Fujita argues that the main problem about these cases is that some groups appropriate systems that constrain the mind and spirit of the victims by appealing to them through religious rhetoric and "religious threats." "Religious threats" in this case refers to rhetoric that forces the victims to hand over money or property under the guise of appeasing the suffering or vengeful spirits (Fujita 2008, 99).

Concerning the Unification Church in particular, Fujita discusses fourteen court cases judged by March 2008 in which the illegality of actions of the group was confirmed (ibid., 124–127), and other fourteen cases that remained in dispute as of April 2008 (ibid., 128–131). In these cases, Fujita argues, the Unification Church first utilizes fortunetelling or palmistry for recruitment without revealing their true identity until the mind and spirit of the recruits are firmly constrained. With regard to the problem about this method of recruitment, a former member sued the Unification Church in 1987 at a district court in Sapporo. Other lawsuits followed in six district courts nationwide. Until around 1999 the plaintiffs lost the cases, but from 2000 onward, the Supreme Court has acknowledged the illegality of that particular method of recruitment and other activities of the Unification Church in five cases (ibid., 154–160).

In the field of sociology of religion, Yoshihide Sakurai has continued to discuss the cult problems in contemporary Japan for the past ten years or so. He has been working in a close relationship with lawyers, journalists, and activists who are working for the prevention of cult problems and for recovery of victims. He seems to be critical about the earlier standpoint of the professed objectivity of religious studies and sociology of religion that could not prevent the problems from emerging nor answer the question why the problems emerged.[7]

In a recent monograph coauthored with Hiroko Nakanishi on the Unification Church, Sakurai explicates the idiosyncrasy and illegality of their activities specifically in Japan. Sakurai points out that the 1980s was a turning point for the Unification Church in Japan, in that they changed their way of proselytizing and moneymaking around that decade. According to Sakurai, members began to proselytize by hiding or disguising their identities. This new method began as a kind of a culture course and ended as an initiation program of the Unification Church (Sakurai and Nakanishi 2010, 95). They made money by selling various products, including ginseng tea and marble vases made in Korea, as goods that would bring good fortune or would appease the suffering or vengeful spirits.

I have not summarized all the arguments developed in detail by Fujita and Sakurai, instead focusing on several important points in their writings. At least on the legal level, some of the activities of the Unification Church and other religious groups in Japan have been confirmed as unlawful in the past decade or so, although the cult issue is not commonly regarded as a problem by the majority of the scholars of religious studies and sociologists of religion. But since the critical judgments on this problem have been accumulated in several courts nationwide, it is expected that scholars in religion in Japan will be increasingly required to present expert commentary on this matter.

CONTROVERSIES CONCERNING THE YASUKUNI SHRINE

The second case I want to discuss is a multi-faceted problem related to Yasukuni Shrine. Regarding this topic, the former Prime Minister Jun'ichirō

Koizumi played a conspicuous role. His visits to Yasukuni Shrine during his position as Prime Minister from 2001 through 2006 not only triggered numerous lawsuits, but also caused diplomatic friction between Japan and its neighboring countries. Before delving into the recent controversies, I will summarize here the history of Yasukuni Shrine based on my earlier research.[8]

Yasukuni Shrine was a national facility until 1945 and has been a private religious corporation since then. This shrine was originally established to enshrine the war dead who lost their lives during the wars that were carried out internally in modern Japan in order to unify the nation, and externally to achieve its imperial and colonialist interests in Asian countries and Pacific regions.[9]

A decision carried out by Yasukuni Shrine in 1978 has complicated the issue tremendously. The decision was for Yasukuni Shrine to enshrine class "A" war criminals, who were not ordinary fallen soldiers but those who were regarded as having committed "crimes against peace."[10] Of the 28 prosecuted class "A" war criminals, 25 were convicted (two of these 28 died of illness during the Tokyo Trial and one was discharged due to mental illness).[11] Of these 25, seven were executed, five died of illness in prison after the trial,[12] and the other 13 were imprisoned but released afterwards. Since Yasukuni Shrine has enshrined these class "A" war criminals with the other war dead, visiting the Shrine to pay respect to the war dead in general necessarily looks like paying respect to the war criminals at the same time. This has become the grounds for protest for the Chinese and the Korean governments whenever the Japanese prime minister visits Yasukuni Shrine.

On a domestic level, politicians' visits to Yasukuni Shrine have been challenged primarily because they can be regarded as a violation of the Constitutional principle of the separation of religion and state.[13] There were several court cases concerning Yasukuni Shrine before 2001, but Koizumi's regular visits since that year stimulated disputes both for and against the shrine and led to the court cases discussed below.[14] These recent court cases have brought up unsolved problems surrounding Yasukuni Shrine with regard to former Japanese colonialism and post-war freedom of religion, in addition to the problem of the separation of religion and state.

Cases Demanding Annulment of Enshrinement

In June 2001, 252 Koreans who were former soldiers and civilian workers in the Japanese army, or their bereaved family, filed a suit against the Japanese state for redress. In this case, the plaintiffs understood that the enshrinement of Korean soldiers and workers at Yasukuni Shrine[15] was processed with the active involvement of the Japanese government, and they demanded that it be annulled.[16] The Japanese government has denied responsibility for the redress because Koreans who were Japanese subjects under the pre-war through inter-war Japanese regime are no longer Japanese citizens. They also claim that the after-war relationship between Japan and Korea has been regulated and the related problems have been solved by inter-governmental treaties. In May 2006 the Tokyo district court dismissed the case, the plaintiffs appealed, and the Tokyo high court dismissed the case in October 2009. The plaintiffs appealed and the case is now pending at the Supreme Court.

In February 2007, eleven Koreans, among whom eight were the plaintiffs of the suit mentioned above, filed another suit against Yasukuni Shrine as well as the Japanese state for annulment of the enshrinement, apology, and redress. This case is pending at the Tokyo district court. In addition to these cases filed by Koreans and Taiwanese, another suit was filed in August 2006 at the Osaka district court against the Japanese state and Yasukuni Shrine, demanding the annulment of enshrinement in the same line as the Korean and Taiwanese court cases. A Catholic priest, Toshihiko Nishiyama, learned in 2005 that his father, also Christian, is enshrined at Yasukuni Shrine. Nishiyama filed a lawsuit with eight other plaintiffs, demanding that the enshrinement of his father and those of other family members be annulled by specifically deleting their names on the list of souls enshrined (Nishiyama 2006, 122–125). In February 2009, all the demands were dismissed. The plaintiffs appealed and the case is now pending at the Osaka high court. Nobumasa Tanaka, a journalist who is highly critical of Yasukuni Shrine, edited and published a volume containing the statements of the plaintiffs in this case, a testimony by a university professor specializing in this subject, and the summary of the ruling of the district court (Tanaka 2009).

Another suit against the Japanese state and Yasukuni Shrine was filed at the Naha district court in Okinawa in March 2008 by the bereaved families of the soldiers and civilian workers for the military at the Battle of Okinawa, demanding the annulment of enshrinement. This case is pending at the Naha district court.

Cases against Prime Minister Koizumi's Visits to Yasukuni Shrine

When Prime Minister Jun'ichirō Koizumi visited Yasukuni Shrine in August 2001, a heated debate arose about the constitutionality of the Prime Minister's visits under a separation between religion and state. The first court case against this visit was filed in November 2001, and until February 2003, there were a number of other suits that were filed in the district courts at Fukuoka, Osaka, Matsuyama, Tokyo, Chiba, and Naha.

The case filed on November 2001 at the Osaka district court includes around 120 Chinese and Koreans among the total 639 plaintiffs, and is referred to as the Yasukuni Asian Case. The case filed in February 2003 also at the Osaka district court includes 124 Taiwanese among the total 236 plaintiffs, and the case is referred to as the Yasukuni Taiwanese Case.

Among these 124, 34 are indigenous Taiwanese including a Taiwanese leg-islator Ko Kim Sò-mûi and a former actress, May Chin, who was cast in a 1993 movie *The Wedding Banquet*.[17]

On April 7, 2004, the Fukuoka district court judged that the prime minister's visit to Yasukuni Shrine was unconstitutional, but dismissed the demand for compensation. The judge explained the reason for this seem-ingly contradictory judgment as follows: The prime minister's visit in this case was made without consideration about its constitutionality. One would expect that it would be repeated if the court avoided its judgment about its unconstitutionality. Therefore this court took its responsibility to deliver this judgment (Tanaka 2007, 126).

After the dismissal at the district court, on September 30, 2006 the Osaka high court made a judgement in the Yasukuni Taiwanese Case that the prime minister's visit was unconstitutional, though the compensation was dismissed. Although Koizumi visited Yasukuni Shrine just after this judgment, on October 17, he seemingly tried to be less religious in his style of visit. According to an attorney for the plaintiffs of the case, this change of style was because Koizumi apparently became conscious about the judg-ment (Nakajima 2006, 172–173). In other cases the plaintiffs in Osaka (the Yasukuni Asian case), Chiba, Matsuyama, Tokyo, and Naha appealed to the Supreme Court, but the judgments at the Supreme Court dismissed all the appeals by April 2007.

The above cases show that there are at least two legal problems related to Yasukuni Shrine. First, Yasukuni Shrine has enshrined the souls of fallen soldiers and military civilian workers—whether they were Japanese, Kore-ans, or Taiwanese—based on the understanding that they lost their pre-cious lives for the then-Japanese empire, without obtaining any consent of the bereaved family.[18] As a private religious corporation, Yasukuni Shrine can perform any religious activity, and their act of enshrinement is con-sistent with their own understanding regarding the lives lost for the state. But at stake here is whether or not it is admissible to enshrine someone whose bereaved family does not wish him or her to be enshrined. In more general terms, one form of dealing with the dead by a private religious group is challenged by another private group—which actually consists of family members of the dead—that regards enshrinement as a violation of their own right of cherishing the dead family member peacefully. However, even Nobumasa Tanaka, who is very supportive of the suits that demand the annulment of the enshrinement mentioned previously, is conscious of the difficulties in questioning Yasukuni Shrine's right to enshrine people. As a private religious corporation Yasukuni comes under same freedom of religion legislation as everyone else (Takahashi and Tanaka 2006, 44). On what grounds can one stop a private religious group from dealing with souls of the dead in some specific way? If one wants to regard the attitude of Yasukuni Shrine as violation of the right of the bereaved family, one should elaborate this right more subtly.

Secondly, it has been questioned whether or not the Prime Minister's visits to Yasukuni Shrine have been constitutional. The visits' unconstitutionality has not been fully settled, but under the current situation, the Prime Minister and other ministers in the present and future need to consider the possibility of the unconstitutionality of their relationship with Yasukuni Shrine as well as with other religious facilities. In my own provisional thought, the visits to Yasukuni Shrine by politicians will always be questioned under the present constitutional separation between religion and state, and whether class "A" war criminals are enshrined or not will not affect this issue. Even if the class "A" criminals should be taken away, as insisted by some proponents, as long as Yasukuni Shrine is a religious facility, politicians should refrain from visiting there.

CONCLUSION

The Aum Affair in 1995 made the general public aware of the problematic—in this case destructive—potential of religion. In the aftermath of the affair, a number of lawyers and journalists have paid increasing attention to the potential "cult problem" in Japan. The response from scholars in religious studies and sociology of religion has been slower, but they are being drawn into the discussion about the limits of the freedom of religion and conscience. At stake here are questions like whose freedom, what kind of freedom, and how to compromise conflicting freedoms.

The Yasukuni problem is another point where religion, state, and society converge. In the past few years foreign nationals have joined the Japanese in challenging the actions of Yasukuni Shrine and the Japanese government. In this sense the problems of the enshrinement of the war dead and government officials' visits to the shrine have become part of a wider international discussion about the relationship between Japan and its neighbors—and not only relating to the past and present, but also to the future. While the "cult problems" make it necessary to rethink the role of religion in contemporary society, with the "Yasukuni problem" the whole issue of how to construct the future of Japan is on trial.

NOTES

1. For data and analysis of general attitudes toward religion among Japanese people based on public opinion polls conducted after World War II, see Ishii 2007.
2. Another important case of a religious corporation sometimes under legal trial, although it is not always referred to as a "cult problem" per se, is the case of Soka Gakkai. This chapter will not deal with this influential religious corporation, but in terms of its relation to politics. See Okuyama (forthcoming).
3. Asahara (b. 1955) is the founder of Aum Shinrikyo, and was revered as the Guru by his followers. His real name is Chizuo Matsumoto. Asahara

organized a Yoga group with some dozen members in 1984, which developed into "Aum Shinsen no Kai [The group of Aum divine ascetics]" in 1986, and was renamed as Aum Shinrikyo in 1987. In spring 1995, they held around 10,000 followers, 1,100 among whom were ascetics in their communes (Shimazono 1995, 5).

4. The doctrine of Aum Shinrikyo is characterized as a mixture of several religious or spiritual ideas, such as esoteric Buddhism, Hinduism, spiritualism, and eschatology. They thought highly of supernatural experiences among their followers, so much so that they eventually used drugs to evoke such experiences instantly. After a number of conflicts between their communes and local communities outside, their antagonism against society intensified, resulting in a series of physical attacks in 1995.

5. A most influential example in this regard has been Soka Gakkai. The group formed and supports a political party. This party was established as the Komei Political League in 1961, renamed as Komeito in 1964, and reorganized as New Komeito in 1998. New Komeito joined in the coalition government with the Liberal Democratic Party (and sometimes another party) from 1999 through 2009.

6. These cases included in the first category of Fujita's argument did not necessarily occur within registered religious corporations. As such they cannot strictly be regarded as religious problems within the current framework. For Fujita, however, these cases should be regarded as religious incidents, although he does not present any definition of religion.

7. In Sakurai's assumption, compared to the scholars in religious studies and sociology of religion, scholars in psychiatry, psychology, or law were more eloquent in discussions dealing with the problems related to cults (Sakurai 2009, ii).

8. For an outline of the history of Yasukuni Shrine and its current problem, see Okuyama 2005; 2007; 2008; 2009a; 2009b. The following discussion is based on my earlier arguments.

9. After it became a private religious corporation, the character of Yasukuni Shrine as the site of commemoration and praise for the war dead was not questioned for decades. Until the mid 1970s emperor Showa and the imperial family, politicians, as well as the general public visited Yasukuni at different occasions during the year. Later, especially after the enshrinement of the class "A" war criminals, Yasukuni became a politically contested site.

10. The concept of "crimes against the peace" was introduced in the International Military Tribunal (1945–1946) against Nazi Germany, also known as Nuremberg Trials.

11. The Tokyo Trial (The International Military Tribunal for the Far East) opened in 1946 and concluded in 1948. Twenty-eight former military or political leaders of the Empire of Japan were prosecuted for "crimes against the peace."

12. The 14 dead, including the two who died during the trial, were enshrined at Yasukuni in 1978.

13. For a general backdrop related to religion and Japanese Constitutional Law, see Okuyama 2006.

14. For an outline of these cases, see Tanaka 2007.

15. 27,863 Taiwanese and 21,181 Koreans are included among around 2,466,000 enshrined souls at Yasukuni Shrine (Tanaka 2007, 42).

16. A documentary film, *Annyong, Sayonara*, directed by Kim Tae-il and co-directed by Kato Kumiko (2005), features a representative of the plaintiffs, Heeja Lee, and a Japanese supporter, Masaki Furukawa. Lee's father was conscripted by the Japanese army in 1944 and had been missing since that

year. She heard from the Japanese Agency of the Defense only in 1996 that her father died in 1944 in China and is enshrined at Yasukuni Shrine, which led her to join in this lawsuit (Tanaka 2007, 188–193). For the implications of this film, see Okuyama 2009b.
17. For details about the Taiwanese Yasukuni Case with historical background of the Japanese colonization of Taiwan, see Nakajima 2006.
18. In addition to this, the involvement of the Japanese government in the process of the enshrinement is also under critical scrutiny these days.

REFERENCES

Fujita, Shoichi. 2008. *Shukyo saiban no uchigawa: seishin o jubaku sareru hito-bito.* [Inside the Religious Incidents: On the People whose Mind and Spirit is Constrained by Religion] Tokyo: Iwanami Shoten.
Ishii, Kenji. 2007. *Deetabukku gendai Nihonjin no shūkyō* [Databook on Religions of Contemporary Japanese]. Revised and enlarged edition. Tokyo: Shin'yō-sha.
Nakajima, Mitsunori. 2006. *Kanga Sorei: Taiwan genjū minzoku to Yasukuni jinja* [May my Ancestors' Souls Return to Mme: Indigenous Taiwanese and Yasukuni Shrine]. Tokyo: Hakutakusha.
Nishiyama, Toshiyuki. 2006. *Yasukuni gōshi torikeshi soshō no chūkan hōkoku: Shinkyō no jiyū no kaifuku o motomete* [A Progress Report on the Case for the Annulment of the Enshrinement at Yasukuni Shrine: In Search of the Recovery of the Freedom of Religious Faith]. Tokyo: San Paolo.
Okuyama, Michiaki. 2005. Historicizing Modern Shinto: A New Tradition of Yasukuni Shrine. In *Historicizing "Tradition" in the Study of Religion*, edited by Steven Engler and Gregory P. Grieve. 93–108.Berlin and New York: Walter de Gruyter.
———. 2006. Religion and Japanese Constitutional Law. *Academia Humanities and Social Sciences* 83(June): 133–147.
———. 2007. Discourses on Shinto in Divergence: Disinterested Description and Political Polemics. *Academia Humanities and Social Sciences* 85 (June): 1–20.
———. 2008. The Politics of Commemoration and Grief: Disputes over the War Dead in Contemporary Japan. *Academia Humanities and Social Sciences* 86 (January): 1–13.
———. 2009a. Disputes over Yasukuni Shrine and Its War Dead in Contemporary Japan. *Religion Compass* (online) 58–71.
———. 2009b. The Yasukuni Shrine Problem in the East Asian Context: Religion and Politics in Modern Japan. *Politics and Religion* 3(2): 235–251. (http://www.politicsandreligionjournal.com/images/pdf_files/engleski/volume3_no2/Analiza%201.pdf) (Accessed 28/08/10).
———. 2010. Soka Gakkai as a Challenge to Japanese Society and Politics. Politics and Religion, 4(1): 83–96. (http://www.politicsandreligionjournal.com/images/pdf_files/engleski/volume4_no1/6%20-%20okuyama%20michiaki.pdf) (Accessed 28/08/10)
Sakurai, Yoshihide. (ed). 2009. *Karuto to supirichuaritii: Gendai nihon ni okeru "sukui" to "iyashi" no yukue* [Cult and Spirituality: Trends of "Salvation" and "Healing" in Contemporary Japan]. Kyoto: Minerva Shobo.
Sakurai, Yoshihide and Hiroko Nakanishi. 2010. *Tōitsu kyōkai: Nihon senkyō no senryaku to kannichi shukufuku* [The Unification Church: Their Proselytization Strategy in Japan, and the Matrimonial Bliss of Korean Men and Japanese Women]. Sapporo: Hokkaido Daidaku Shuppankai.

Shimazono, Susumu. 1995. *Aum Shinrikyo no kiseki* [Traces of Aum Shinrikyo]. Tokyo: Iwanami Shoten.

Takahashi Tetsuya and Tanaka, Nobumasa. 2006. *"Yasukuni" to iu mondai* [The Problem "Yasukuni"]: Tokyo: Kin'yōbi.

Tanaka, Nobumasa. 2007. *Document, Yasukuni soshō* [Documents, Yasukuni cases]. Tokyo: Iwanami Shoten.

———. (ed) 2009. *Koreni masu kanashiki kotono nanika aran: Yasukuni goshi kyohi Osaka hanketsu no syatei* [Is There any Grief Deeper than This? Implications of the Ruling at Osaka District Court of the Case for the Annulment of the Enshrinement at Yasukuni]. Tokyo: Nanatsumori Shokan.

Yamaguchi, Hiroshi, Shuji, Nakamura, Hiroshi, Hirata, and Masaki, Kito. 2000. *Karuto shukyo no toraburu taisaku* [Countermeasures to Troubles Caused by Cults and Religions]. Tokyo: Kyoiku Shiryo Shuppankai.

12 George W. Bush and Church-State Partnerships to Administer Social Service Programs

Cautions and Concerns

Derek H. Davis

During his eight-year tenure as President of the United States (2001–2009), George W. Bush embarked upon an aggressive plan to enlist the aid of the American religious community to improve delivery of social services to American citizens in need. Although it is customary for many countries to lean on churches and other religious groups to alleviate hunger, poverty, and sickness, the Bush plan was unique in that it involved substantial government monetary sums being placed in the hands of religious organizations and was thus a bold challenge to well-entrenched American ideals of church-state separation.

This chapter examines the difficulties the Bush administration encountered in furthering his "faith-based initiative," especially the constitutional questions it posed. It is suggested here that the Bush plan, while noble in its aims, was not successful because it ignored church-state constitutional safeguards designed to protect religion and religious institutions from being compromised. Since taking office in 2009, President Barack Obama has not abandoned the Bush "faith-based initiative" entirely, but has promised to apply constitutional standards that preserve church-state separation in administering the program. But as of the date of this writing, no one is quite sure exactly what form the Obama plan will take.

THE BUSH FAITH-BASED INITIATIVE

Within days after his January 2001 inauguration as the 43rd president of the United States, George W. Bush announced his plan to provide government money for churches and other houses of worship that offer social services for Americans in need. The president stated, "When we see social needs in America, my administration will look first to faith-based programs and community groups, which have proven their power to save and change lives" (Davis 2001, 411). The president drew a line between what the initiative would support and what it would not. He added, "We will not fund the religious activities of any group, but when people of faith provide social services we will not discriminate against them" (Davis 2001, 411). As to his administration's commitment to the initiative the president confidently declared, "It's going to be one of the most important initiatives that my administration not only discusses, but also implements" (Davis 2001, 411).

Subsequently, President Bush issued executive orders to establish the Office of Faith-Based and Community Initiatives to coordinate the program. The next day, Bush charged the Congress to pave the way for faith-based organizations to "compete with secular agencies for government dollars." The president signed another executive order committing five cabinet departments—justice, housing and urban development, health and human services, labor, and education—to "investigate ways to make it easier for faith-based groups to compete for government contracts" (Davis 2001, 411). He followed that up with another executive order that eventually established faith-based and community offices at eleven federal agencies. The president's plan earmarked between $8 billion and $10 billion to be spent on faith-based initiatives during his first year in office. While that much money apparently was never spent in any single year of the Bush administration, grants to faith-based charities during the Bush years, more than 1300 total awards (Chao 2008), averaged more than $2 billion annually, unprecedented government spending on religion in a nation that had always prided itself on the separation of church and state. Was the nation heading toward transforming itself from a secular to a religious state?

No previous president had been as bold in crafting a specific program that would so dramatically challenge the American principle of church-state separation. Exactly how much money was spent on the faith-based initiative in the Bush years is anyone's guess. Accurate numbers are hard to come by. Bush officials routinely stated that it was hard to keep track of how much money was channeled to religious organizations because their "nondiscriminatory" plan no longer distinguished secular and religious groups. Documentation of results achieved by the president's faith-based initiative is still sorely lacking. Bush officials made it a practice frequently to parade "success stories" before the American people, but they said little about how much money was wasted, stolen, or simply used to no good end. Accountability was clearly lacking, especially since the grants were overseen by agencies under the control of the Bush administration rather than Congress.

Public accountability took another hit when in 2007 the U.S. Supreme Court ruled in *Hein v. Freedom from Religion Foundation* that taxpayers who do not have a direct connection to a government grant to a religious organization have no standing to sue. An earlier precedent, *Flast v. Cohen,* was held to be inapplicable because it permitted taxpayer lawsuits only when Congressional action was under challenge. Because the Bush grants were sanctioned pursuant to executive order, no taxpayer suit could force a challenge of a particular grant under Bush's Faith-based Initiative. The Court's decision greatly reduced the chances that successful challenges of the Bush plan could be waged. In fact, no successful challenges were lodged during the Bush years.

Arguably the greatest subterfuge associated with the Bush plan was the way it was touted as a plan to end discrimination against religion generally and against various religious groups specifically. When the Bush plan was first announced in 2000, well-known evangelical leaders such as Jerry Falwell and Pat Robertson voiced objections to the plan because it threatened "Christian America" since groups like Scientology, the Unification Church, and Wicca might receive government money. But this concern proved toothless, since according to one study in November 2006 reported by the *Boston Globe*, 98.3% of all Bush administration grants to faith-based agencies from the Office of Faith Based Initiatives were awarded to Christian groups (Kranish 2006). The practice of excluding non-Christian groups was confirmed by a former staffer in the White House Office of Faith-Based and Community Initiatives. David Kuo, in *Tempting Faith: An Inside Story of Political Seduction* (2006), asserted that applications for federal faith-based funds were often rejected by reviewers because they came from non-Christian applicants. Kuo reported being told by one grant reviewer, "When I saw one of those non-Christian groups on the set I was reviewing, I just stopped looking at them and gave them a zero. A lot of us did." (Americans United Press Release, October 12, 2006).

Eventually, Bush's faith-based initiative spread to a host of federal, state and local government agencies; by the end of the Bush term, at least 35 governors and 70 mayors, both Democratic and Republican, had established state and local programs modeled after the Bush federal program. Ironically, Congress still had never passed legislation sanctioning or in any way adopting the Bush plan (Berkowitz, 2008). Meanwhile, the Bush administration allowed and openly encouraged faith-based groups to discriminate in their hiring practices. This violated traditional law that prohibited recipients of government money to discriminate on the basis of religion; in the pre-Bush years religious organizations had to make employment available to persons of all faiths if government money was being dispensed. The Bush administration never observed this longstanding rule, telling religious grant recipients instead that they were free to "hire their own."

On June 26, 2008 Bush appeared at a Washington, D.C. conference sponsored by the very Office of Faith-Based and Community Initiatives that he had created, where he told an audience of over 1,000: "You've helped revolutionize the way government addresses the greatest challenges facing our society. . . . I truly believe the Faith-Based Initiative is one of the most important initiatives of this administration." Journalist Bill Berkowitz suggested that Bush was perhaps motivated by the need, mere months before the election of a new president, to locate something that might qualify as his lasting "legacy." Since he had failed in crafting what he sought to be his perduring legacy—bringing democracy to Iraq and Afghanistan—perhaps Berkowitz's insight has merit. (Berkowitz 2008).

While the Bush years have passed, the effects of the Bush plan to embrace faith-based agencies in the network of government funding are still under discussion. No one doubts that many people were helped by the plan. Aiding American citizens to get relief from drug and alcohol dependency, be fed a decent meal, locate adequate housing, receive clothing for one's children, receive needed pregnancy counseling, etc—and faith-based agencies administered all of these kinds of programs with government funding during the Bush years—is not to be taken lightly. But hard questions need to be asked. What are we to make of the church-state separation principles that the Bush faith-based funding violated? Will evasion of these principles come back to haunt the nation and its citizens? Are there actually good reasons to deny government funding to faith-based groups? Should church-state separation be altered to conform to the Bush initiative, or would that weaken the structure of the American democratic order? These are questions that should be given careful consideration.

QUESTIONING THE BUSH FAITH-BASED INITIATIVE

Without doubt, due to constitutional restrictions on government funding of religious institutions in the United States, Bush's plan was a bold challenge to the principle of church-state separation. Traditionally, churches and other faith-based organizations in the United States have been prohibited from receiving direct government grants, not because the government chooses to discriminate against religion, but because the courts have understood the constitutional purpose for restrictions on funding of religion to be grounded in the notion that religion functions more effectively if it is autonomous, not tied to government, and not threatened by government supervision and control. It is true, of course, that some religiously affiliated organizations have received government funding for decades. However, these groups are legally separate in structure from churches and other houses of worship, and they are neither allowed to proselytize their clients nor discriminate on the basis of religion in hiring. These rules are designed to protect the religious liberty of clients and to further the nation's commitment to nondiscrimination when using government dollars to finance a program. Successful organizations like Catholic Charities and Lutheran Social Services have operated effectively with these rules for years. Under these rules, there is much less concern for the nature of religious activity engaged in by faith-based social service providers, and they are prohibited from using religious criteria in hiring. But under the Bush plan, religious organizations received government funding directly rather than having to establish insulated social service organizations. Also, while the Bush plan technically did not permit the use of government money to proselytize, there was no prohibition against a house of worship using its own money to proselytize. Thus, by way of example, a church could set up a program requiring a client to hear a sermon before accessing social service benefits.

It is suggested here that, under Bush's lead, the notion that America's need to enlist the aid of government to assist churches and other faith-based institutions to administer social service programs began softening the nation on one of its founding principles—the separation of church and state. For many this "softening" was a welcome change. Legal scholar Carl Esbeck states that "[t]o increasing numbers of Americans, strict separation presents a cruel choice between suffering funding discrimination or forced secularization." (Esbeck 1998, 13). These supposed coercive and discriminatory elements of church-state separation are common arguments among those favoring greater governmental accommodation of religious institutions of all kinds. (Davis and Hankins 1999; Kennedy and Bielefeld 2006). As will be seen, however, the evidence proves that church-state separation has served to benefit rather than harm American religious vitality.

The arguments set forth in this chapter will perhaps appear melodramatic. Many may ask how simply altering America's course from a system of church-state separation to government accommodation of religion could possibly reconstitute the United States in such a way as to cause it injury? But the best intentions of government often result in its greatest blunders. It is suggested here that offering government aid to religion as a social good is a blunder that can have serious adverse consequences on the vital role that religion plays in American society.

To comprehend the potential damage to American religious vitality done by government benevolence, one first must recognize that the durability of a nation's spirit is conditioned heavily by the maintenance of separation between its two dominant institutional forms—the political and the religious. Baron de Montesquieu, recognizing the horrors of the church-state monism of eighteenth-century France, observed that the way to kill the vitality of religion is through government "favor." Similarly, Alexis de Tocqueville, having surveyed the American cultural landscape a century later, expressed his insight that "[s]o long as a religion derives its strength from sentiments, instincts, and passions . . . it can brave the assaults of time"; however, "when a religion chooses to rely on the interests of this world, it becomes almost as fragile as all earthly powers." (de Tocqueville 1969, 296). For de Tocqueville, it was not coincidental that it is in America "where the Christian religion has kept the greatest real power over men's souls." (de Tocqueville 1969, 291). The potential damage of the Bush initiative to the preservation of the unique American ethos only can be discerned through recognition that the American constitutional system is uniquely susceptible to institutional subtleties, especially those that attempt to benefit religion through favor. There is considerable irony in the fact that the American church-state structure is able to withstand sledgehammer assaults like the great cultural schisms precipitated during the Civil and Vietnam Wars, and the official attacks on liberal and pacifist denominations during the McCarthy era.[1] Yet church-state separation in the United States might not always be so resilient. The protections that are accorded to religious organizations in America might be threatened by the Bush plan.

THE CONSTITUTION AND THE BUSH PLAN

The provisions in the Bush plan that funded faith-based institutions on the same basis as their secular counterparts are often referred to generically as "charitable choice." The "charitable choice" nomenclature comes from Section 104 of the 1996 Welfare Reform Act which allows a state to contract with "charitable, religious and private organizations" to provide various social services. This enables a beneficiary to choose between obtaining aid from either a "secular" or "charitable" provider, hence "charitable choice." At first glance, these provisions do not seem too remarkable, since under certain judicial decisions, religiously affiliated organizations can receive government money to administer social programs, provided they are not "pervasively sectarian." The "pervasively sectarian" category, carved out by the Supreme Court in a series of cases handed down beginning in the early 1970s, includes churches and other religious organizations whose religious character is so pervasive that it would be impossible for them to carry out "secular" functions, thus violating the Establishment Clause's prohibitions against advancing religion (Sandin 1990, 24–27).

Under these rules, churches and other houses of worship were by definition "pervasively sectarian" and therefore disqualified from receiving government funds to administer social programs. Some churches, however, creatively resorted to setting up separate organizations to receive government funding to administer social programs. While maintaining some ties to the churches and other houses of worship that spawned them, these organizations nevertheless did not proselytize, discriminate on religious grounds, or otherwise advance their own religious tenets. This method appropriately allowed churches and other sectarian organizations to cooperate with government in delivering social services without forfeiting their own religious freedom or denying it to those whom they served. Obviously, there are a great number of organizations across the country that operate within this framework. For example, a hospital might operate under the auspices of a Roman Catholic charity, a drug and alcohol rehabilitation center might have a close association with Methodist bodies, or a day-care center might function under an affiliation with the United Presbyterian Church, all receiving government funding because they operate, at least presumptively, without running afoul of the Establishment Clause.

But "charitable choice" ignores the nuances in the law that prohibits government funding of churches, synagogues, and other pervasively sectarian organizations. Indeed, the Bush plan, following the "charitable choice" framework, seemed to place no restrictions whatsoever on the kinds of organizations that could receive government funding. Under an "equal treatment" or "neutrality" theory, anyone could apply to become a contracting party. It remains uncertain whether the Bush initiative, if and when it is challenged, will withstand judicial scrutiny.

The Bush initiative faced another constitutional hurdle in permitting faith-based institutions to practice religious discrimination in hiring even though they were receiving federal funds. This violated a longstanding American legal tradition. Bush claimed that churches and other faith organizations must be protected under the Free Exercise Clause to be able to hire only those that are compatible with their own faith objectives, but case law in the United States has not traditionally supported this contention. *Corporation of Presiding Bishop v. Amos* (483 U.S. 327, 1987) makes it clear that religious organizations, even when no particular religious qualifications are necessary to the performance of a job, may discriminate in hiring on the basis of religion, but this rule has not been applied when the worker is paid with government funds. The Bush initiative, suffice it to say, boldly challenged a large body of traditional case law intended to keep a safe distance between religious and governmental institutions.

THE BUSH PLAN AND THE "EQUAL TREATMENT" DOCTRINE

The foregoing analysis has focused on a few constitutional considerations that, based on traditional Supreme Court doctrine, are certain to receive close attention in any future review of the Bush faith-based initiative. Such a review would probably (or at least should) result in a finding that significant parts of the plan violate the Establishment Clause. Thus, a finding in support of the Bush faith-based initiative would require a less traditional analytical framework. The leading candidate for such a framework is the Court's so-called "equal treatment" doctrine (sometimes called the "neutrality" or "nondiscrimination" doctrine), an approach that increasingly has been utilized by the Court in cases dealing with religious speech, but which might easily be expanded to embrace a range of government funding issues.

What is the equal treatment doctrine, and will it support the constitutionality of the Bush initiative?[2] Even though President Bush's term in office has passed, the question remains relevant because churches and other houses of worship continue to receive government funds to administer social programs under the Bush plan—a plan operating under executive orders that the current president did not issue. Basically, the "equal treatment" doctrine surfaced in a line of cases in which the Supreme Court seemed satisfied to equate religious speech with other forms of secular speech, so that it adjudicated the cases strictly pursuant to a free speech analysis. This approach emphasized that religious speech is not in a privileged position vis-à-vis political, philosophical, or other forms of speech, leading the Court to justify its decisions on an "equal treatment" principle. But the equal treatment principle subsequently emerged in funding cases in which free speech issues were wholly absent.For example, the Court's equal treatment approach was applied in the 2000 case of *Mitchell v. Helms*. The *Helms* decision enabled federal funds to go to state and local education agencies that in turn lend educational materials and equipment to public and private elementary and secondary schools to implement "secular, neutral, and nonideological" programs. In *Helms*, roughly one-quarter of the available funds went to private religious schools.

The Supreme Court held that as long as eligibility for government funds are assessed without regard to religion, that is, as long as private religious schools, private nonreligious schools, and public schools are given "equal treatment" in their eligibility for aid, there is no violation of the Establishment Clause. *Helms* suggests that many of the Supreme Court justices no longer care whether government funds are diverted to religious purposes. These justices are now supportive of an equal treatment principle that makes government accountable only for neutral allocations of government funds.

The "equal treatment" doctrine received another vote of confidence in the 2002 case of *Zelman v. Simmons-Harris*, which dealt with the constitutionality of voucher programs. Vouchers are designed to provide parents with alternatives to public education by providing tuition from public funds to enable parents to send their children to private schools. Ohio's Pilot Project Scholarship Program became the test case for the constitutionality of vouchers.

Attorneys for the plaintiffs argued that 96% of students participating in the program enrolled in schools with religious affiliations, proving a bias toward religion. Nevertheless, the Supreme Court ruled 5–4 that the Ohio program does not violate the Establishment Clause, holding that "a government aid program is not readily subject to challenge under the Establishment Clause if it is neutral with respect to religion and provides assistance directly to a broad class of citizens who, in turn, direct government aid to religious schools wholly as a result of their own genuine and independent private choice." Justice David Souter sought to look to the effect of the program (that 96% of the recipients of funds attended religious schools), but the majority rejected this line of reasoning, saying that percentages were not relevant to the constitutional question of whether money should or should not go to religious institutions.

In *Helms and Zelman*, neutrality has come to mean providing religious groups with the same treatment that other groups get. But the future path of the equal treatment doctrine is uncertain. Since the doctrine is virtually indispensable to the survival, in the post-Bush era, of President Bush's faith-based initiative, the election of Barack Obama as the 44th president of the United States obviously raises the question of how he will handle the matter of government-funded faith-based services. During the presidential campaign that resulted in his election in November 2008, Obama made it known that he is not opposed to the Bush scheme in principle. He knows that neither religious institutions nor government alone can solve America's poverty problem or adequately aid impoverished communities and families. He sees the need for some kind of "partnership." Early in his administration he changed the name of the Bush office to Office of Faith-Based Initiatives and Neighborhood Partnerships and appointed a director, 26-year-old Pentecostal pastor Joshua DuBois. Thus, it seems that Obama wants to move the faith-based initiative forward, but in a different manner. He apparently has no problem with government supplying significant sums of money to faith-based institutions. He made it clear in his presidential campaign, however, that he wants the money used strictly for secular programs and that religion should not be used as a factor in hiring. This latter point angered many religious conservatives, but Obama seems to want to focus on devising quality services rather than on *who* is providing those services.

Obama stated in his campaign that his Faith-Based Office would undertake as its first order of business the creation of a $500 million per year program to provide summer education for at least one million poor children. As one editorialist wrote during the presidential campaign, "As a community organizer who was funded by Roman Catholic charities in the early 1980s, Obama saw the vital role that churches can play in revitalizing neighborhoods. As a former law professor who taught Constitutional law, he understands the First Amendment pitfalls of funding religious groups." (*Mercury News* 2008). Implementing these correctives would move the nation back closer to the legal structure of government-funded religion before charitable choice and the Bush faith-based initiative moved into the picture. Previously, religious groups could not use religion as a basis for discriminatory hiring; this principle, circumvented by one of Bush's executive orders, would be restored. Previously, religious groups were required to set up independent entities to receive government funding so as not to comingle government and private funds. Obama is apparently willing to allow direct funding of religious groups, saying only that he will require that the program administered with government funds be "secular," which is perhaps another way of mandating that public and private funds not be mixed. So, all things considered, Obama seems much more respectful toward a traditional interpretation of the Establishment Clause that respects church-state separation.

But the Bush initiative and the legal doctrines that undergird it might still prevail. If the Bush faith-based initiative is to withstand constitutional scrutiny, it will likely be on the basis of the Supreme Court's equal treatment theory.

CONCLUSION

The Bush plan was frequently advanced, especially by George W. Bush himself during his tenure as president, as necessary to end the pattern of discrimination against religion in America. But there are serious problems attending a framework of nondiscriminatory distribution of government benefits to religious institutions. First, a nondiscriminatory program should be expected to operate in a genuinely nondiscriminatory way. As there are now approximately two thousand identifiable religions and sects in the United States, it would be impossible to fairly and equitably distribute government monies among them all. Under the Bush initiative, those with the most financial resources and political clout received the largest share of the pie; smaller, less popular faith groups were forced to the periphery in a climate of destructive competition among America's communities of faith.

Second, making religion the servant of government is now perhaps inaugurating the decline of religion's current role as the nation's "prophetic voice" and conscience against ill-advised governmental policies. Religion with its hand out can never fulfill its prophetic role in society. The Bush initiative in some ways proves the point that many in America still fail to understand that religion is better off without government money. President Barack Obama will hopefully return to the basic pre-Bush framework for religion-government partnerships. After all, what is so wrong with a system of requiring religion to rely upon its supporters and, ultimately, upon God for sustenance rather than government? Benjamin Franklin's counsel is surely appropriate here: "When a Religion is good I conceive that it will support itself; and when it cannot support itself, and God does not care to support it, so that its Professors are obliged to call for the help of the Civil Power, 'tis a sign, I apprehend, of its being a bad one!" (Sparks 1882, 8: 505).

The Bush plan unnecessarily invoked a host of church-state issues of fundamental importance. The new president and Congress should steer clear of First Amendment problems by limiting the scope of potentially participating organizations in government benefits to private organizations, including religiously affiliated organizations that have an organizational charter or bylaws establishing their secular function. Houses of worship and other religious groups could then participate in various welfare programs, performing their contractual responsibilities with the state in a secular setting and without proselytization. This arrangement would protect both church and state from encroachment by the other.

The Bush administration seemed convinced that meeting the needs of the nation's poor and needy could only be achieved by enlisting the aid of faith-based institutions. But why does this also require an infusion of government money, with all of the attendant problems, both practical and constitutional? If a lack of financial resources hinders faith-based institutions from a full participation in social programs, Congress would do better to allow all taxpayers to deduct their charitable contributions, even those who do not itemize. Congress could also offer economic incentives (e.g. tax credits and multiple write-offs) to corporate America for donations to faith-based institutions. The possibilities here are endless, but the notion of corporations adopting and providing the financial means for charities, churches, and other faith-based organizations to administer social programs—in effect creating a new strain of partnerships to solve problems that government cannot solve—is an attractive prospect.

But apart from these possibilities, and even in the new world of "equal treatment" of religion, houses of worship and other religious organizations can still exercise the same option that has always been open to them: assist the poor and needy on their own terms, with their own financial resources, in an expressly religious environment, and with complete freedom to proselytize and teach their own religious beliefs. America's tradition of religious liberty could never be more faithfully or effectively exercised.

NOTES

1. Robert S. Ellwood contends that McCarthyism not only attempted to subvert churches supposedly sympathetic to communism but tried to establish "an anti-Communist state church." See Robert S. Ellwood, *The Fifties Spiritual Marketplace: American Religion in a Decade of Conflict* (New Brunswick, NJ: Rutgers University Press, 1997).
2. For a more extended argument for "equal treatment" theory in the provision of faith-based social services, see Stephen V. Monsma, *When Sacred and Secular Mix: Religious Nonprofit Organizations and Public Money* (Lanham, MD.: Rowman and Littlefield, 1996), and Stephen V. Monsma and J. Christopher Soper, eds., *Equal Treatment of Religion in a Pluralistic Society* (Grand Rapids, MI: William B. Eerdmans, 1998).

REFERENCES

Americans United for Separation of Church and State Press Release, "Bush 'Faith-Based' Initiative Was Used For GOP Campaigns, Former White House Official Charges In New Book," October 12, 2006.

Berkowitz, Bill. "A President Desperately Seeking a Legacy," *Scoop Independent News*, July 14, 2008. http://scoop.co.nz/stories/HL0807/S00117.htm (Accessed July 31, 2008).

Chao, Elaine L. Secretary of Labor, speech delivered June 28, 2008. Washington, D.C.

Davis, Derek H. 2001. President Bush's Office of Faith-based and Community Initiatives. *Journal of Church and State* 43(Summer): 411–422.

Davis, Derek, and Hankins, Barry. (eds). 1999. *Welfare Reform and Faith-Based Organizations*. Waco, TX: J. M. Dawson Institute of Church-State Studies, Baylor University.

de Tocqueville, Alexis. 1969[1835 and 1840]. *Democracy in America*. Translated by George Lawrence, edited by J. P. Mayer. Garden City, NY: Doubleday.

Ellwood, Robert S. 1997. *The Fifties Spiritual Marketplace: American Religion in a Decade of Conflict.* New Brunswick, NJ: Rutgers University Press.

Esbeck, Carl. 1998. Equal Treatment: Its Constitutional Status. In *Equal Treatment of Religion in a Pluralistic Society*, edited by Stephen V. Monsma and J. Christopher Soper. Grand Rapids, MI: William B. Eerdmans.

Kennedy, Sheila Suess, and Bielefeld, Wolfgang. 2006. *Charitable Choice at Work: Evaluation Faith-Based Job Programs in the States.* Washington D.C.: Georgetown University Press.

Kranish, Michael. (2006). "Democrats Inspect Faith-Based Initiative", *Boston Globe*, December 4. http://www.boston.com/news/nation/washington/articles/2006/12/04/democrats_inspect_faith_based_initiative/. (Accessed August 2, 2010.)

Kuo, David. 2006. *Tempting Faith: An Inside Story of Political Seduction.* New York: Simon and Schuster.

Mercury News. 2008. "Obama Advocates Faith-Based Plan that Trumps Bush's," *Mercury News Editorial*, July 14. http://www. mercurynews.com/opinion/ci_9875321 (Accessed July 31, 2008).

Monsma, Stephen V. 1996. *When Sacred and Secular Mix: Religious Nonprofit Organizations and Public Money.* Lanham, MD: Rowman and Littlefield.

Monsma, Stephen V. and Soper, J. Christopher. (eds). 1998. *Equal Treatment of Religion in a Pluralistic Society.* Grand Rapids, MI: William B. Eerdmans.

Sandin, Robert T. 1990. *Autonomy and Faith: Religious Preference in Employment Decisions in Religiously Affiliated Education.* Atlanta, GA: Omega Publications.

Sparks, Jared. (ed). 1882. *The Works of Benjamin Franklin*, 8 volumes. Chicago: MacCoun.

COURT CASES

Corporation v. Presiding Bishop, 483 U.S. 327 (1987).
Hein v. Freedom from Religion Foundation, 127 S. Ct. 2553 (2007).
Flast v. Cohen, 392 U.S. 83 (1968).

13 The Cult as a Social Problem

Eileen Barker

Jesus was undoubtedly a problem—as were the early Christians, Mohammed and the early Muslims, and Wesley and the early Methodists. Today, L. Ron Hubbard and the Church of Scientology, Louis Farrakhan and the Nation of Islam, Li Hongzhi and Falun Gong; Osama bin Laden and Al Qaida have all been considered a threat not only to their individual followers but also to the very fabric of society. Indeed, throughout history, religious leaders and the movements to which they have given rise have been perceived to be social problems by those who are sure that they know another, truer Truth, and a different, better way of life than that proposed by the new religion.

This chapter is concerned not so much with religion *per se* being considered a problem, but with constructions of images of "wrong" or "bad" religions as social problems. Indeed, an integral part of these constructions usually implies the contemporaneous existence of "good" and "true" religion as something to be protected and clearly differentiated from bad or false religions, which, in order to avoid confusion, can be denied the label religion and, in the popular parlance of the day, branded as cults or (more commonly for French-speakers) sects.

CULTS, SECTS, AND NEW RELIGIOUS MOVEMENTS

Most lay understandings of the terms "cult" and "sect" begin with an assumption that the movements are social problems. Exactly what kind of problems they are thought to pose may vary, but these can include imputations of heretical beliefs, political intrigue, child abuse, criminal activity, financial irregularity, the breaking up of families, sexual perversion, medical quackery, and/or the employment of mind control or brainwashing techniques.

Social scientists have tended to start from a more neutral perspective, using "cult" and "sect" as technical terms to refer to religious groups in tension with the wider society. Around the early 1970s, however, a number of scholars who were studying organizations such as the Children of God, the Church of Scientology, ISKCON (the International Society for Krishna Consciousness) and the Unification Church decided to abandon use of the terms cult and sect, at least in public discourse, largely because they wanted to avoid the negative connotations now widely associated with these words. Instead, they opted for the term "new religious movement" (NRM) in the hope that this would provide a generic label for the phenomena they were researching without prejudging whether or not they were social problems.

There has been (and continues to be) considerable debate among sociologists, historians and religious studies specialists as to what exactly constitutes the phenomena that are covered by the term NRM. Many of the organizations to which the term is applied are not obviously religious, others are not altogether new, and yet others are hardly movements. However, while not suggesting that any one meaning is more correct than another, it can be argued that a *useful* approach is to start from a conception of an NRM as a religious or spiritual association with a predominantly first-generation membership (Barker 2004).[1]

As one person's cult is likely to be another person's religion, sturdy boundaries need to be constructed in order to keep the two unambiguously differentiated, and these distinctions have had to be defended against anyone who constructs a different boundary, with a variety of methods being brought into play to clarify and justify the antagonists' distinctions between a cult and a "genuine religion" (Barker 1991). There have, of course, been "cult wars" throughout history. Schisms, alternative interpretations of Scripture, and new religions have long been labeled as heresies, and the heretics have frequently died at the hands of those who labeled them thus (Jenkins 2000; Versluis 2006). So far as the more recent wave of NRMs is concerned, starting in the early 1970s a number of people who, for one reason or another, were opposed to the movements began to organize themselves into what came to be known generically as the anti-cult movement (ACM).[2]

From an anti-cultist perspective the reason why the NRMs are considered a social problem is, quite simply, because the movements *are* a social problem: their beliefs and practices are perceived as anti-social and a danger to individuals and to society. From another perspective (especially that of the NRMs themselves), it has been argued that, left to their own devices, the movements would not pose any kind of real threat: it is the purely the way that they are portrayed by their opponents that results in their being perceived as a social problem. Using the language of constructionism, the former position sees *primary* constructions (that is, the actions of the members) as the social problem; the latter position considers it is *secondary* constructions of the movements which result in their being perceived as a social problem.

PRIMARY AND SECONDARY CONSTRUCTIONS OF REALITY

All social life involves the construction of images. Social reality itself is a human construction. On the one hand, it is a reality in the sense that it exists independently of any individual person's volition—that is, one has to take it into account; one can accept it, try to reject it or change it, but, as with a brick wall, one cannot wish it away or ignore it without facing the consequences. On the other hand, unlike physical reality, social reality exists only in so far as it is recognized by individuals. This means that social reality has both an objective and a subjective character; it can, consequently, have a more or less recognizably stable structure, yet it is always an on-going, ever-changing process.

NRMs are part of social reality. They are constructed through the actions and interactions of their individual members. The founder of a movement and his or her followers create, maintain and change the movement through proclaiming their beliefs, giving their community a special name, identifying themselves as a more or less distinguishable unit and behaving in ways that reinforce (yet may eventually destroy) the movement as a recognizable social entity.[3] Such actions can be called *primary constructions*—they involve the creation, continuance and demise of the phenomenon itself.

A *secondary* construction occurs when people (be they participants or non-participants in the primary construction of the NRM) not only recognize the existence of the movement, but also construct an image of it that can be transmitted to others. There are always some features of a social reality that are agreed upon by those who perceive it (otherwise it would not be a *social* reality), but no two individuals' perceptions are ever exactly the same. The differences in their images are not, however, random. The various positions (geographical, psychological and social) from which a phenomenon is perceived can account in part for *systematic differences* between alternative depictions of the phenomenon. While people may tell the truth, and nothing but the truth, it is impossible for anyone to tell the *whole* truth. Everyone (more or less consciously) selects what is to be included or excluded from their picture of reality according to a number of criteria—one criterion being what is relevant to their interests.

Thus it is that members of an NRM (who are likely to have an interest in persuading people how good their movement is and, probably, in gaining new converts) will select for inclusion what they consider (and/or assume others will consider) to be positive features, while keeping silent about any skeletons that may be lurking in the cupboard. The movement's opponents, on the other hand, are more likely to select what they consider to be bad or harmful actions in their depiction of the movement. In this they may be aided and abetted by the media who are anxious to attract and keep the attention of an audience more interested in the novel and sensational than in the normal and everyday (Barker 2003).

Rather than arguing that the reason NRMs are perceived as a problem *either* because of their actions *or* because their opponents see them as such, I shall suggest reasons why it is possible that *both* the NRMs themselves *and* their opponents' secondary constructions that can be at least partly responsible. Furthermore, it will be suggested, the interaction between the different constructors can exacerbate the situation, resulting in the movements becoming seen as increasingly problematic.

POTENTIALLY PROBLEMATIC CHARACTERISTICS OF NRMS

There are some new religions that have performed what, to most members of society, would be unequivocally problematic actions. Take, for example, the apparently senseless murders of Sharon Tate and others by members of The Manson Family in 1969. In 1978 the world was horrified by the murder of Congressman Leo Ryan and his companions and the mass suicide/murders at Jonestown, Guyana, by members of the Peoples Temple. The 1990s saw the suicides and murders of members of the Solar Temple between 1994 and 1997, the release of sarin gas in the Tokyo underground by members of Aum Shinrikyo in 1995, and the Heavens Gate suicides in 1997.

It should, however, be stressed that such atrocities are rare occurrences considering the hundreds of law-abiding NRMs that have emerged during the past century or so.[4] Generalizing about NRMs is fraught with dangers as nearly every generalization can be disproved by at least one of their number. Nonetheless, first-generation religions are likely to exhibit certain characteristics merely because they *are* new in this sense, and several of these characteristics can contribute towards antagonistic relationships between the movement and non-members, resulting in the former being defined as a social problem.

First, the very fact that the membership of an NRM is made up of converts can in itself lead to friction. Converts to any religion tend to be far more enthusiastic, even fanatic, than those born into a religion. It is not always easy to reason or even to communicate with converts who are enthused by their new-found faith, and who, not having totally internalized the beliefs and practices, might do little more than reiterate slogans that mean nothing to their listeners—or who may be so preoccupied that they do not even attempt to explain their new beliefs and behavior.

Secondly, new religions do not attract a random sample of the population. Although the movements may differ from each other in a number of significant ways, each of them appeals disproportionately to particular sections of society. While in the past, new religions have frequently appealed to the socially, economically and/or politically oppressed, NRMs that became visible in the West in the latter part of the twentieth century appealed disproportionately, although not exclusively, to well-educated, white young adults. This meant that "normal" society was presented with a very visible picture of young people abandoning the widely sought-after opportunities they had been given and, instead, embracing apparently inexplicable behavior, such as devoting their lives to some foreign guru, selling flowers or candles on the street for up to 18 hours a day, living in relative poverty, changing their outward appearance, marrying someone who has been chosen for them, and possibly severing connections with their former life, including their family and friends.

Thirdly, the founders and/or leaders of NRMs are frequently granted charismatic authority by their followers. This means that they are relatively unconstrained by either tradition or rules, and are, thereby, both unpredictable and unaccountable to anyone except, perhaps, to God. This in turn means that they can be seen as more dangerous than those in more established leadership positions whose actions can, generally speaking, be anticipated in advance. Later, there might develop a hierarchical authority structure with commands issuing from the top to the lower levels, giving the movement a strength and control over individuals who might be expected to sacrifice themselves for a greater good, which, they are told, is God's will and, therefore, unquestionable.

Fourthly, NRMs may be considered a social problem because many of them declare the rest of the world to be the social problem. It is not uncommon for the movements to operate with a dichotomous world-view, erecting a sharp boundary between "us" (the insiders) and "them" (the outsiders)—a distinction that may be reinforced not only through shared beliefs and values but also through the employment of a special language, dress, diet, music and/or other types of distinguishing behavior. As a result, non-members may be encouraged to see the NRM as "other."

Fifthly, as has already been intimated, NRMs have characteristically given rise to suspicion, fear and, not infrequently, discrimination and/or persecution. New movements offer an alternative way of viewing the world and, quite often, an alternative way of living one's life. It is not surprising that they are unlikely to be welcomed by those with a vested interest in preserving the *status quo*—or even by those who accept that statistically normal, taken-for-granted beliefs and practices are both ethically correct and desirable. Early Christians were thrown to the lions; Cathars were burned at the stake; Bahá'ís have been executed in Iran and Ahmadis in Pakistan; Jehovah's Witnesses were gassed in Auschwitz; and there are numerous examples of NRMs being imprisoned, tortured and put to death in parts of today's world (US Commission 2009; Pew 2009). In what follows, however, it is some of the more subtle methods of discrimination that will be considered—methods which are, nonetheless, directed towards creating a perception of the movements not only as "different" but also as a social problem.

But first it should be added that a sixth and often ignored characteristic of NRMs is that they are likely to change far more rapidly and fundamentally than older, more traditional religions. Inevitable demographic changes occur with the arrival of second and subsequent generations; converts typi-cally lose some of their initial enthusiasms as they mature; founding leaders age and eventually die, which frequently results in the authority structure becoming more traditional and bureaucratic and, thereby, more predictable and accountable. The movements' beliefs may become less sharply defined and more open to qualification, and the strong boundary that distinguishes members from non-members may become more permeable with greater interaction taking place between the members and the wider society.

THE ANTI-CULT MOVEMENT (ACM)

Organized opposition to contemporary NRMs in the West arose early in the 1970s. It started with the concerns of parents of converts to the Chil-dren of God, a branch of the "Jesus Movement" that had emerged during the 1960s. These parents, together with Ted Patrick, the originator of forc-ible "deprogramming," founded FREECOG (Free the Children of God), which was to be the first formal cult-watching group in the United States (Patrick 1976; Shupe and Bromley 1980, 89ff). Before long there appeared a cluster of other groups similarly concerned about the practices of NRMs.[5] The composition of the ACM has varied; in its early days it consisted pre-dominantly of middle-class parents who were in a position to protest and to be heard, but soon the parents were joined by professionals such as lawyers, deprogrammers, therapists, mental health practitioners and, increasingly, former members.

The Cult Awareness Network (CAN) was formed from a merger of sev-eral small groups and became the foremost anti-cult coalition until 1996, when it was bankrupted as the result of an illegal kidnapping case (*Scott v. Ross*) in which it was found guilty of referring a parent to the depro-grammer (Shupe and Darnell 2006, 180–188). The subsequent purchase of the name of CAN by the Church of Scientology left the American Family Foundation (AFF) as the largest cult-watching group in North America. Founded in 1979 as a research and education organization (Langone 2002, 5), AFF membership had had considerable overlap with CAN so far as its Board and attendance at conferences were concerned (Shupe and Darnell 2006, 115), but the AFF was less strident than CAN, and, as an orga-nization, has not promoted forcible deprogramming, preferring instead the non-violent "exit counseling" and, later, "thought reform counseling" (Giambalvo et al. 1998).

Meanwhile, concern about the movements had also been growing in other parts of the world. Some of the most active opposition to NRMs in Western Europe has been in France, which, having established a number of anti-cult groups in the 1970s,[6] commissioned government reports on the perceived problem, first in the early 1980s, then again in the mid 1990s. This second report was the cause of considerable controversy (Introvigne and Melton 1996), not least because it contained a list of 172 sects which were presumed to be dangerous due to their exhibiting at least one of ten characteristics. These included mental destabilization, exorbitant financial demands, breaking with one's original environment, indoctrination of children, anti-social speech, disturbances of law and order, and infiltrating the public authorities (Guyard 1995, 15). Needless to say, it was widely remarked that most traditional religions could find themselves included under such a definition.

Since its publication there have been numerous allegations by movements listed in the report that they have suffered from discrimination merely on the grounds that they were on the list (Lheureux et al. 2000). Two years later, the Belgian government produced a report that had attached to it a list of 184 movements which included the Society of Friends (Quakers) and the YWCA (Young Women's Christian Association). Although this report explicitly stated that the list was only of names brought up in evidence and did not imply that the commission considered the movement to be a sect or, *a fortiori*, dangerous, the very fact that a movement is on the list has led to occasions when it has allegedly been discriminated against and/or assumed to be a social problem.

Regardless of the status of any particular movement, it was clear that both the French and Belgian governments considered the movements as a whole to constitute a social problem, and accordingly they both established organizations that would monitor the movements' actions. The French organization is currently named MIVILUDES,[7] and the Belgian one is known as the CIAOSN.[8]

By the end of the 1980s, small groups had surfaced throughout all Western Europe. In England, for example, the first anti-cult group, FAIR (Family Action Information and Rescue) had been founded in 1976,[9] and further groups followed during the 1980s. There was also a growing number of groups in Australia, Japan and other Asian locations. Then, following the fall of the Berlin Wall in 1989 and the subsequent flood of movements taking advantage of the new freedoms in Eastern Europe and the former Soviet Union, worried parents and the traditional churches that had been repressed under atheistic regimes organized themselves to fight the cults, which became widely perceived as a threat to the new post-communist society. In this they were encouraged by Western anti-cultists and their literature (Shterin and Richardson 2000); some were also eager to play a role as members of FECRIS, an umbrella organization for European anti-cultists, founded largely through the endeavors of UNADFI in Paris in 1994.[10]

STATE ATTITUDES TOWARDS NRMS

The success of the ACM in lobbying support from those in positions of power has varied from time to time and from place to place. In some societies their existence is irrelevant, but elsewhere the evidence of "cult-watching groups" can tip the balance one way or the other. Societies governed by the principles of atheistic socialism are unlikely to consider NRMs a particular problem because all religions are considered a social problem; in Saudi Arabia, all religions apart from the state religion are considered a social problem. At the other end of the spectrum, the USA has a Constitution forbidding the government to discriminate between religions. There are, however, many states that do discriminate between religions, sometimes giving special privileges, sometimes imposing restrictions on minority or unpopular religions. In France, legislation has been introduced clearly indicating that the state feels the need to protect its citizens from the social problem of dangerous sects (Altglas 2008, 56–57; Rolland 2003). Sometimes legislative discrimination is directed towards a named NRM, as is the case in China where Falun Gong, explicitly defined as a social problem, has been banned as an "evil cult" and practitioners have to undergo "re-education" (Ownby 2008; Palmer 2007).

Rather than elaborating further on the structural or organizational aspects of the ACM (Altglas 2008; Beckford 1985; Chryssides 1999; Shupe and Bromley 1980; 1994; Shupe and Darnell 2006), or the varied reactions by governments and in courts of law (Richardson 2004), what follows will concentrate on the construction of cult images as one (but, it must be recognized, only one) of the methods employed by the NRMs' opponents in their attempts to persuade others (and, perhaps, themselves) that the movements are, in one way or another, a social problem.

CONSTRUCTING IMAGES OF NRMS AS A SOCIAL PROBLEM

It needs to be stressed that the issue being addressed here is not whether one set of images is superior to another set. I have argued elsewhere (Barker 2003) that the *methodology* of the social sciences can result in more reliable (objective) secondary constructions than other methods. It should, however, be noted that objectivity is not necessarily the main concern of all secondary constructors, just as it should be noted there are those who are associated with the anti-cultist camp who espouse a scientific approach, and that there are academics whose work falls lamentably short of the standards of science.

Just as it is impossible to generalize about NRMs, it is impossible to generalize about the ACM. One distinction that can be drawn, however, is that between those whose main concern is helping the people (such as relatives and former members) who have experienced harm because of direct or indirect contact with the movements, and those whose main concern is to expose the movements as harmful cults—a position that may be motivated by the experience of personal suffering, a firm conviction that any deviation from a socially accepted norm is problematic, or, possibly, financial interests in, say, a lucrative deprogramming practice. Generally speaking, members of the first group are more likely to want their secondary constructions to reflect the primary constructions so that they can better understand and deal with the problems, whilst members of the latter group are more likely to want to emphasize only negative features and may resort to various ruses to ensure that their images unambiguously depict cults as a social problem.

Language, Brainwashing and Mind Control

As has already been suggested, one of the most common and effective means by which an NRM is depicted as a social problem is simply through using the term "cult." There are, however, many other ways that language can convey a negative image. Nouns, adjectives, and adverbs can all contain evaluative overtones, and grammar, particularly the use of the passive tense, can support imputations of brainwashing or mind control. "I converted to a new religion" becomes "he was recruited into a cult"; "I've chosen a life of sacrifice and dedication to God" becomes "she's being exploited by the guru."[11]

The brainwashing debate is one of the more heated battles in the cult wars. Parents who saw their (adult) children apparently change overnight into completely different people embracing strange beliefs and life-styles found the suggestion that they had been subjected to brainwashing or mind-control techniques the only comprehensible explanation. The theory absolved both relatives and "victims" from any responsibility; it also justified the use of forcible deprogramming as it was alleged that the victims were unable to escape by themselves but needed rescuing (Patrick 1976, 70, 276). On the other hand, NRM scholars have found that, although many of the NRMs certainly try to influence potential converts by various means, the vast majority of those subjected to such practices have resisted the pressure—and the majority of those who have joined have tended to leave of their own accord within a relatively short period (Barker 1994; Bromley and Richardson 1983). With the passage of time and further research, more sophisticated understandings of the processes involved in joining the movements have been embraced by both "sides," but, perpetuated in large part by the popular media, the metaphor of brainwashing continues to form an enduring element in the popular image of cults.

Generalizing

Indeed, the role of the media cannot be over-estimated. Analyses of "cult stories" have repeatedly uncovered ways in which NRMs are portrayed as social problems by, for example, including frequent references to unrelated "suicide cults," with vivid pictures of the tragedies accompanying the article (Beckford 1999; van Driel and Richardson 1988). Thus a programme about Soka Gakkai in the UK, which had not succeeded in unearthing any particularly problematic details, started and ended with footage of firemen removing bodies from the Tokyo underground after the release of sarin gas by members of Aum Shinrikyo—an NRM which, apart from its Japanese origins, bears no similarity to Soka Gakkai.

This is a variant of the inductive logic that, if one member of a class of phenomena is known to have committed a criminal act, it can be assumed that all members of that class have done likewise. It is not always necessary for anyone to suggest that all cults are guilty of crimes; the very fact that the media report a crime when it has been committed by a cultist can result in the reader/listener/watcher concluding there is a strong connection between cults and crime. They are less likely to notice that the media do not report the religious affiliation of Anglicans when they commit crimes, yet the Anglican crime rate might be twice that of NRMs. A slightly different assumption is that an action that is true of NRMs is peculiar to NRMs but not the rest of the population. Thus it may be "discovered" that members of NRMs sometimes cried as children, which, while undoubtedly true, is hardly peculiar to those who join NRMs.

Imputing Negative Motives and Double Standards

Both sides in the cult wars have a tendency to define their own actions as being carried out for the best of motives, while imputing the worst of motives to their opponents. Even (perhaps especially) when NRMs perform what would normally be regarded as "good works," these may be dismissed by the ACM as nothing but devious PR enterprises designed to gain (illegitimate) legitimacy. A related practice is to condemn actions performed by the "other side" while the very same action performed by one's own side is described as justifiable or even praiseworthy. The accounts by Ted Patrick (1976) of deprogrammings he conducted provide copious examples of this strategy, ranging from the use of deception to the use of physical violence.

Labeling and Deviance Amplification

Criminologists have long recognized that labeling people in a negative way can result in a self-fulfilling prophecy, encouraging them to behave as they have been labeled (Becker 1963). They have also observed what has come to be known as a spiral of "deviance amplification" when a society's negative reaction towards a movement that is perceived as deviant may result in the movement becoming *more* deviant, thereby provoking further condemnation—and so on . . . (Young 1973, 350). Escalating hostility between the FBI and the Branch Davidians, and between the Chinese People's Republic and Falun Gong, provide examples of this kind of negative polarization within the "cuit scene" (Bromley and Melton 2002). It should, however, be noted that the spiral can work in the opposite direction, decreasing tensions through mutual accommodation.

PROTECTING IMAGES

ACM activists need not only to construct but also to *defend* their constructions in a market place of competing images (Barker 2003). Part of their
defensive strategy can involve challenging conflicting depictions, especially
those of NRM scholars whom they may try to dismiss by labeling them as
"cult-apologists." The final section of this chapter offers examples of some
of the ways those who are concerned to defend their images of cults as a
social problem do so by attacking what they consider to be "the other side."
Several illustrations are of a personal nature, if only because my work has
invoked a formidable array of examples!

Whilst publications by NRM scholars are frequently ignored, there
are two ways in which they do get "used" by their antagonists in the cult
wars: data deemed to be positive (or even neutral) are taken to "prove" the
scholar is a cult-apologist; data deemed to be negative are taken to show
that *even* cult-apologists have to admit that the cults are a social problem.

This kind of "tails-you-lose, heads-I-win" approach was adopted by an
ACM reviewer when she reported, "the author focuses almost exclusively
on her positive reframing and apologetic reframing [of the movements]"
then concluded:

> Ultimately, I suppose we can thank Palmer for giving us more ammuni-
> tion in the academic (and sociocultural) battle between those of us who
> believe that such groups are potentially harmful . . . and those who line
> up with the cult apologists. (Lalich 1997, 159–161)

Sometimes what has been written is taken completely out of context. In
an article designed to demonstrate that "apologist NRM scholars" have
collaborated with the movements by presenting only positive images, one
critic wrote:

> Barker (1991, 11) noted the "considerable economic advantages to be
> gained from being defined as a religion", but has not suggested that
> this may motivate any specific NRMs or their leaders. (Beit-Hallahmi
> 2001, 57)

In fact, the entire paragraph from which the citation was lifted was devoted
to suggesting that very thing.

A posting on a cult-watching website offers an interesting example of
selective perception. It consists of an account of a lecture I had given, but
bears little relation to my actual position or to what I had said, including a complaint that I had presented "a graphic image of the bombing
of an ISKCON temple [but] no images of atrocities committed by cultic
groups."[12] In fact, my PowerPoint presentation had contained two graphic

images of dead bodies in Jonestown; one of the Branch Davidians compound in flames; a collage of bodies in the Tokyo underground and Aum Shinrikyo's leader, Asahara; and a photo of the blazing Twin Towers. It was only after showing these that I had shown the picture of the bombed ISKCON temple—which was followed by a further picture of bunk beds containing the bodies of Heaven's Gate members who had committed suicide.

I have no reason to believe that the complainant was deliberately lying. I suspect he just had not remembered my showing the other pictures, which would have merely confirmed his taken-for-granted dichotomous worldview of *"cults=bad vs. rest-of-society=good"*. A proponent of cognitive dissonance theory might conclude that the inclusion of the unfamiliar ISKCON picture threatened his picture of reality and, to protect this, he had to reject the apparent inconsistency by proclaiming I was a cult apologist who presented only information defending the cults (Festinger et. al 1956).

Perhaps less forgivable are occasions when complainants presumably know that they are fabricating the evidence. On an internet discussion group an avowed anti-cultist has attacked one of my books (Barker 1994), stating that I used methodological techniques I had explicitly not used, and giving a ridiculously inaccurate account of my findings. When another list member challenged the woman's statements, she defended herself by saying that she had not read the book as, she claimed, she had tried to get it from Amazon "but even a used copy is more than $100." On checking Amazon that same day, I saw several copies on offer for under $5.

Then there are those who apparently consider any direct familiarity with my work would involve contamination. One of my students, attending a FAIR meeting, found herself being told about the terrible things I had written. The student, somewhat surprised, asked her informant where she had read these things, whereupon the woman replied in a shocked voice that she wouldn't dream of reading any of my work.

One of the criticisms sometimes leveled against NRM scholars is that they are too academic; they cannot understand the situation because they have never lost a child to a cult.[13] Several years ago I was asked to write a pamphlet for the Catholic Truth Society about the new religions. This I did, but it was rejected because, I was told, it was too objective. Another Catholic publication, *The Clergy Review,* did publish an article I wrote for them, whereupon the then-Chair of FAIR telephoned the editor demanding the right "to redress the balance as Barker's article was so balanced!" When I asked another of FAIR's Chairmen to give me examples of errors in my publications, he responded that he didn't think I was wrong, just that by presenting two or more points of view I was "muddying the waters." It was, he said, much easier for the FAIR membership if they had an uncomplicated picture of the situation.

CONCLUDING REMARKS

"Cult wars" are likely to continue so long as there are new religions. What has been suggested in this chapter is that if we want to understand why there is a widespread perception of cults as a social problem it is necessary to study not only the NRMs, but also the various interests, methods and techniques involved in secondary constructions of the movements. This chapter has briefly introduced the complexity of the constructions of social life—but there is much, much more to be written on the subject

NOTES

1. To adopt for definitional purposes the presence of the independent variable of being in tension with the society can be useful for other purposes (Langone 1993, 5; Melton 2004), but would be to beg the question in this chapter, when the point is to enquire how new (in the sense of first-generation) religious movements may *come to be perceived* in negative terms.
2. For reasons of clarity, in what follows, NRMs will be referred to as "movements" while their opponents' organizations will be referred to as "groups." When the term "cult" is used, this will be indicating that a movement is being viewed from the perspective of its opponents.
3. Drawing heavily on Berger and Luckmann (1967), I have discussed the construction of images of NRMs in greater detail elsewhere (Barker 2003).
4. Inform (www.inform.ac) has information on just under a thousand different movements currently active in the UK.
5. Around the same time, there was also the growth of the counter-cult movement (CCM) which, although overlapping to some extent with the ACM, was more concerned with exposing what its members considered to be the theologically incorrect beliefs of NRMs (Cowan 2003).
6. ADFI, the most influential of these, was founded in 1974, then, uniting the growing number of branches, it became known under the umbrella term of UNADFI (National Union of the Association for the Defense of Families and the Individual) in 1982.
7. Inter-Ministerial Mission of Vigilance and Fight against Sectarianism; http://www.miviludes.gouv.fr/.
8. Information and Advice Center on Harmful Sectarian Organizations; http://www.ciaosn.be/.
9. FAIR changed its name to Family Action Information and Resource in 1994, when it was decided that the illegal practice of involuntary deprogramming carried out by some of its members was no longer acceptable.
10. *Fédération Européenne des Centres de Recherche et d'Information sur le Sectarisme.* Member organizations are listed at: http://www.fecris.org/.
11. NRM scholars have been accused of dismissing the testimonies of former members by labeling these as apostates' atrocity tales (Bromley 1998; Langone 1993, 32).
12. http://dialogueireland.wordpress.com/2009/11/06/question-and-answers-from-maynooth-conference-mick-farrell-2-eileen-barker/.
13. I have been greeted with this criticism on numerous occasions, particularly since founding Inform (www.Inform.ac), with the express aim of helping those who were seeking reliable information about the movements. http://www.inform.ac/aboutInform.pdf/.

REFERENCES

Altglas, Véronique. 2008. French Cult Controversy at the Turn of the New Millennium. In *The Centrality of Religion in Social Life*, edited by Eileen Barker. 55–68. Aldershot: Ashgate.

Barker, Eileen. 1991. "But is it a Genuine Religion?" *Report from the Capital* April: 10–14.

Barker, Eileen. 1994. *The Making of a Moonie: Brainwashing or Choice?* Aldershot: Ashgate. (Originally published Oxford: Blackwell 1984).

Barker, Eileen. 2003. The Scientific Study of Religion? You Must Be Joking. In *Cults and New Religious Movements: A Reader*, edited by Lorne Dawson. 7–25. London: Blackwell.

Barker, Eileen. 2004. What Are We studying? A Sociological Case for Keeping the "Nova". *Nova Religio* 8(1):88–102.

Becker, Howard S. 1963. *Outsiders: Studies in the Sociology of Deviance*. New York: Free Press.

Beckford, James A. 1999. The Mass Media and New Religious Movements. In *New Religious Movements: Challenge and Response*, edited by Bryan Wilson and Jamie Cresswell. 103–119. London: Routledge.

Beckford, James. 1985. *Cult Controversies: The Societal Response to the New Religious Movements*. London: Tavistock.

Beit-Hallahmi, Benjamin. 2001. "O Truant Muse": Collaboration and Research Integrity. In *Misunderstanding Cults: Searching for Objectivity in a Controversial Field*, edited by Benjamin Zablocki and Thomas Robbins. 35–70. Toronto: University of Toronto Press.

Berger, Peter, and Luckmann, Thomas. 1967. *The Social Construction of Reality*. London: Allen Lane.

Bromley, David. (ed). 1998. *The Politics of Religious Apostasy: The Role of Apostates in the Transformation of Religious Movements*. Westport CT and London: Praeger.

Bromley, David and Melton, J. Gordon. (eds). 2002. *Cults, Religion and Violence*. Cambridge: Cambridge University Press.

Bromley, David and Richardson, James. (eds). 1983. *The Brainwashing/Deprogramming Controversy*. New York: Edwin Mellen Press.

Cowan, Douglas 2003. *Bearing False Witness? An Introduction to the Christian Countercult*. Westport, CT: Praeger.

Chryssides, George 1999. Britain's Anti-Cult Movement. *New Religious Movements: Challenge and Response*, edited by Bryan Wilson and Jamie Cresswell. 257–274. London: Routledge.

Festinger, Leon, et al. 1956. *When Prophecy Fails*. Minneapolis: University of Minnesota Press.

Giambalvo, Carol, et al. 1998. From Deprogramming to Thought Reform Consultation." AFF Conference, Chicago. http://www.csj.org/infoserv_indexes/index_tpcol_definitionalissues.htm (Accessed August 27, 2010).

Guyard, Jacques (Rapporteur). 1995. Les Sectes en France. Paris: Assemblée Nationale.

Introvigne, Massimo and Melton J. Gordon. (eds). 1996. *Pour en finir avec les sectes: Le débat sur le rapport de la commission parlementaire*. Turin and Paris: CESNUR.

Jenkins, Philip. 2000. *Mystics and Messiahs: Cults and New Religions in American History*. Oxford: Oxford University Press.

Lalich, Janja. 1997. Review of *Moon Sisters, Krishna Mothers, Rajneesh Lovers*. *Cultic Studies Journal* 14(1):158–161.

Langone, Michael. 2002. History of the American Family Foundation. *Cultic Studies Review* 1(1):3–50.

Langone, Michael. (ed). 1993. *Recovery from Cults: Help for Victims of Psychological and Spiritual Abuse*. New York: W. W. Norton.
Lheureux, N. L., et al. 2000. *Report on Discrimination against Spiritual and Therapeutical Minorities in France*. Paris: Coordination des Associations et Particuliers Pour la Liberté de Conscience.
Melton, J. Gordon. 2004. Toward a Definition of "New Religion", *Nova Religio* 8(1):73–87.
Ownby, David. 2008. *Falun Gong and the Future of China*. Oxford: Oxford University Press.
Palmer, David. 2007. *Qigong Fever: Body, Science, and the Politics of Religion in China, 1949–1999*. London: Hurst.
Patrick, Ted. 1976. *Let Our Children Go*. New York: Ballantine.
Pew Forum on Religion and Public Life. 2009. *Global Restrictions on Religion*. Washington DC: Pew Research Centre. http://pewforum.org/newassets/images/reports/restrictions/restrictionsfullreport.pdf
Richardson, James. (ed). 2004. *Regulating Religion: Case Studies from around the Globe*. Dordrecht: Kluwer Academic/Plenum.
Rolland, Patrice. 2003. La loi du 12 juin 2001 contre les mouvements sectaires portant atteinte aux droits de l'homme. *Archives de Sciences Sociales des Religions* 48(121):149–166.
Shterin, Marat, and Richardson, James. 2000. Effects of the Western Anti-Cult Movement on Development of Laws Concerning Religion in Post-Communist Russia. *Journal of Church and State* 42(2): 247–271.
Shupe, Anson and Bromley, David. 1980. *The New Vigilantes: Deprogrammers, Anti-Cultists, and the New Religions*. Beverly Hills: Sage.
Shupe, Anson, and Bromley, David. (eds). 1994. *Anti-Cult Movements in Cross-Cultural Perspective*. New York: Garland.
Shupe, Anson and Darnell, Susan. 2006. *Agents of Discord: Deprogramming, Pseudo-science, and the American Anticult Movement*. New Brunswick, NJ: Transaction.
US Commission on International Freedom. 2009. *Annual Report 2009*. Washington DC.van Driel, Barend, and Richardson, James. 1988. Print Media Coverage of New Religious Movements: A Longitudinal Study." *Journal of Communication* 38(3): 37–61.
Versluis, Arthur. 2006. *The New Inquisitions: Heretic-Hunting and the Intellectual Origins of Modern Totalitarianism*. Oxford: Oxford University Press.
Young, Jock. 1973. The Amplification of Drug Use. In *The Manufacture of News*, edited by Stanley Cohen and Jock Young. 350–359. London: Constable.

14 Other Religions as Social Problem
The Universal Church of the Kingdom of God and Afro-Brazilian Traditions

Steven Engler

The Igreja Universal do Reino de Deus (Universal Church of the Kingdom of God—UC) is a Brazilian Neo-Pentecostal church, founded in Rio de Janeiro in 1977.[1] According to census data, the UC grew from 269,000 members in 1991 to 2.1 million in 2000, making up for 12% of all Pentecostals in Brazil, with a growth rate three times the average among all Pentecostal denominations (Jacob et al. 2003, 42). It draws disproportionately on poorer, less educated, non-white sectors of Brazilian society; and it has founded hundreds of churches in dozens of other countries (Freston 2001, 198–200). The dramatic growth of the UC has been characterized by its consistent opposition to Afro-Brazilian religions. Denigration of these competing religions is prominent in its theology and rituals. The same spiritual entities that play central, positive, healing roles in Umbanda and Candomblé are present, under the same names, in UC rituals: but they are reframed as "demons"; they are blamed for financial, interpersonal, psychological and other problems; and their ritual exorcism is central to the church's conception of salvation. In other words, the UC frames Afro-Brazilian spirit possession as a social problem in order to claim that it has a monopoly on the means of addressing that problem.

By analyzing this case in terms of social problems theory, I propose to make two symmetrical contributions. First, social problem theory offers useful leverage for conceptualizing these aspects of the discourse and practice of this church. It helps to clarify the relation (not clearly conceptualized in the existing literature) between religious agency (control of healing) and discursive agency (definition of norms) in the UC. As such, it offers a valuable characterization of the "neo" in "Neo-Pentecostalism." Second, this example contributes to social problems theory by clarifying certain aspects of a weak constructionist perspective, namely the importance of social and cultural context. In the case of the UC, deviance and norm are both strategic constructs that emerge in the relative positioning of religious traditions in a specific cultural context and religious market. That is, this case illustrates a particularly dynamic inter-relation between construction of a "problem" and of the "norms" by which it is measured; and, as a result, it illustrates the function of claims-making, not just in constituting a social problem, but in strategies of group formation in a specific cultural context. The UC's othering of Afro-Brazilian religions is not simply a matter of market positioning; it self-consciously re-frames "normal" or "non-problematic" relations between religion and healing for millions of people.

NEO-PENTECOSTALISM IN BRAZIL

Neo-Pentecostalism is a recent and prominent development on the Brazilian religious landscape. It is important to distinguish "Neo-Pentecostal" here from earlier uses of the same term to refer to the charismatic movement (Corten 1999, 165–168). The history of Protestantism in Brazil can be divided into four phases: (i) early false starts by Protestant colonizers from France and Holland in the sixteenth century; (ii) nineteenth-century immigration (e.g. by German Lutherans to the south of Brazil); (iii) conversion due to missionary work, primarily American, during the late nineteenth and early twentieth centuries; (iv) large-scale conversions in the late-twentieth century (Freston 1993; Mendonça 2008; Mendonça and Velasques Filho 1997). Pentecostalism arrived in Brazil in 1910 and evolved in three waves over the twentieth century: (i) initial establishment of missionary churches, primarily the Assembléia de Deus (1910) and the Congregação Cristã do Brasil (1911); (ii) the founding and growth of new healing-focused and media-savvy churches in the 1950s and early 1960s (e.g. Igreja do Evangelho Quadrangular [1951], Brasil para Cristo [1955], and Igreja Pentecostal Deus é Amor [1962]); and (iii) the founding and growth of the Neo-Pentecostal churches in the late 1970s and 1980s (e.g. Igreja Universal do Reino de Deus [1977], Igreja Internacional da Graça de Deus [1980], Cristo Vivo [1986], and Renascer em Cristo [1986]) (Freston 1995, 1996; Mariano 1999a, 28–32). The first wave is sometimes called "traditional Pentecostalism" and the second, "autonomous Pentecostalism," in contrast with Neo-Pentecostalism, though some have suggested that issues of origin, characteristics, and class make this more a spectrum than a clear division (Mariano 1999a, 32–34; Freston 1999, 145–152).

The "neo" of Neo-Pentecostalism marks both its recent emergence and certain distinguishing characteristics. Like many of the second-wave churches, Brazilian Neo-Pentecostal churches are national, autonomous, emotionally expressive, strongly focused on healing, and make effective use of communications media. More distinctively, the Neo-Pentecostal churches are aggressively militant, attempt little ethical control of congregants, are even more strongly focused on healing (with a corresponding de-emphasis on speaking in tongues), aggressively encourage tithing in the context of a gospel of prosperity, have a correlated inner-worldly conception of salvation, have distinctive rituals (e.g. seven- and nine-day prayer "chains"), use contemporary marketing concepts and strategies, and have a very hierarchical and centralized form of organization (including management of finances and pastoral personnel), with the opening of new temples being comparable to a franchising operation. Most significantly, for the purposes of this chapter, Neo-Pentecostal churches view the devil as the source of the world's evils and of congregants' personal problems, and position themselves explicitly against Afro-Brazilian religions, especially Umbanda and Candomblé, and to a lesser extent against Kardecist Spiritism: "the gift of healing" is the result of relabeling and exorcizing the very same spirits who play central, generally healing, roles in these competing religions. It is, of course, no coincidence that the Neo-Pentecostal churches emerge in Rio de Janeiro and spread primarily in São Paulo and Bahia, where this particular religious competition is more marked than in other regions of Brazil (Freston 1995, 130; 1996, 131; see Jacob et al. 2006).

This characterization of Neo-Pentecostalism becomes complicated, however, when we recognize that many of these supposedly distinctive characteristics were present in second-wave churches: uniformed workers, interviews with demons, and cries of "burn" at the moment of exorcism were found in Deus e Amor; seven- and nine-day prayers chains, insistent preaching on the importance of paying tithes, and Friday exorcism services were prominent in the Igreja Quadrangular in Minas Gerais in the early 1970s; and, most importantly, ritual interviews with "demons" identified with Afro-Brazilian traditions were an important element of the Igreja da Nova Vida (founded in 1960, and the original denomination of the founders of both the UC and the Igreja Internacional da Graça de Deus) (Freston 1993, 93; Mariano 1999a, 41–43). In sum, simply listing basic characteristics of the Neo-Pentecostal churches is not sufficient to distinguish them in anything but very general terms: at this level, their family-resemblance to other Pentecostal churches in Brazil is quite strong. To distinguish Neo-Pentecostalism, we need to look not just at the characteristics themselves, but also at the way they interact.

Social problems theory allows us to more effectively characterize the UC as an example of Neo-Pentecostalism. Several of the characteristics in the list above converge in a way that is quite distinct from second-wave Pentecostalism. By accepting Afro-Brazilian and Kardecist spiritual entities into the church as demonic forces to be exorcized, the UC both elides and reinforces two distinctions: between the church and its competitors in the religious marketplace; and, more generally, between Christianity and popular religiosity (Birman 1997, 63–64; Mariano 1999b).[2] The Neo-Pentecostal churches appropriate theological and ritual elements from competing religions, a characteristic also found among some second-wave churches. However, the Neo-Pentecostal churches are unique in the manner and extent to which they reframe these appropriations, i.e. in how they portray their competitors as a principle source of the world's evils and of congregants' personal problems. In other words, Neo-Pentecostalism is distinguished by the extent to which it claims that other religions are a social problem.

ASSERTING THE SOCIAL IN SOCIAL PROBLEMS

For the Universal Church of the Kingdom of God (UC), possession by the spirits of Afro-Brazilian religions is a social problem. To be more specific, from this particular theological perspective, the influence of demonic entities meets the following sociological definitions of "social problem": "a substantial discrepancy between widely shared social standards and actual conditions of social life"; "conditions that are widely believed to cause avoidable and remediable misery or frustration"; "when organized society's ability to order relationships among people seems to be failing; when its institutions are faltering, its laws are being flouted, the transmission of its values from one generation to the next is breaking down, the framework of social expectations is being shaken"; "the activities of groups making assertions of grievances and claims . . . about some putative conditions" (Merton 1971, 799; Beckford 1990, 1 n.1; Raab and Selznick cited in Spector and Kitsuse 2001, 1–2; Spector and Kitsuse 1973, 146).

Specific, narrow social problems can be analyzed in terms of their reflecting more general, broader social problems (see Beckford 1990, 4–6). For example, rape is part of a larger social problem of violence against women which itself can be (from certain perspectives) subsumed under a still larger, or more fundamental, social problem of gendered inequity. In effect, the UC has subsumed a series of social problems (unemployment, marital breakdown, depression, substance abuse, etc.) under a larger umbrella by framing them as effects of a more fundamental social problem, i.e. spirit possession. Similarly, some Christian, Muslim, Jewish, and Hindu creationists claim that the theory of evolution is the root cause of a variety of social problems (Engler forthcoming). In sum, granted the UC's theological premises regarding the nature of reality, spirit possession is a social problem by virtue of causing social dysfunction and violating community norms.

At the same time, however, most non-members would discount the UC's claim that this "problem" even exists. On the one hand, this turns our attention to the specific social context, a point I develop below. On the other hand, this example simply underlines a basic tension in social problems theory. Theoretical approaches to social problems necessarily inhabit the middle ground between objective conditions and subjective evaluations (Hjelm 2009, 927). This is clear in a classic definition:

> A social problem is a condition which is defined by a considerable number of persons as a deviation from some social norm which they

cherish. Every social problem thus consists of an objective condition and a subjective definition. The objective condition is a verifiable situation. . . . The subjective definition is the awareness of certain individuals that the condition is a threat to certain cherished values. (Fuller and Myers 1941, 320)

In this section of the chapter I argue that, in analyzing these two aspects (objective conditions and subjective evaluations), it is also necessary to pay attention to social context.

Since the early twentieth century, there have been tensions between at least five distinct approaches to defining social problems (see Blumer 1971; Davis 1972; Kitsuse and Spector 1973; Spector and Kitsuse 2001, 23–58; Schneider 1985). Functionalist approaches define social problems as conditions that lead to an empirically verifiable social pathology, social disorganization, or dysfunction. Normative approaches define social problems as objective conditions that violate broadly held normative standards.

Value-conflict approaches define social problems as conditions that are defined as such by a sufficient number of competent observers within a society. (The main difference from the normative approach was to let go of any insistence on objective conditions, further emphasizing subjective evaluations.) The labeling theory of deviance extended the emphasis on subjective evaluations by shifting attention to the social processes of definition that labeled certain people and behaviors coming to be considered deviant. Social-constructionist approaches define social problems with an even greater emphasis on subjective evaluations, bracketing assertions regarding the existence of objective conditions or the objective status of the norms used to make judgments. In a classic 1962 paper, John I. Kitsuse sought "to shift the focus of theory and research from the forms of deviant behavior to the *processes by which persons come to be defined as deviant by others*"; "The notion that social problems are a kind of *condition* must be abandoned in favor of a conception of them as a kind of *activity*"; the analytical focus shifts to "the emergence, nature, and maintenance of claims-making and responding activities . . ." (Kitsuse 1962, 248, original emphasis; Spector and Kitsuse 2001, 73, 76, original emphasis).

I review these perspectives in order to make two claims. First, none of these theoretical approaches exemplifies a pure emphasis on either objective conditions or subjective evaluations. All occupy a position on a spectrum of possible positions between those extremes. On the one hand, it would be patently impossible to secure unquestionable empirical support for, or universal agreement that, some specific set of conditions *just is*, objectively, a social problem: whether defined in functionalist or normative terms. Requisite conceptions of structure or the basis of universal norms would sever their relation to the necessarily embedded nature of social problems by virtue of their very universality. It is entirely possible, of course, for some group of people to hold that certain conditions are objectively and universally a social problem, but the sociologist must qualify this claim precisely as the perspective of a group. A theory can place great emphasis on objective conditions, but some element of subjective evaluations necessarily remains, if only because the very concept of a "problem" is inherently normative. On the other hand—as is indicated by the fact that most social problems theorists offer weak readings of Kitsuse's strong constructionist views—a strict constructionism relies inevitably on at least some objectivist assumptions (Best 1993). A theory can place great emphasis on subjective evaluations, but some element of objective conditions necessarily remains, if only because the resulting analysis of language games cannot ignore the social context of that language use. In sum, it is not possible to focus solely on social problems as objective facts nor solely on the language of claims about social problems; some analysis of social context seems inescapable.

Second, the UC's view of spirit possession illustrates the importance of a second meta-theoretical axis in social problems theory. At one end of the spectrum, we can analyze social context and conditions in order to illuminate social problems; at the other, we can analyze social problems in order to cast light on social issues. Work on social problems, even as it has moved away from an emphasis on objective conditions, has understandably been clustered at one end of this spectrum: eyes fixed on the problems, however defined. The example of Neo-Pentecostalism in Brazil lends itself to working at the other end of the spectrum: we can analyze claims-making not as a constitutive element of the social problem but as a strategy of group formation.

To take this down from the meta-theoretical to the theoretical level, social problems are necessarily situated, to a greater or lesser extent. Claims regarding the nature and existence of objective conditions and subjective assessments of their positive or negative impact can play a role in distinguishing social groups.[3] Work on social problems has, of course, explored the "social" end of this spectrum as well as the "problems" end: for example, the social constructionist perspective emphasized group dynamics early on (e.g. "Value groups may find that as they raise a condition as a social problem, they gain as allies other groups who have a vested interest in their position"; Kitsuse and Spector 1973, 415; see also Spector and Kitsuse 2001, 88); case studies analyze how different groups use distinct language to frame claims regarding a given social problem (e.g. showing how a university administration and conservative Christian ministers in the U.S. characterized homosexuality on campus in terms of a Constitutional discourse of rights and a biblical discourse of sin, respectively: Cohn and Gallagher 1984); and other studies explore the cultural and attitudinal factors that shape the views of specific groups regarding specific social problems (e.g. arguing that White American Conservative Protestants have distinctive explanations of racism, emphasizing individual rather than structural factors: Emerson, Smith, and Sikkink 1999).

Paying attention to these two meta-theoretical spectra allows us to foreground the issue of social context. Immediately following their definition of "social problem," cited above, Fuller and Myers add an important note of clarification: "The objective condition is necessary but not in itself sufficient to constitute a social problem. Although the objective condition may be the same in two different localities, it may be a social problem in only one of these areas . . ." (1941, 320). This statement must be qualified in two ways. First, variations in both the objective conditions and the subjective evaluations of social problems vary not just by "localities" but also by nation, culture, and social group. Second, the objective condition is neither necessary nor sufficient: a perception, construction or claim of an objective condition is necessary, but its existence is a separate issue (Kitsuse and Spector 1973, 413–414; Spector and Kitsuse 2001, 76). Whether possession by demonic spirits is an empirically verifiable phenomenon or not, the fact that millions of Brazilians consider it to be a major social problem is worthy of investigation; and it is useful to investigate what claims-making and responding activities tell us not just about the "problem" but about the formation and maintenance of Neo-Pentecostal churches as social groups in that specific social and cultural context. My discussion below, then, takes a weak constructionist approach.

SPIRIT POSSESSION AS SOCIAL PROBLEM

The Universal Church of the Kingdom of God (UC) offers a distinctive narrative logic of salvation, one that varies according to its different national contexts and audiences (Freston 2001; Oro and Samán 2001; Mora 2008; see Corten 1999, 168–174). This section addresses the discourses and practices of the church in its Brazilian context.

The exorcism of Afro-Brazilian spirits lies at the heart of the UC's conception of salvation. The devil and his demons are the primary cause of the entire gamut of social problems: "demons 'cause' disease, adultery, homosexuality and all other harms in life. This . . . explains, in an exhaustive manner, misery and poverty, sickness and pain, family and social conflicts, in sum, everything that leads us to characterize life as something bad" (Gomes 1996, 236). In the words of the UC's leader, Edir Macedo, the demons "constantly possess those without the protection of God," and they are able to do so, in large part, due to their prominence in other religions, "from the most primitive African sects to the salons of modern society . . . [,] in eastern religions and in those western ones linked to occultism. They continually try to penetrate even into Christian religions, where they have achieved some success" (Macedo 2001, 19, 25). Exorcism thus becomes an accessible and repeatable technique for resolving social problems: "These demons become maladies that, once they have been named by their victims, can be exorcised away" (De Temple 2005, 221). The most prominent demons—called upon by name and interviewed by microphone-wielding pastors on stage as part of "unloading sessions"—are the very same spirits that possess people in Afro-Brazilian religions, especially Umbanda.[4] According to the UC's doctrine—as verified by the statements of demons interviewed during exorcism rituals—the two main causes of possession are direct participation in Afro-Brazilian rituals and the solicitation of "works" in those religions, rituals through which malevolent people can send a demon to possess a given individual. As a result, the existence and agency of these Afro-Brazilian spirits is acknowledged within the UC, but they are valued differently (positive healing forces in Umbanda and Candomblé; demonic causes of social problems in the UC): "As a result, the efficacy of the UC's vision . . . does not rest on the creation of a new model of relation with the supernatural, but precisely in the repetition of an already existing model" (Soares 1990, 87–89; see Campos 1999, 345; Mariano 1999a, 127; Oro 2006). This "religiophagic" character results in the UC's ritualistic as well as doctrinal convergence with its Afro-Brazilian competitors (Oro 2007, 32–38). As Edir Macedo notes, "In many of our meetings . . . we see a dark and sombre scene, a true display of hell. If someone were to arrive at the moment in which these people are being liberated, they might even think that they are in a centre of *macumba* [Afro-Brazilian religion], and it really does look like it" (Macedo 2001,108). The ritual necessity of the manifestation of spirits/demons makes the UC similar to Umbanda but unlike Pentecostalism (Gomes 1996, 243): "In traditional Pentecostalism, the demons are rather kept at a distance; in the UC, they are sought out and confronted. The pastors call the demons, under the names of the various umbanda entities, to manifest themselves in people present, so they can then be exorcised" (Freston 1995, 130). In other words, a crucial discursive move in the claims-making process of Neo-Pentecostalism—one that distinguishes it from second-wave Pentecostalism—is its inverted acceptance of much of the worldview of its competitors, the Afro-Brazilian religions. The UC shares their central doctrinal and ritual emphasis on spirit possession; it accepts their pantheon of possessing spirits; but it inverts the valuation of those spirits, calling them demons; and it insists that these demons are in control in those other rituals, while the pastors have the upper hand in the UC's own rituals. The agency of demons in Afro-Brazilian religion hinders human agency; the agency of UC pastors liberates it. The UC accepts the descriptive claims of other religions, in order to characterize the basic objective condition of social problems; but it imposes a distinct subjective evaluation, inverting the normative framework of those claims, and subverting the claims to agency of participants in the competing religions.

　　A potential counter-argument to framing this as a case of claims-making regarding social problems is that these claims are part of an insider discourse, not an appeal to the public or to institutions or agencies whose acceptance of these claims is seen as a step toward resolving the social problems. Thus, for example, a "letter from a constituent to a member of congress urging support of some measure is a claim" (Spector and Kitsuse 2001, 78). Where the UC portrays demonic possession as the primary cause of all social problems, it separates out (in social and functional terms) two elements that are linked by social constructionist approaches to social problems: (i) the descriptive and normative dimensions of *characterizing* the problem; and (ii) the *activity* of directing a claim (i.e. a demand) to an agent with the power to address the problem. In the case of the UC (i) is addressed to members and potential members and (ii) is addressed to God. This is clearest in the fact that the monetary tithe, offering, or sacrifice is also called a *desafio*, a "challenge" to God (Gomes 1996, 238–239; see Roca 2007): "When we pay the tithe to God, He is obligated . . . to keep His Word, reprimanding the devouring spirits that disgrace human life and that cause diseases, accidents, vices, social degradation and all aspects of human activity that make us suffer" (Macedo 2005, 64).

Separating out these two dimensions of claims-making allows us to make two points. First, social problems theory hasn't taken supernatural beings into account as actors to whom claims are often directed. Second, the unquestioning association of these two aspects of claims-making reflects a limiting presupposition. To illustrate this, let's return to the point made above: both the objective conditions and the subjective evaluations of social problems vary not just by "localities" but by culture. Failure to take this into account is a source of potential bias. Concepts of structure and norms can presuppose specific cultural or national perspectives. Most work on social problems is by American sociologists addressing American social issues. It presumes American social structures in its definitions of "function" and "dysfunction" as well as in its determination of the communities whose norms shape assessments of "problem" and "deviance." This is often explicit in definitions of both objective conditions and subjective evaluations: "When members of the American public use the term *social problems*, we most frequently are interested in these as objective characteristics of the social environment"; "How many Americans must be 'poor' . . . before we worry about 'poverty'?"; social problems are defined by the judgment of "a determining number of the American people" (Loseke 2003, 7, 15, original emphasis; Nisbet 1971, 12).

More specifically, the two dimensions of claims-making that are separated out in the UC case (characterizing the problem and demanding a solution) tend to be seen as *necessarily* connected in two separate ways in the social problems literature. However, one of these ways is, in fact, *contingent*. On the one hand, characterizations of social problems tend to implicitly contain some conception of solutions (and vice versa). The two dimensions of claims-making are indeed necessarily linked at this conceptual level. The UC case illustrates this well: defining social problems in terms of demon possession already invokes exorcism as the solution (and vice versa). On the other hand, however, the two dimensions of claims-making are contingently linked at social and functional levels. Describing social problems and calling for solutions can be directed at distinct audiences and fulfill distinct functions.

This is not a radical critique by any means, but it suggests that a more nuanced account can help us to understand the role of claims-making in group dynamics. To clarify, Spector and Kitsuse build a sense of entitlement into their concept of claims-making that is foreign to many cultural contexts: "Claims-making is always a form of interaction: a demand made by one party to another that something be done about some putative condition. A claim implies that the claimant has a right at least to be heard, if not to receive satisfaction" (Spector and Kitsuse 2001, 78). This political dimension is framed in terms of "recognition by some official organization, agency, or institution," "established procedures," "bureaucratic handling," and "response or lack of response of the agency or institution" (Spector and Kitsuse 1973, 147; see Spector and Kitsuse 2001, 79–81). The culturally-specific (largely U.S.-centric) assumptions here are that certain institutional channels are broadly recognized as potentially effective means of addressing social problems, and that the social capital of a group making claims regarding what it sees as a social problem typically translates into political leverage. The social constructionist literature on social problems tends to link the two dimensions of claims-making because, in the North Atlantic context, conceptions of democracy, political agency, and the public sphere lead to a sort of practical syllogism in which broad public acknowledgement of the existence of a problem typically leads to efforts to address that problem. On this view, knowing leads to acting; the descriptive side of claims-making is seen as having normative force. Persuading someone that a problem exists is a necessary (though not sufficient) step in solving it, because the discursive frame, "social problem," automatically carries the force of a demand for solutions. The missing premise here is that the "social" in "social problems" is public—according to a very culturally-specific sense of "public."

However, this linkage between recognizing and acting on "public" issues is not so prominent in many parts of the world, given historical, social, cultural, and political differences (the distinction being not black-and-white, of course, but one of degrees). On the American view, everyone has a stake in social problems; on a more relational view, only the problems of those in my group are my problems, and they call for action not because I necessarily agree that they are problems, but because petitions from with my network demand a response. The case of the UC underlines these differences. In specific terms, Pentecostals in Latin America operate within a very different political and cultural system—reflecting different tensions between public and private spheres, shaped by personal relations rather than impersonal bureaucracy, and dominated to a greater extent by power-brokers in the context of patron-clients relations—and, as a result, their claims-making is not a matter of lobbying (Petersen 2004, 301–303).[5] In more general terms, the Latin American context forces us to more clearly separate the two dimensions of claims-making (in social and functional, though not in conceptual, terms). The American view that describing claims and demanding solutions are pragmatically linked rests on an epistemological assumption: i.e. if a condition is *truly* a social problem, it demands a response. The force of this epistemological assumption undergirds many of the debates between functionalist and constructionist approaches to social problems (see, e.g. Best 1993, 112–114). The issue of whether perceptions and reality match up in the case of social problems fades into the background when we let go of this presupposition. As a result, bracketing this epistemological assumption—i.e. separating the two sides of claims-making in pragmatic, though not conceptual, terms—aids in shifting our theoretical focus from "problems" to their social context. In the context of patronage relations, doing someone a favor can have as its primary goal incurring future obligations, cementing relationships, demonstrating power and status, etc. Solving problems can be instrumental and secondary, and the actual existence of objective conditions is not essential; the core issue is the context of social relationships between clients and patrons, not whether there *truly* is a problem. Where perception leads to petition, perception is enough. Claims-making as description can mark horizontal boundaries of inclusion in a relevant social group; claims-making as demand can mark vertical relations of allegiance, authority, and asymmetrical reciprocity.

Following this line of critique—i.e. recognizing that the link between the two dimensions of claims-making is culturally contingent—leads us to conclude that the UC's claims-making is precisely what we should expect: a description of the problems that serves to demarcate and constitute a social group; with a petition to an agent best characterized in terms of the distinction between patron and client, not public and private. The UC's theology reconceptualizes and redistributes agency: the participants of Afro-Brazilian traditions are wrong to think they have agency, because only the demons are true agents there; those demons have the power, through possession, of hindering the agency of human beings; the UC's pastors have the power of removing that blockage, thus liberating human agency and allowing it to become aligned with the Will of God; and members of the church can then exercise their liberated agency by acting to "challenge" God in an escalating cycle of exchange relations, as marked by tithing (see Lima 2007: 2008). This claims-making activity redefines the relation between religious agency (control of healing and gifting) and discursive agency (definition of norms) in this particular social context. The UC is distinguished from earlier types of Pentecostalism by virtue of this particularly Brazilian mode of claims-making, that is, by its framing other religions as a basic social problem.

A CONCLUDING NOTE

The study of social problems and the study of religion share a curious feature. Each is characterized not in terms of its theoretical or methodological commitments, but in terms of a specific subject matter; and the nature of both "social problem" and "religion" came under increasing scrutiny over the latter decades of the twentieth century, especially from constructionist perspectives. The same sort of critique offered above—of cultural bias in "claims-making" as a defining characteristic of social problems—also offers purchase on the concept of "religion." One of the legacies of debates over secularization and reenchantment has been a general acceptance that religion—whatever its state of health—is aligned in some fundamental way with tensions between the public and private spheres. Recognizing to a greater extent that this and related distinctions are culturally specific could potentially lead us to qualify a variety of claims: e.g. that "it is basically correct to describe the prevalent form of modern religion as 'thematic' rather than [doctrinally] systematic" (Beckford 1990, 8). The UC's doctrine and rituals are both systematic and thematic in ways that make more sense in terms of patronage and group formation than privatization and invisible religion. Cross-cultural studies of the social and cultural context of religion—like that of social problems—offer one means of re-examining our conceptual presuppositions.

NOTES

1. Research for this chapter was supported, in part, by the Fundação de Amparo à Pesquisa do Estado de São Paulo (FAPESP), the Coordenação de Aperfeiçoamento de Pessoal de Nível Superior (CAPES), and Mount Royal University's Research Reserve Fund. All translations are mine. Thanks to Titus Hjelm for very helpful formal and substantive comments on the initial draft.
2. This claim must be considered against a broader backdrop: there is a close relation in Brazilian culture between religion and healing, extending from popular Catholicism, through an entire "spectrum" of spirit-possession religions—Afro-Brazilian, Spiritist, and NRMs—to new Christianities, including the UC (Camargo 1961; see Engler 2009c, 20).
3. Along these lines, the relation between claims-making and identity formation is a core issue in discussions of the overlap between social problems theory and social movements theory (Kitsuse and Spector 1973, 417; Schneider 1985, 225–226; Best 1993, 124 n.4).
4. A YouTube search for "*sessão do descarrego*" will result in videos of this ritual. For ethnographic descriptions see Kramer 2005; Almeida 2009, 63–98; and Engler 2009a. On ritual parallels and differences between possession in Umbanda and the IURD see Engler 2009a.
5. On hierarchy and patron–client relations see, e.g. Oliveira Vianna 1933; Buarque de Holanda 1999; Freyre 2005; Faoro 1998; Banfield and Fasano 1958; Queiroz 1976; Uricoechea 1980; DaMatta 1983; Morse 1988; Graham 1990; Souza 2003. I have argued elsewhere that the possession rituals of

Umbanda rehearse these aspects of Brazilian social relations (Engler 2009b). Of course, it would be wrong to think that patronage relations are the whole story in Latin America, to characterize the region as undemocratic or corrupt, or, generally, to define it in terms of a lack of certain American or European characteristics. A more nuanced consideration of difference in the context of alternative modernities is required (see, e.g. Avritzer, 2000; Auyero, Lapegna and Poma 2009; Domingues 2009).

REFERENCES

Almeida, Ronaldo de. 2009. *A Igreja Universal e seus demônios: um estudo etnográfico*. São Paulo: Editora Terceiro Nome.
Auyero, Javier, Lapegna, Pablo, and Poma, Fernanda Page. 2009. Patronage Politics and Contentious Collective Action: A Recursive Relationship. *Latin American Politics and Society* 51(3): 1–31.
Avritzer, Leonardo. 2000. Democratization and Changes in the Pattern of Association in Brazil. *Journal of Interamerican Studies and World Affairs* 42(3): 59–76.
Banfield, Edward C. and Laura Fasano. 1958. *The Moral Basis of a Backward Society*. Glencoe, IL: The Free Press.
Beckford, James A. 1990. The Sociology of Religion and Social Problems. *Sociological Analysis* 51(1): 1–14.
Best, Joel. 1993. But Seriously Folks: The Limitations of the Strict Constructionist Interpretation of Social Problems. In *Constructionist Controversies: Issues in Social Problems Theory*, edited by Gale Miller and James A. Holstein. 109–127. New York: Aldine De Gruyter.
Birman, Patrícia. 1997. Males e malefícios no discurso pentecostal. In *O mal à brasileira*, edited by Patrícia Birman, Regina Reyes Novaes and Samira Crespo. 62–80. Rio de Janeiro: EdUERJ.
Blumer, Herbert. 1971. Social Problems as Collective Behavior. *Social Problems* 18(2): 298–306.
Buarque de Holanda, Sérgio. 1999[1936]. *Raízes do Brasil*. São Paulo: Companhia das Letras.
Camargo, Cândido Procópio Ferreira de. 1961. *Kardecismo e Umbanda: uma interpretação sociológica*. São Paulo: Pioneira.
Campos, Leonildo Silveira. 1999. *Teatro, templo e mercado: organização e marketing de um empreendimento neopentecostal*. 2nd ed. São Paulo: Vozes.
Cohn, Steven F. and Gallagher, James E. . 1984. Gay Movements and Legal Change: Some Aspects of the Dynamics of a Social Problem. *Social Problems* 32(1): 72–86.
Corten, André. 1999. Pentecôtisme et «néo-pentecôtisme» au Brésil. *Archives de Sciences Sociales des Religions* 44(105): 163–183.
DaMatta, Roberto. 1983. *Carnavais, malandros e heróis: para uma sociologia do dilema brasileiro*. 5 ed. Rio de Janeiro: Zahar.
Davis, Nanette J. 1972. Labeling Theory in Deviance Research: A Critique and Reconsideration. *The Sociological Quarterly* 13(4): 447–474.
De Temple, Jill. 2005. Chains of Liberation: Poverty and Social Action in the Universal Church of the Kingdom of God. In *Latino Religions and Civic Activism in the United States*, edited by Gastón Espinosa, Virgilio Elizondo and Jesse Miranda. 219–231. Oxford and New York: Oxford University Press.
Domingues, José Maurício. 2009. Modernity and Modernizing Moves: Latin America in Comparative Perspective. *Theory, Culture and Society* 26(7–8): 208–227.

Emerson, Michael O., Smith, Christian, and Sikkink, David. 1999. Equal in Christ, but Not in the World: White Conservative Protestants and Explanations of Black-White Inequality. *Social Problems* 46(3): 398–417.

Engler, Steven 2009a. Brazilian Spirit Possession and Theory of Ritual. *ARC: The Journal of the Faculty of Religious Studies, McGill University*: 1–28.

———. 2009b. Ritual Theory and Attitudes to Agency in Brazilian Spirit Possession. *Method and Theory in the Study of Religion* 21(4): 460–492.

———. 2009c. Umbanda and Hybridity. *Numen* 56(5): 545–577.

———. Forthcoming. Criacionismo. In *Teologia e ciência*, edited by Eduardo R. Cruz. São Paulo: Paulinas.

Faoro, Raymundo. 1998[1958]. *Os donos do poder: formação do patronato político brasileiro*. 13 ed. São Paulo: Globo.

Freston, Paul C. (1993). Protestantes e política no Brasil: da constituinte ao impeachment, Universidade Estadual de Campinas (UNICAMP).

———. 1995. Pentecostalism in Brazil: A Brief History. *Religion* 25: 119–133.

———. 1996. Breve história do pentecostalismo brasileiro *Nem anjos nem demônios: interpretações sociológicas do pentecostalismo*. Petrópolis: Vozes.

———. 1999. "Neo-Pentecostalism" in Brazil: Problems of Definition and the Struggle for Hegemony. *Archives de Sciences Sociales des Religions* 44(105): 145–162.

———. 2001. The Transnationalisation of Brazilian Pentecostalism: The Universal Church of the Kingdom of God. In *Between Babel and Pentecost: Transnational Pentecostalism in Africa and Latin America*, edited by Andre Corten and Ruth Marshall-Fratani. 196–215. Bloomington and Indianapolis: Indiana University Press.

Freyre, Gilberto. 2005[1933]. *Casa-grande e senzala: Formação da família brasileira sob o regime da economia patriarcal*. 50th ed. São Paulo: Global Editora.

Fuller, Richard C. and Myers, Richard R. . 1941. The Natural History of a Social Problem. *American Sociological Review* 6(3): 320–329.

Gomes, Wilson. 1996. Nem anjos nem demônios: o estranho caso das novas seitas populares no Brasil da crise *Nem anjos nem demônios: interpretações sociológicas do pentecostalismo*. 225–270. Petrópolis: Vozes.

Graham, Richard. 1990. *Patronage and Politics in Nineteenth-Century Brazil*. Stanford, CA: Stanford University Press.

Hjelm, Titus. 2009. Religion and Social Problems: A New Theoretical Perspective. In *The Oxford Handbook of the Sociology of Religion*, edited by Peter Clarke. 924–941. Oxford: Oxford University Press.

Jacob, Cesar Romero, Rodrigues Hees, Dora, Waniez, Phillippe, and Brustlein, Violette. (eds). 2003. *Atlas da filiação religiosa e indicadores sociais no Brasil*. São Paulo: Edições Loyola.

———. 2006. *Religiao e sociedade em capitais brasileiras*. Rio de Janeiro and São Paulo: PUC-Rio/Edições Loyola.

Kitsuse, John I. 1962. Societal Reaction to Deviant Behavior: Problems of Theory and Method. *Social Problems* 9(3): 247–256.

Kitsuse, John I. and Spector, Malcolm. 1973. Toward a Sociology of Social Problems: Social Conditions, Value-Judgments, and Social Problems. *Social Problems* 20(3): 407–419.

Kramer, Eric W. 2005. Spectacle and the Staging of Power in Brazilian Neo-Pentecostalism. *Latin American Perspectives* 32(1): 95–120.

Lima, Diana Nogueira de Oliveira. 2007. "Trabalho", "mudança de vida" e "prosperidade" entre fiéis da Igreja Universal do Reino de Deus. *Religião e Sociedade* 27(1): 132–155.

———. 2008. "Prosperidade" na década de 1990: etnografia do compromisso de trabalho entre Deus e o fiel da Igreja Universal do Reino de Deus. *Dados* 51(1): 7-35.

Loseke, Donileen R. 2003. *Thinking about Social Problems: An Introduction to Constructionist Perspectives.* 2nd ed. New York: Aldine De Gruyter.

Macedo, Edir. 2001. *Orixas, caboclos e guias: deuses ou demônios?* Rio de Janeiro: Editora Gráfica Universal.

———. 2005. *Nos passos de Jesus.* Rio de Janeiro: Editora Gráfica Universal.

Mariano, Ricardo. 1999a. *Neopentecostais: sociologia do novo pentecostalismo no Brasil.* São Paulo: Loyola.

———1999b. O futuro não será protestante. *Ciencias Sociales y Religión/Ciências Sociais e Religião* 1(1): 89-114.

Mendonça, Antônio Gouvêa 2008. *O Celeste porvir: a inserção do protestantismo no Brasil.* 3rd ed. São Paulo: EdUsp.

Mendonça, Antônio Gouvêa and Filho, P. Velasques. 1997. *Introdução ao protestantismo no Brasil.* São Paulo: Loyola.

Merton, Robert K. 1971. Social Problems and Sociological Theory. In *Contemporary Social Problems* edited by Robert K. Merton and Robert Nisbet. 793-845. New York: Harcourt Brace Jovanonich.

Mora, G. Cristina. 2008. Marketing the "Health and Wealth Gospel" across National Borders: Evidence from Brazil and the United States. *Poetics* 36: 404-420.

Morse, Richard M. 1988. *O espelho de Próspero: cultura e idéias nas Américas.* Translated by Paulo Neves. Rio de Janeiro: Companhia das Letras.

Nisbet, Robert. 1971. The Study of Social Problems. In *Contemporary Social Problems* edited by Robert K. Merton and Robert Nisbet. 1-25. New York: Harcourt Brace Jovanonich.

Oliveira Vianna, Francisco José de. 1933[1918]. *Populações meridionaes do Brasil: historia, organização, psycologia.* 3 ed. São Paulo: Companhia Editora Nacional.

Oro, Ari Pedro. 2006. O neopentecostalismo "macumbeiro". In *Orixás e espíritos: o debate interdisciplinar na pesquisa contemporânea,* edited by Artur Cesar Isaia. 115-127. Uberlândia: Edufu.

———. 2007. Intolerância religiosa iurdiana e reações afro no Rio Grande do Sul. In *Intolerância religiosa: impactos do neopentecostalismo no campo religioso afro-brasileiro,* edited by Vagner Gonçalves da Silva. 29-69. São Paulo: EdUSP.

Oro, Ari Pedro, and Samán, Pablo. 2001. Brazilian Pentecostalism Crosses National Borders. In *Between Babel and Pentecost: Transnational Pentecostalism in Africa and Latin America,* edited by Andre Corten and Ruth Marshall-Fratani. 181-195. Bloomington and Indianapolis: Indiana University Press.

Petersen, Douglas. 2004. Latin American Pentecostalism: Social Capital, Networks, and Politics. *Pneuma: The Journal of the Society for Penteeostal Studies* 26(2): 293-306.

Queiroz, Maria Isaura Pereira de. 1976. *O mandonismo local na vida política brasileira e outros ensaios.* São Paulo: Editora Alfa-Omega.

Roca, Roger Sans.i 2007. Dinheiro Vivo: Money and Religion in Brazil. *Critique of Anthropology* 27(3): 319-339.

Schneider, Joseph W. 1985. Social Problems Theory: The Constructionist View. *Annual Review of Sociology* 11: 209-229.

Soares, Mariza de Carvalho. 1990. Guerra santa no país do sincretismo. In *Sinais dos tempos: diversidade religiosa no Brasil,* edited by Leilah Landim. 75-104. Rio de Janeiro: ISER.

Souza, Jessé. 2003. *A construção social da subcidadania: para uma sociologia política da modernidade periférica.* Belo Horizonte/Rio de Janeiro: Editora UFMG/IUPERJ.

Spector, Malcolm and Kitsuse, John I. 1973. Social Problems: A Reformulation. *Social Problems* 21(2): 145–159.

———. 2001. *Constructing Social Problems.* New Brunswick, NJ and London: Transaction Publishers.

Uricoechea, Fernando 1980. *The Patrimonial Foundations of the Brazilian State.* Berkeley: University of California Press.

15 Islam and Integration in German Media Discourse

Yasemin El-Menouar and Melanie Becker

The assassination of Dutch film maker Theo van Gogh in 2004, riots of French adolescents of Maghrebinian background in 2005, an honor killing in Sweden in 2002 which led to changes in law, violent protests against caricatures of Mohammad published by a Danish newspaper, terrorist attacks in London by "normal" British adolescent Muslims. The chain of events that has confronted Europe in recent years has raised questions of religious fanaticism, migration, and failed integration—and kept the media busy with a new issue: Islam and Muslims. Also in Germany, a country with around three million Muslims (most of them migrants with Turkish nationality or descent) there is an ongoing and very vivid public discourse about integration and the impact of Muslim faith on it. Although Muslims have been living in Germany since the late 1960s, the integration of the so called "guest workers" into German society was not a major topic in public and media debate until the pivotal point of 9/11 and the subsequent global reframing of Islam.

In this chapter, we will explore how the discourse on the integration of Muslims into German society has evolved in the media. The analysis shows a change from a discourse that centered on rather specific social problems linked to Muslim religiousness into a discourse that poses the general question of a failure of integration.

The findings presented below are based on an analysis of articles from the German weekly news magazine *Der Spiegel*. This magazine is generally considered a leading magazine that sets the agenda for other media (Noelle-Neumann and Mathes 1987; Weischenberg, Maik, and Scholl 2006). The political background of *Der Spiegel* is generally considered as centre-left, although currently more centre-right. We included in our sample articles that focused either on issues related to Islam in Germany and/or articles that focused on social problems related at least in part to migrants of Muslim origin.[1] The analyzed material covers all relevant articles between 1996 and 2007. The aim of the analysis is to determine the kind of social problems that are associated with Islam and the specific way in which Islam is considered related to those problems.

MUSLIMS IN GERMANY

There are currently more than three million Muslims—about 4% of the total population—living in Germany. About 90% of them are of Turkish origin and this is also the largest immigrant group in Germany. Approximately 80% of German Muslims are Sunnis and one-fifth belongs to the Alevis, which is a fraction of the Shiites. Within these two main Muslim groups there are many other denominational divisions which are hardly covered statistically as is the case for Muslims in general. Besides Muslims of Turkish origin, other Muslims living in Germany come from Bosnia (approximately 150,000), Iran (approximately 115,000, mostly Shiites), Morocco (approximately 80,000) and many other countries. There are also about 100,000 to 150,000 German converts.

Islam in Germany is represented by mosque associations, umbrella, and head organizations. Due to the diversity of countries of origin and confessions, the existing Islamic associations are very heterogeneous. There are four main head organizations, all of which represent mainly Muslims of Turkish descent. These are (1) the DITIB (*Türkisch-Islamische Union der Anstalt für Religion* e.V.), which is assigned to a more liberal and secular Islamic position, (2) the IGMG (*Islamische Gemeinschaft Milli Görüs*), which is currently under observation by the Federal Office for the Protection of the Constitution because of suspicion of Islamist tendencies, (3) the ZMD (*Zentralrat der Muslime in Deutschland* e.V.) and (4) the VIKZ (*Verein islamischer Kulturzentren*). Efforts to centralize the decentralized and highly scattered landscape of Islamic associations are currently in progress. The main contact for the German government in this respect is the DITIB (Spuler-Stegemann 2002).

Most of the Muslims came to Germany as uneducated guest workers ("Gastarbeiter") in the late 1960s. This population still differs highly from the German average population in the areas of education and socioeconomic status, a fact that is thought to have a big impact on the ongoing discourse about integration. Residents of Turkish origin are mostly less educated then Germans, also in the second and third generation, and the amount of unemployment is twice as high as in the German population on the average (Münz, Seufert, and Ulrich 1997).

INTEGRATION AND RELIGIOSITY OF MUSLIMS IN GERMANY

According to the classical assimilation theory of the "race-relations-cycle", immigrants should improve their adaptation to the host society with every generation (Bogardus 1930; Park 1950). Accordingly it is expected that the third immigrant generation has gained equal access to the opportunity structure of society and adapted to the host culture (Price 1969). Contradictory to these assumptions there is a persistent social and cultural inequality between migrants with a Muslim background and the German population (Diefenbach 2005; Granato and Kalter 2001; Kalter 2006; Kecskes 2000; 2001; Kristen 2002; Haug 2003). Against the expectations of adaptation theorists, Muslims of the third generation are allegedly subjects of "Re-Islamization". As empirical studies have discovered, particularly this generation of Muslims has returned to Islam. A recurring survey carried out among residents with a Turkish migration background between 2000 and 2006 demonstrates a steady increase of people expressing that they are quite or very religious. A formerly existing age effect on religiosity (older people tended to state higher religiousness) was diminished over time so that there is no significant difference between migrants of the first and migrants of the third generation (Sauer 2007; Sen and Sauer 2006).

Since the 1990es there has been a growing interest in research on the religiousness of Muslim migrants in Germany. Although the study by Thomä-Venske in 1981 made a first step to establish a link between Islam and integration, the public didn't get alarmed until 16 years later when the results of an empirical study from Heitmeyer, Müller, and Schröder (1997) with the title *Verlockender Fundamentalismus* ("Tempting Fundamentalism") was published. This quantitative study on Turkish adolescents discovered a turn to Islam and a great potential of religious radicalization among the youngsters. According to the study, adolescents with relatively low educational degrees and problematic family contexts are particularly receptive to radical ideologies. Today there is more skepticism about the conclusions of the Heitmeyer study and its results have often been criticized, mainly for methodological reasons (Bukow 1999; Pinn 1999). At the time of its publication, however, it had a significant impact on German society, although later studies have found no significant relation between religiousness, education, neighborhood, and other indicators for integration (Kecskes 2000). According to another study, deviant behavior does not seem to be influenced by Muslim religiosity (Brettfeld and Wetzels 2003).

Unlike the Heitmeyer study, these later studies have interpreted the growing importance of Islam for third generation Muslims as a sign of successful integration (e.g. Klinkhammer 2000; Nökel 2002; Tietze 2001). According to this view, Islam is an element of a certain lifestyle and the adolescents simply develop their unique identities, thereby meeting the expectations of a modern society. This seems to be supported by the fact that they interpret Islamic faith in a highly individualized way, distancing themselves from the traditional forms of religiosity of their parents. In these studies a pluralization of Islamic lifestyles, which is characterized by flexible treatment of religious rules and aestheticization, was observed among young Muslims (Klinkhammer 2000). These "Neomuslims" are seen as developing into modern individuals by practicing purifying self-techniques such as strictly planning and structuring their daily life (Nökel 2002).

All studies presented previously have one thing in common although arriving at different and often contradictory conclusions. They share a specific understanding of what integration means. Integration is understood as cultural adaptation to the host society according to classical theories of immigrant assimilation.

ISLAM AND THE CONSTRUCTION OF SOCIAL PROBLEMS

As has been shown in the previous section, socioeconomic and cultural integration of Muslim migrants in Germany has been increasingly discussed in the social sciences in recent years, mainly within the framework of their religiousness. The exact relationship between integration deficits and religious conviction, however, is yet far from clear. Is Islamic religiousness a causal factor with strong impact that can explain the emergence of integration problems? Does it aggravate negative developments, or does it merely result from failed integration that is actually caused by non-cultural conditions? Or could it even play an ambivalent role, being both cause and effect of the problem depending on its form?

From a social scientific point of view, the relationship between Islam and social problems is unclear. Thus, there is no objective framework available with which to compare whether media representations are either "biased" or "correct". Research therefore cannot simply rely on a preconceptualized, closed research instrument, derived from scientific findings. The design must be an exploratory, qualitative design that is able to *reconstruct* rather than evaluate or compare media images and framings of social problems and the attributed role of Islam. So far, there has not been any research on media representation of Islam from the perspective of a social problems approach. There are some studies which analyze the depiction of Islam from other perspectives, but the findings of these studies are rather fragmentary and do not complement each other, due to different research questions, concepts and methods applied. Therefore, they are not an adequate base for our research (e.g. Schiffer 2005; Jung, Niehr, and Böke 2000; Müller 2005; Pinn 1997; on public discourse see also Halm 2008).

In this paper, an exploratory approach of media analysis will be applied that follows two objectives: Firstly, we will outline and reconstruct which social problems Islam is typically associated with in the media. Secondly, we will trace the role that is attributed to Islam in the presentation and discussion of these social problems. The term "attributed" is crucial here, as this analysis follows the tradition of the social constructionist approach which was prominently formulated by Kitsuse and Spector in the late 1970s. We apply an updated version of it that follows the ideas of Schetsche (2008) and is best described as a sociology of knowledge approach to social problems. This perspective holds that social problems are the product of claims making activities, definition activities and specific framing of collective actors. Media play a prominent role in the process of formation and distribution of social problems and their specific framings. In the case of problems that are distant from the every day experience of the public, they serve as the main information and knowledge resource. Media can frame and construct social problems themselves, but they also serve as an arena for the framing and claims making activities of collective actors such as experts, victims, advocates, problem users and many more (see Schetsche 2008 for actors typically involved in the construction of social problems).

MEDIA COVERAGE OF MUSLIM INTEGRATION IN GERMANY

There is a clear change in the number, length and quality of articles dealing with Islam before and after the terrorist attacks of September 11, 2001. In each of the years after 2001, there are more articles than in the five previous years altogether. Immediately after the terrorist attacks the number of articles increases sharply. In the period right after the event, most articles only dealt with the question of Islamist terrorism. Questions of integration of Muslim migrants into German society were not yet addressed. Once Islam was discovered as a recurring topic, however, the scope of the debate widened and other Islam related issues were brought up.

Three social problem issues can be distinguished in the media debate: (1) the oppression of women, (2) fundamentalist indoctrination in mosques and Quran schools, and (3) the comprehensive issue of a development of so called "parallel societies" (*Parallelgesellschaften*). These issues comprise several sub issues that were taken up when specific events occurred[2]. In the following sections, we will analyze how these three social problem issues are presented in the magazine.

OPPRESSION OF WOMEN: THE VEIL, FORCED MARRIAGE, AND HONOR KILLING

The question of relations between men and women in Muslim migrants' families is a core issue of the integration debate. Many articles discuss the living conditions of oppressed Muslim women in Germany. Although the discourse often pays lip service to the notion that not all women live under problematic conditions and that oppression is not the rule in Muslim families, the articles focus almost exclusively on problems. Women are presented as victims of their traditionalist and religious husbands and families. The reader is told that women are kept away from their social environment, that they have to suffer from physical and sexual violence, and that they are forced into marriages with men they do not know. This general issue comprises several subtopics, such as the meaning and legitimacy of the veil, the issue of forced marriages, and the issue of the so called "honor killings".

The most frequently mentioned symbol for the oppression of Muslim women is the veil. In Germany, the veiling discourse was intensified with the emergence of a political debate over Muslim teachers' right to wear a veil in the classroom.[3] The discussion is not centered on legal aspects, but instead deals with the political interpretation of Islam, women's rights, and questions of integration of Muslim women and girls. Therefore, the debate is not limited to the initiating question whether teachers should be allowed to wear a veil. The veil is rather discussed as a key symbol of resistance to integration and many other negative aspects attributed to Islam, like in the following excerpt from an interview with a Moroccan author living in Paris:

> The veil is the rejection of laicism . . . the veil is anything but harmless . . . If you tolerate this, then as the next step the father or the brother of the student will tell her "You won't participate in music or art lessons anymore, it would corrupt morality." (18/2003, "Islam Shows a Totalitarian Tendency")

Another often debated issue is the phenomenon of forced marriages. Young girls, many underage, are married to husbands they neither love nor know, forced by the pressure and threats by the families who choose the husband. Forced marriage is seen as a patriarchal religious tradition that enslaves women and girls. It binds them forcefully to the family clan and its archaic norms of an "honorable" life which for many means pain and martyrdom.

> Their names are Emine, Zeynep or Fadime, they grew up in Turkey and typically they were wedded by their parents to a mostly unknown fellow countryman or distant relative at an age of 16, 17 or 18. Here they are then fully committed to their families—mostly without contact to German society and without the chance to live a self-determined life. (4/2005, "Alarming Insight")

The reader is not only told that Muslim women are victims of patriarchal traditions, but is also informed what might happen to those women who refuse to stay a victim. They will be abandoned by their families and in the worst case they may even pay for their freedom with their lives.

This discourse about oppression of women was fueled again when in February 2005 a young Muslim woman named Hatun Sürücü, who had struggled to live a self-determined and free life, was killed by her brother in the name of honor. Although honor killing is a rare crime, articles frame the event with already familiar interpretations of the oppression of women in Muslim families and thus make it appear rather symptomatic than exceptional and singular. It is presented as the tip of an iceberg of the underlying problems:

> Crimes in the disguise of honor, pride and religion are long omnipresent . . . The problems of the Sürücüs are typical (17/2006, "Crimes in

the Name of Honor"), "For us, laws do not apply", 19 year-old Aylin says, "girls are not of age until they are married." And if they don't comply, death is imminent (47/2004, "For Us, Laws Do not Apply")

The articles do not only describe the various forms in which women are oppressed, but the reader is also informed of how Islam is related to oppression. The argumentation is somewhat blurred though. Sometimes the problem is derived directly from an alleged Islamic understanding of rights of men and women, other times it is derived from cultural forms in which religion works as a legitimation and in which religious traditions guide social behavior comprehensively. It is claimed that women suffer from oppression because they are subject of a paternalistic culture that forces them to integrate into a collectivistic and paternalistic community. According to the articles, many migrants from Turkey live in segregated neighborhoods with dense social control networks that exert collective pressure on women to make them conform to strict religious rules.

FUNDAMENTALIST INDOCTRINATION? MOSQUES, QURAN SCHOOLS, AND AFTER SCHOOL CARE

Mosques and Quran schools are another issue that is frequently discussed in *Der Spiegel*. In these articles mosques frequently appear in the context of religious fundamentalism and integration problems. In this context, they are presented as hiding places for Islamic fundamentalists and as a place of uncontrolled "hate preaching." Mosques are portrayed as a source of Islamistic conspiracy and as a recruiting ground for fundamentalists and terrorists, but they are also portrayed as a threat for integration. In some mosques, so the articles tell us, there is agitation against the West and its values, and attendants are instilled with false information about non-Muslims.

Many articles focus particularly on the allegedly dangerous religious indoctrination of children that takes place in mosques. Quran schools and after school care by mosques are presented as a major problem for the integration of Muslim children. The reader is informed that parents send their children to Quran schools or after school care to mosques, where they are taught nothing valuable for their better integration into German society. They only learn to recite suras by heart (the reader is told that learning about the Quran means reciting and not questioning it), and in the worst case they are taught hostility against a free society. According to cited experts, institutions that claim to promote integration actually do the opposite, namely drag children into a Islamic parallel world and alienate them from the world outside. Children are told to avoid contact with non-Muslims and girls are taught archaic ideas of how a woman must behave. The articles conclude that this enhances their feeling of being torn apart between two cultures.

> [T]here is agitation against the West, assertions of superiority, ghettoization is promoted . . . in some Quran schools children are accommodated the whole day, under constant surveillance of the Hodschas, the religious teachers, with little contact to the outside world . . . Quran schools aggravate the inner conflict of Muslim youth . . . they dragged the children back powerfully into the world of their parents and grandparents . . . Quran lessons are stupefying and authoritarian . . . (32/2002, "If Allah Pleases")

[T]hese homes are impeding integration . . . children get indoctrinated into a rigid, Sharia-orientated Islam. (46/2006, "And Quran at Night Time") Official Islamic religious education in public schools is discussed in some articles as a measure to prevent Muslim school kids from the influence of Quran schools. But existing Islamic education in public schools seems to rather achieve the opposite:

> [S]chool has to contrast false statements in mosques with something. (32/2002, "If Allah Pleases")

> [B]ut Marion Berning, headmaster, . . . has observed . . . that "girls have become shyer and increasingly wear veils." Boys, on the other hand . . . "pick fights on the school yard more often now and don't take homework and punctuality seriously anymore". (40/2003, "The Crux of Quran")

The role of Islam regarding these problems seems obvious. Anti-western values that inhibit integration are conveyed to pious migrants and their children through orthodox Islam. The religious values are conceptualized as problematic as such and they unfold their problematic potential by working as a comprehensive guide for action and attitudes through indoctrination and socialization.

PARALLEL SOCIETIES: IDENTITY PROBLEMS, DELINQUENCY, AND TERRORISM

The issues presented in the previous section ultimately merge in the articles. They are increasingly presented as interrelated problems that lead to the question of an alleged failure of integration of Muslims into German society. This question is often posed by using the catch phrase concept of "parallel societies."

"Parallel societies" is a term borrowed from sociological discourse. Here they are defined as spatially and socially segregated communities in which rules and values are in opposition to "German values" (Meyer 2002) and are allegedly passed unnoticed from one generation to the next. Those general characterizations are adopted (though not literally) in the media discourse. One symptom of parallel societies that is mentioned frequently is the existence of an ethnic infrastructure. This is often considered to serve as a connection between social problems and Muslim communities. Turkish shops, restaurants, cafés, doctors and the like can be found in most neighborhoods with a relatively large Turkish community. The following section of an article on parallel societies is a typical example:

> Whole districts in Germany are German only by name. Those who live here educate their children according to the norms of their native country, shop at their fellow countrymen's, listen to native music, watch native television and solve their problems among each other, and it is not unusual that the archaic norms of the father dominate and not the German law. (12/ 2006, "Who is Germany?")

The term "parallel society" or "parallel world" was used first in media reports on the terrorist attacks in Madrid and the assassination of the Dutch filmmaker Van Gogh. Many articles were published dealing with the radicalization process of terrorists born and grown up in Europe. The argument is that only in the context of a parallel society a radicalization can develop unnoticed.

Identity problems are mentioned as the main cause for being receptive to fundamentalism and Islamist ideologies. The "career" of a terrorist therefore is said to typically start with other forms of delinquency:

> ... an involvement in "petty crimes" would be characteristic: young Arabs who eke out a living as passport faker, drug dealer or guns dealer before they discover Islam as an anchor and jihad as a steam valve for their delinquent energy. (12/2004, "As You Are in War")

> Young men like those from Leeds and Aylesbury possibly live in Paris, Madrid, Rome and other European cities. But these men feel at home in the Muslim world, not in European culture. They perceive each other as belonging to one group, which empowers them but makes for some rivalry as well. Each of them aiming to be a small Osama, each of them a successor of Mohammad Atta. . . . They have grown up in Europe, live there, but see nothing but enemies all around them. (29/2005, "The Second Front")

Usually the topics on "oppression of women" and "fundamentalism" are covered separately in *Der Spiegel*. Within the debate on so called "parallel societies" all these topics are incorporated. These social problems are not just connected with each other in this debate but also generalized and expanded. On the one hand relatively rare social problems like crimes of honor and forced marriages are presented as general practices in districts with relatively high proportions of Muslim residents. On the other hand typical social problems in disadvantaged neighborhoods like youth violence and delinquency are portrayed as a consequence of problematic Islamic values. The following section of an article is a typical example:

> Crime under the pretext of honor, pride and religion has been long present, but the merciless violence, which comes from young, mostly Muslim immigrants, wasn't noticed for a long time . . . The life of the immigrant family is a tightrope walk between quarter and Quran. Whereas the strong religious parents still don't speak a word of German, the children grow up in between the values of the homeland and the apparently unlimited freedom of the western modern society. Soon the three Sürücü-sons were known to the police, also due to violence and drug delinquency. (17/2006, "Crime in the Name of Honor")

Again identity problems caused by the opposition between religious values at home and democratic values at school are held responsible for delinquency and violence of young Muslims. Within the debate on parallel societies, identity problems are seen as widespread and a typical problem of the Muslim youth living in those disadvantaged neighborhoods. Their parents and their religiosity are held responsible for the problems as they still live in their country of origin mentally and are not able or willing to integrate themselves and their children into German society. The lack of language skills and knowledge about Germany together with the different norms at home lead to identity problems of the children which, as a consequence, makes them more open for influence in mosques and Quran schools:

> A lot of Muslim adolescents have an identity crisis today . . . That makes them susceptible to radical preachers. (30/2005, "The Virus of Fear")

Violence in general, and violence against women and children in particular, is portrayed as a major problem in Muslim families by *Der Spiegel*. As a consequence of this, children allegedly adapt this mentality and cultivate it at school. A vivid example of these problematic consequences is the case of the "Rütli-School," a school in a disadvantaged neighborhood in Berlin. Muslim male pupils were described as extremely violent and having no respect for teachers. The concept of honor was made responsible for their behavior. Other schools with a high proportion of Muslim pupils are mentioned to have similar problems. Here again we find the connection between honor, violence, and Islam, although in a more general context compared to the more specific problem of honor killings.

Nevertheless, an indirect connection is often drawn between violence of Muslim youth and terrorism. This is emphasized in the following example:

A conflict because of a veiled girl escalates to a knifing at a school in Hamburg. Do teenagers already carry out religious conflicts with violence . . . This case shows a strange mixture of infantile power struggles (*Kraftmeierei*), adolescent disorientation and a liability to violence. And in all of this Islam played a decisive role. (51/ 2006, "Sisters in Faith")

A more direct association between Islamist terrorism and a lack of integration can be found in the following statement:

Almost three million Muslims live in the country, but we don't have any relationship to the diverse Muslim community although it is an inherent part of our society . . . Otherwise we will not cope with the challenge of integration and the threat of international terrorism. If we want to prevent attacks we need more information and a better integration. (28/ 2006, "There is a Problem")

The integration policy of the "multicultural society" is held responsible for the development of parallel structures. According to this view, Muslims have withdrawn completely from German society and isolated themselves in order to live unrestrictedly according to their own rules, which are often contradictory to democratic values. A wrong understanding of tolerance has resulted in the establishment of intolerance:

How much tolerance do Muslims claim for a practice of intolerance? (4/2005, "Alarming Insight")

THE ROLE OF ISLAM: A CULTURALIST FRAMEWORK OF FAILED INTEGRATION

The relationship between religiousness and social problems is hardly ever defined or analyzed clearly in the news on Islam. Most of the articles limit the alleged conjunction to associations of concepts, that is, to proximity in semantic fields, which the media itself reproduces. The reader is informed about the impacts and characteristics of Islam when it comes to core values such as the equality of gender, modernity, liberalism, peace, and tolerance. In these issues Islam is associated with anti-modernist values. The associations can either be affirmative (in statements that depict Islam as anti-modernist), critical of prejudice (in statements that refuse the notion that Islam is anti-modernist), or ambivalent (in statements that discuss the issue from multiple perspectives). No matter if affirmative or denying, the association with anti-modernist values is the framework in which Islam is presented.

It remains unclear how the attributed characteristics of Islam influence the practice of specific problematic conduct, i.e. how abstract moral values promoted by a religion can influence complex and concrete integration processes. Three vague problem frames can be distinguished in the media discourse, all of them implicitly equating integration with "cultural integration" and therefore showing a somewhat tautological logic:

> a) The idea that Islam actualizes its potential to resist integration in traditions which are brought from the countries of origin and upheld unchanged. This idea is typically symbolized by pejorative expressions like "medieval East-Anatolia" (self-exclusion frame), b) the idea that Muslim faith transforms into resistance to integration by indoctrination (alienation frame), c) the claim that "misleading understanding of tolerance" on behalf of the German society, politics and judiciary has facilitated the formation of Muslim parallel societies. Multiculturalist conceptions have impeded cultural assimilation (facilitated exclusion frame).

The presented measures to fight the integration problems that are discussed in the selected *Der Spiegel* articles are numerous. They include many abstract solutions that correspond to the role assigned to Islam in a culturalist framework, such as commitment of Muslims to basic values (this demand ranges from their commitment to a German "mainstream culture" ["*Leitkultur*"] to just a commitment to constitutional principles), a reformation process of Islam ("Euro-Islam"), control and regulation of religious activities, and more integration efforts on behalf of the migrants.

Apart from religion, other factors that inhibit integration are named as well, such as socioeconomic deprivation, and failures of integration policy. They are typically not presented as elements of competing problem frames, however, but rather as additional factors. Also, integration aspects other than cultural are underrepresented (though not neglected), for example educational participation, integration into the labor market or political participation.

Vellenga's (2008) observation that in the Netherlands culture (equated with religious values, faith and practice) is given an enormously strong emphasis in the integration debate may be transferred to the German case. Failed integration on various levels is mainly associated with a lack of cultural integration instead of other factors such as socioeconomic deprivation, injustice of the educational system, recursive processes of discrimination and retreat, or the like. Cultural integration, the implicit assumption seems to be, is not the result but rather the basis for other forms of integration.

CONCLUSION

The problem of Islam and integration has received increasing coverage in *Der Spiegel* after the terrorist attacks of September 11, 2001. As we have shown, at first selected sub issues are presented separately in various articles, such as the opression of women, the indoctrination in Quran schools and honor killings. In the development of the discourse, however those issues are comprised in the overarching issue of "parallel societies", complemented by further aspects like juvenile delinquency and fundamentalism. The discourse is increasingly centering on the core question of integration of Muslims into German society. Our exploratory analysis therefore opens up three conclusions and adjacent thoughts:

The problem issues are increasingly merged and related to Islam. Formulation of how exactly problems are interrelated and how exactly Islam must be assessed in its role as a problem factor remains vague in many articles, though. Links are established in the discourse but the nature of these links is hardly ever traced and expatiated upon profoundly.

In the course of the years, the stream of articles has established an increasingly clearly cut culturalist problem frame. It can be assumed that this problem frame (especially if it resonates with public discourse in general) becomes more and more familiar to the readers. Familiarity of frameworks can be achieved by constant repetition and reformulation of the predictable and reliable set of issues, topics, symbols, and attributes they comprise.

The clearest and most prototypical representation of the culturalist frame can probably be found in the overarching issue of Muslim parallel societies. This may have a high moral and emotional impact for both Muslim and non-Muslim publics. Following the problem theory of Schetsche, the issue of parallel societies can be considered a "consensual issue" (Schetsche 2008, 76ff) which means that basic assumptions about the existence of the issue are widespread and shared.

If we look at the political actions taken in order to improve the integration of Muslims into German society the same tendency can be observed. They are mostly related to the integration of Islam rather than solving the socioeconomic problems of Muslims: education of Imams at German universities, efforts to integrate religious education in public schools, efforts to change the institutional structure of Muslim organizations, and finally the setting up of the German Islam Conference. As Tezcan (2008) points out, it seems that a "(. . .) domesticated Islam is expected to take over the task of integration." Therefore not only the social problems are framed in a culturalist way but also the solutions. "(. . .) Integration appears as a matter of moral values (. . .)" (Tezcan 2008).

It requires more detailed research to evaluate if a uniform, culturalist interpretation of the problem(s) is biased or "justified." Nevertheless,

242   *Yasemin El-Menouar and Melanie Becker*

establishing a broader scientific discourse on the issue based on the falsification principle would be a worthwhile project. The alternative would be leaving the field to the media which tends to favor the principle of affirmation of everyday knowledge and is often moralistic rather than analytic in its approach.

NOTES

1. The sample was preselected by a keyword search in electronic archives of the newsweekly, and therefore excludes all articles in which the terms "Islam" or "Muslim" do not appear. We consider loss of relevant articles by this process improbable.
2. These issues and sub issues can only be separated analytically, as articles often deal with more than one issue.
3. This debate emerged when a Muslim teacher on probation was interdicted to wear a veil in the classroom. She started proceedings that were taken as high as to the constitutional court which finally determined that it was in the competence of the federal states governments to administer this matter.

REFERENCES

Bogardus, Emory S. 1930. A Race-Relations-Cycle. *American Journal of Sociology* 35: 612–617.
Brettfeld, Katrin and Wetzels, Peter. 2003. Junge Muslime in Deutschland: Eine kriminologische Analyse zur Alltagsrelevanz von Religion und Zusammenhängen von individueller Religiosität mit Gewalterfahrungen, -einstellungen und -handeln. In *Islamismus. Texte zur Inneren Sicherheit*, ed. Bundesministerium des Inneren. 221–316. Bonn: BMI.
Bukow, Wolf-Dietrich, and Ottersbach, Markus. (eds). 1999. *Fundamentalismusverdacht. Plädoyer Plädoyer für eine Neuorientierung der Forschung im Umgang mit allochthonen Jugendlichen*. Opladen: Leske+Budrich.
Diefenbach, Heike. 2005. Determinanten des Bildungserfolges unter besonderer Berücksichtigung intergenerationaler Transmission. In *Aspekte der Integration. Eingliederungsmuster und Lebenssituation italienisch- und türkischstämmiger junger Erwachsener in Deutschland*, edited by Sonja Haug and Claudia Diehl. 133–158. Wiesbaden: VS Verlag für Sozialwissenschaften.
Granato, Nadia and Frank Kalter. 2001. Die Persistenz ethnischer Ungleichheit auf dem deutschen Arbeitsmarkt: Diskriminierung oder Unterinvestition in Humankapital. In *Kölner Zeitschrift für Soziologie und Sozialpsychologie* 53: 497–520.
Halm, Dirk. 2008. *Der Islam als Diskursfeld. Bilder des Islams in Deutschland*. Wiesbaden: VS Verlag für Sozialwissenschaften.
Haug, Sonja. 2003. Interethnische Freundschaftsbeziehungen und soziale Integration. Unterschiede in der Ausstattung mit sozialem Kapital bei jungen Deutschen und Immigranten. In *Kölner Zeitschrift für Soziologie und Sozialpsychologie* 55: 716–736.
Heitmeyer, Wilhelm, Müller, Joachim, and Schröder, Helmut. 1997. *Verlockender Fundamentalismus. Türkische Jugendliche in Deutschland*. Frankfurt a.M.: Suhrkamp Verlag.

Jung, Matthias, Niehr, Thomas, and Böke, Karin. 2000. *Ausländer und Migranten im Spiegel der Presse. Ein diskurshistorisches Wörterbuch zur Einwanderung seit 1945*. Wiesbaden: Westdeutscher Verlag

Kalter, Frank. 2006. Auf der Suche nach einer Erklärung für die spezifischen Arbeitsmarktnachteile von Jugendlichen türkischer Herkunft. In *Zeitschrift für Soziologie* 35: 144–160.

Kecskes, Robert. 2000. Soziale und identifikative Assimilation türkischer Jugendlicher. *Berliner Journal für Soziologie* 10: 61–78.

Kecskes, Robert. 2001. Die starken Gründe, unter sich zu bleiben. Zur Begründung der Entstehung ethnisch homogener sozialer Netzwerke unter türkischen Jugendlichen. In *Zeitschrift für Türkeistudien* 14: 161–185.

Klinkhammer, Gritt. 2000. *Moderne Formen islamischer Lebensführung. Eine qualitativ-empirische Untersuchung zur Religiosität sunnitisch geprägter Türkinnen in Deutschland*. Marburg: Diagonal Verlag.

Kristen, Cornelia. 2002. Hauptschule, Realschule oder Gymnasium? Ethnische Unterschiede am ersten Bildungsübergang. In *Kölner Zeitschrift für Soziologie und Sozialpsychologie* 54: 534–552.

Meyer, Thomas. 2002. Parallelgesellschaft und Demokratie. In *Die Bürgergesellschaft. Perspektiven für Bürgerbeteiligung und Bürgerkommunikation*, edited by Thomas Meyer and Reinhard Weil. 343–372. Bonn: J. H. W. Dietz Verlag.

Müller, Daniel. 2005. Die Darstellung ethnischer Minderheiten in deutschen Massenmedien. In *Massenmedien und die Integration ethnischer Minderheiten in Deutschland*, edited by Rainer Geißler and Horst Pöttker. 83–126. Bielefeld: Transcript.

Münz, Rainer, Seufert, Wolfgang, and Ulrich, Ralf. 1997. *Zuwanderung nach Deutschland. Strukturen, Wirkungen, Perspektiven*. Frankfurt: Campus Verlag.

Noelle-Neumann, Elisabeth, and Mathes, Rainer. 1987. The "Event as Event" and the "Event as News": The Significance of "Consonance" for Media Effects Research. *European Journal of Communication* 2: 391–414.

Nökel, Sigrid. 2002. *Die Töchter der Gastarbeiter und der Islam. Zur Soziologie alltagsweltlicher Anerkennungspolitiken. Eine Fallstudie*. Bielefeld: Transcript.

Park, Robert Ezra. 1950. *Race and Culture*. Glencoe, IL: The Free Press.

Pinn, Irmgard. 1999. Verlockende Moderne? Eine Replik auf die Studie "Verlockender Fundamentalismus" von W. Heitmeyer. *Die Brücke* 110: 11–17.

Pinn, Irmgard. 1997. Muslimische Migranten und Migrantinnen in deutschen Medien. In *Wissenschaft Macht Politik. Interventionen in aktuelle gesellschaftliche Diskurse*, edited by Garbriele Ruth, Ina Cleve, Ernst Schulte-Holtey and Frank Wichert. 215–234. Münster: Verlag Westfälisches Dampfboot.

Price, Charles. 1969. The Study of Assimilation. In *Migration*, edited by J. A. Jackson. 181–237. Cambridge: Cambridge University Press.

Sauer, Martina. 2007. *Perspektiven des Zusammenlebens: Die Integration der achten Mehrthemenbefragung. Eine Analyse im Auftrag des Ministeriums für Generation, Familie, Frauen und Integration des Landes Nordrhein-Westfalen*. Essen: Zentrum für Türkeistudien.

Schetsche, Michael. 2008. *Empirische Analyse sozialer Probleme. Das wissenssoziologische Programm*. Wiesbaden: VS Verlag für Sozialwissenschaften.

Schiffer, Sabine. 2005. *Die Darstellung des Islam in der Presse: Sprache, Bilder, Suggestionen. Eine Auswahl von Techniken und Beispielen*. Würzburg: Ergon-Verlag.

Sen, Faruk, and Sauer, Martina. 2006. *Islam in Deutschland. Einstellungen der türkischstämmigen Muslime. Religiöse Praxis und organisatorische Vertretung türkischstämmiger Muslime in Deutschland. Ergebnisse einer bundesweiten Befragung*. Essen: Zentrum für Türkeistudien.

Spuler-Stegemann, Ursula. 2002. *Muslime in Deutschland. Informationen und Erklärungen.* Freiburg: Herder Verlag.

Tezcan, Levent. 2008. Governmentality: Pastoral Care and Integration. In *Islam and Muslims in Germany,* edited by Ala Al-Hamarneh and Jörn Thielmann. 119–132. Leiden: Brill.

Thomä-Venske, Hanns. 1981. *Islam und Integration.* Hamburg: Rissen.

Tietze, Nicola. 2001. *Islamische Identitäten. Formen muslimischer Religiosität junger Männer in Deutschland und Frankreich.* Hamburg: Hamburger Edition HIS.

Vellenga, Sipco J. 2008. "Huntington" in Holland. The Public Debate on Muslim Immigrants in the Netherlands. *Nordic Journal of Religion and Society* 1: 21–41.

Weischenberg, Siegfried, Malik, Maja, and Scholl, Armin. 2006. Journalismus in Deutschland 2005. Media Perspektiven 7: 346–361.

Contributors

Amy Adamczyk is an Assistant Professor of Sociology at John Jay College of Criminal Justice and the Doctoral Program in Criminal Justice at the Graduate Center, City University of New York. Professor Adamczyk has examined the influence of religion for explaining the decision to obtain an abortion, timing of first sex, marijuana use, and cross-national attitudes about homosexuality. She was recently awarded a grant from the Robert Wood Johnson Foundation to examine the influence of religion-supported after-school programs for young men's health-related behaviors. Before joining the faculty at the City University of New York, Professor Adamczyk was an Assistant Professor of Sociology at Wayne State University. Her work can be found in the *Journal of Health and Social Behavior, Social Science Research, Sociological Quarterly, Justice Quarterly, Sociology of Religion*, and the *Journal for the Scientific Study of Religion*.

Abe W. Ata is a Senior Fellow at the Institute for the Advancement of Research at the Australian Catholic University. His main research areas have been Religion and Ethnic Identity, Christian-Muslim Intermarriage, and Christian-Muslim relationship in Australia. His recent publications include *Mixed Marriages: Catholic and Other Inter-Church Marriages in Australia* (2005), *Attitudes of School Age Non-Muslim Australians to Muslims and Islam: A National Survey* (2007), and *Us & Them: Muslim-Christian Relations and Cultural Harmony in Australia* (2009).

Peter B. Andersen is an associate professor at the History of Religions Section, University of Copenhagen. His main research interests are religion in modern Denmark including immigrant religion and new religious movements, and the religion of the Santals of West Bengal in India. His latest publications include articles on Scientology, majority religion in Denmark, and an edited volume on religion, school, and cultural integration in Denmark and Sweden.

Eileen Barker, PhD, PhD h.c., OBE, FBA, is Professor Emerita of Sociology with Special Reference to the Study of Religion at the London School of

Economics. Her main research interests are 'cults', 'sects' and new religious movements, and the social reactions to which they give rise. She has over 250 publications (translated into 27 different languages), which include the award winning *The Making of a Moonie: Brainwashing or Choice?*, and *New Religious Movements: A Practical Introduction*. In the late 1980s she founded INFORM, a charity based at the LSE which provides information about the new religions that is as accurate, objective and up-to-date as possible.

Melanie Becker is a Lecturer and Research Assistant at the Institute for Social Sciences, University of Duesseldorf. Her main research interests are the sociology of social problems with a focus on the construction of social problems, crime control, and crime related attitudes, and qualitative empirical methods in the social sciences. Currently she is working on the publication of her doctoral thesis on crime related attitudes and on an article which deals with the crimes of the security police in Nazi Germany.

James A. Beckford, Fellow of the British Academy, is Professor Emeritus of Sociology at the University of Warwick. His recent books include *Religion in Prison. Equal Rites in a Multi-Faith Society* (with S. Gilliat, 1998), *Social Theory and Religion* (2003), *Muslims in Prison: Challenge and Change in Britain and France* (with D. Joly and F. Khosrokhavar, 2005), *Theorising Religion: Classical and Contemporary Debates* (edited with J. Walliss, 2006) and *The SAGE Handbook of the Sociology of Religion* (edited with N. J. Demerath III, 2007).

Marian Burchardt is a Research Associate at the Department of Cultural Studies at the University of Leipzig. He received his PhD from the same university and has worked as a visiting fellow at the New School for Social Research in New York City and Stellenbosch University, South Africa. His main academic interests include cultural sociology, social theory, religious pluralism and globalization. His most recent publications are "Ironies of Subordination: Ambivalences of Gender in Religious AIDS-Interventions in South Africa." *Oxford Development Studies*, 38(1): 63–82, (2010) and "Subjects of Counselling: Religion, HIV/AIDS and the Management of Everyday Life in South Africa", in: P. W. Geissler and F. Becker (eds) *AIDS and Religious Practice in Africa* (2009).

Derek H. Davis is Dean of the College of Humanities and Dean of the Graduate School at University of Mary Hardin-Baylor, Belton, Texas, and Director of the UMHB Center for Religious Liberty. He was formerly Director of the J.M. Dawson Institute of Church-State Studies and Professor of Political Science, Baylor University, and Editor of *Journal of Church and State*. He is the author or editor of 16 books, including *Original Intent: Chief Justice Rehnquist & the Course of American*

Church-State Relations (1991), and *Religion and the Continental Congress, 1774–1789: Contributions to Original Intent* (2000). He has also published more than 140 articles in various journals and periodicals. He serves numerous organizations given to the protection of religious freedom in American and international contexts.

Yasemin El-Menouar is a Lecturer and Research Assistant at the Institute for Social Sciences, University of Duesseldorf. Her main research interests are sociology of religion with a focus on Islam, the integration of minorities and qualitative empirical methods in the social sciences. Currently she is working on her PhD on Religiosity among Muslims in Germany and on an article that deals with value differences in Turkey.

Steven Engler is Associate Professor of Religious Studies at Mount Royal University, Calgary, and Adjunct Assistant Professor (Religion in the Americas) in the Department of Religion at Concordia University, Montréal. From 2005-2007, he was Visiting Professor in the Programa de Estudos Pós-Graduados em Ciências da Religião, Pontifícia Universidade Católica de São Paulo (PUC-SP), Brazil. His main areas of specialization are religion in Brazil (with recent articles in *Numen, Method and Theory in the Study of Religion,* and *Nova Religio*) and theory of religion (with recent articles, co-authored with Mark Q. Gardiner, in *Method and Theory in the Study of Religion, Religion,* and in Michael Stausberg (ed.), *Contemporary Theories of Religion: A Critical Companion*).

Gastón Espinosa is an Assistant Professor of religious studies at Claremont McKenna College. His research focuses on Latino religions and politics in the United States. He is the coeditor of *Latino Religions and Civic Activism in the United States* (2005), *Rethinking Latino Religions and Identity* (2006), and *Mexican American Religions* (2007), and editor of *Religion and the American Presidency* (2007). His work has appeared in the *Journal of the American Academy of Religion* and *Social Compass.*

Titus Hjelm is Lecturer in Finnish Society and Culture at University College London. His main areas of expertise are cultural sociology, sociology of religion, social problems, social theory, media, and popular culture. His research focuses on the role of minority religions in contemporary societies and the media treatment of alternative religion. He is currently working on a book on social constructionism (due out in 2011) and has published several books in Finnish and articles in journals such as *Social Compass* and *Journal of Contemporary Religion.*

Sanna Lehtinen is a Researcher in Church and Social Studies at the University of Helsinki, currently working as a doctoral student in the project "Church and Civil Society in the European Context" funded by the Academy of Finland. Lehtinen is interested in the relationship between the Evangelical

Lutheran church of Finland and the European Union. Her research focuses on European Social Fund projects in Finland. She has published her research findings in Finnish in the journal *Diakonian tutkimus.*

Peter Lüchau is a PhD candidate at the History of Religions Section, University of Copenhagen. His main research areas include religion and national identity in Denmark, the Danish national church, the religion of immigrants, and quantitative studies of religion in Europe. His latest publications include articles (in English) on religion and globalization in Denmark and patterns of faith and church attendance in Europe.

Lina Molokotos-Liederman lives and works in London, UK. She has an MSc in Mass Communication from Boston University (1990) and a doctorate in Sociology of Religion from the Ecole Pratique des Hautes Etudes, Paris (2000). She has extensive experience in European projects including "The Religious Factor in the Construction of Europe: Greece, Orthodoxy and the EU", based at the University of Exeter, UK. She has also worked on projects dealing with religion and education, migration, social welfare, and humanitarian aid. These include: the WREP and WAVE projects on religion and social welfare in Europe, an IOM/ ISESCO funded project on "Religion and Migration" and an IOCC survey on Orthodox diakonia worldwide. She is the author of numerous academic articles and book chapters.

Michiaki Okuyama is a Professor at Nanzan University and a Research Fellow of the Nanzan Institute for Religion and Culture, Nagoya, Japan. His works in English includes "Historicizing Modern Shinto: A New Tradition of Yasukuni Shrine," in Steven Engler and Gregory P. Grieve (eds), *Historicizing "Tradition" in the Study of Religion* (2005), and "Camouflage and Epiphany: The Discovery of the Sacred in Mircea Eliade and Oe Kenzaburo," in Bryan Rennie, (ed), *The International Eliade* (2007).

Ignatius Swart currently fills the position of Executive Director: Academic and Research at the Huguenot College in Wellington, South Africa and was until recently Associate Professor in the Department of Practical Theology and Missiology at Stellenbosch University. During his appointment at Stellenbosch he acted as leader of a major team research project on "Faith-Based Organisations, Social Capital and Development" as well as South African project leader of the international research project on "Religion and Welfare" with researchers from the Uppsala Religion and Society Research Centre in Sweden. Amongst his most recent publications is "Development Research as an Emerging Field in South African Practical Theology" in *International Journal of Practical Theology* (2008) and an edited book *Religion and Social Development in Post-Apartheid South Africa* (SUN Press, 2010).

Index

9/11. *See* September 11, 2001

A

abstinence. *See* sexuality
adultery. *See* sex, extramarital
African Americans, 124, 126, 131, 132
Afro-Brazilian religions, 213–228
Agency 213, 220–223
Ahmadis, 202
AIDS. *See* HIV/AIDS.
Alcohol, 4, 16, 18, 21, 24, 27, 28, 124, 189, 191
Aleph, 175
Alienation, 240
Allardt, Erik, 9
Al Qaida, 198
Altruism, 77, 139
American Catholic Sociological Society, 54
Anti-cult movement, the, 8, 176, 199, 203–204, 205, 209
anti-modernism, 239
apartheid, 98–100, 112
Asahara, Shoko, 174–175
assimilation, 138, 230, 232, 240
Association for the Sociology of Religion, 5, 54
atheism, 42, 204, 205
Atta, Mohammad, 237
Aum Shinrikyo, 7, 173, 201, 207, 209

B

Bahá'ís, 202
Barnes, Gerald, 129, 130, 131
Barker, Eileen, 208, 209
Becker, Howard, 3, 123
Beckford, James, 2, 144
Berger, Julia, 82
Berger, Peter L., 8

Berkowitz, Bill, 188, 189
Berning, Marion, 236
Best, Joel, 2, 58,
Beyer, Peter, 5
Blair, Tony, 59
Blumenthal, Sydney, 134
Blumer, Herbert, 123
Bourdieu, Pierre, 6, 146
bin Laden, Osama, 198
biomedicine, 147
Branch Davidians, 207, 209
Brewer, Jan, 124, 135
British Humanist Association, 61
Brownback, Sam, 132, 134
Buchanan, Patrick J., 123
Bush, George W., 7, 8, 122, 126, 127, 128, 130, 132, 133, 134, 138, 186–195

C

Candomblé, 8, 213, 215, 220
Cartoon Crisis, the, 37
Casanova, José, 78
Castellanos, Noel, 131
Cathars, 202
Catholic Church, 84, 85, 90, 129, 130
catholicism, 78, 122
chain graph models, 44–46
Chávez, César, 126, 127, 129, 130
church sector. *See* religious sector
Church Act (Finland), 68
Chin, May, 181
child abuse, 198,
circumcision, 4, 15, 17, 19, 21, 22, 24, 27, 28
civil rights, 58, 122, 124, 125, 126, 127, 129, 131, 134, 136
claims-making, 6, 9, 123, 145, 214, 217, 218, 219, 220, 221, 222, 223, 224, 232, 233

Clinton, Hillary, 132
Colonialism, 179,
Communality, 68, 73, 78
Communism, 83, 84, 85, 86, 95, 204
Congress (USA), 122, 123, 129, 131,
    132, 133, 134, 137, 138, 187,
    188, 195, 196, 221
Conspiracy, 235
Constitution: Denmark, 33; Finland,
    68; Germany, 240; Japan, 7,
    179–182; United States, 8, 137,
    146, 186–197, 205, 218
contingency, 146, 147, 148, 221, 222,
    223
Cooperman, Alan, 134
Cortes, Luis, 131
Council for Ethnic Minorities (Den-
    mark), 33
crime, 1, 57, 62, 124, 128, 130, 135,
    136, 137, 138, 151, 174, 175,
    179, 182, 198, 207, 243, 237,
    238
criminalization, 122, 125, 126, 128,
    129, 131, 135, 136
curriculum, 7, 149, 161, 162, 170,
cult, 197–212 ; cult controversies, 56,
    175; cult apologists, 208, 209
cultural turn, 146
cultural competence, 143, 146

D
de Jesus, Wilfredo, 131
delinquency, 16, 54, 237, 238, 241
demonization, 122, 154
demons, 8, 213, 215, 216, 219–223;
    see also spirit possession.
Department for Communities and Local
    Government (UK), 59, 60
Deuteronomy, 126, 133,
Devil, the, 215, 219
diakonia, 83–96
Diamond, Mark, 130
differentiation, 67, 79
dignity, 78, 79, 129, 130, 131, 134,
    136, 138, 139
DiMarzio, Nicholas, 129
discourse, 6, 8, 9, 33, 34, 56, 100, 117,
    139, 142, 143, 144, 145, 147,
    148, 149, 151, 154, 155, 159,
    170, 199, 213, 218, 219, 220,
    229, 230, 232, 233, 234, 236,
    237, 240, 241, 242,
discrimination, 7, 9, 39, 58, 60, 134,
    153, 160, 161, 162, 163, 175,

    188, 190, 192, 195, 202, 204,
    205, 240; non-discrimination,
    189, 192
disease, 54, 143, 144, 147–150, 219,
    221
diversity, 5, 9, 57, 59, 62, 83, 161, 170,
    230. *See also* religious diversity
drugs, 16, 18, 21, 24, 27, 74, 124, 135,
    189, 191, 237, 238
DuBois, Joshua, 194
Durazo, Maria, 131
Durkheim, Emile, 4, 114, 145,

E
El Cucuy, 131
Equal Treatment Doctrine, 192–194
Erikson, Kai, 8
Esbeck, Carl, 190
ESF. *See* European Social Fund
Establishment Clause, 191–194
ethics, 4, 34, 35–36, 112, 129, 143,
    148, 149–150, 152, 154, 155,
    160, 202, 214
ethnicity, 34, 37, 38, 39, 42, 43, 44, 45,
    46, 47, 57, 59, 62, 83, 85, 86,
    102, 127, 131, 134, 137, 159,
    160, 161, 162, 237
ethnomethodology, 146
Euro-Americans, 122, 123, 124, 125,
    132
Euro-Islam, 240
European Commission, 94
European Social Fund, 67–79
European Union, 5, 67, 83, 95
EU. *See* European Union
Exorcism, 213, 215, 219, 220, 221
expedience, 5, 56, 58–62

F
Faith-based Initiative, 7, 8, 62,
    186–191, 192, 194
Faith-based Organizations, 60, 82, 86,
    90, 93, 98, 124, 126, 128, 148,
    149, 153, 154, 196
Faith Communities Unit (UK), 59, 60
faith communities, 5, 53, 59–62, 116
Falun Gong, 198, 205, 207
Falwell, Jerry, 188
Farrakhan, Louis, 198
FBI. *See* Federal Bureau of Investigation
FBOs. *See* Faith-based Organizations
Federal Bureau of Investigation, 207
Federal Office for the Protection of the
    Constitution (Germany), 230

feudalism, 35
First Amendment, 194, 195
forced marriage, 8, 233–234, 237
fortunetelling, 178
Francis of Assisi, Saint, 127
Franklin, Benjamin, 195
Free Exercise Clause, 192
Frist, Bill, 131, 134
Fuller, Richard, 123, 219
Fujita, Shōichi, 177–178
functionalism, 55, 217, 223
fundamentalism, 231, 233, 235, 237, 241

G
Gandhi, Mahatma, 127
gender, 4, 21, 37, 39, 44, 45, 46, 47, 55, 57, 146, 147, 154, 168, 216, 239
government, 5, 7, 8, 16, 86, 88, 93, 94, 95, 96, 205; Australian, 159, 161, 162; Belgian, 204; British, 53, 56, 59–62; Chinese, 179; Danish, 32, 33, 38; French, 203, 204; German, 233; Japanese, 175, 176, 179, 182; Korean, 179; South African, 99, 103; United States, 125, 128, 186–196, 205; Western Cape Provincial (South Africa), 100–102
globalization, 55, 56, 86
group dynamics, 218, 222
Guardian, the, 134
guest workers, 32, 129, 134, 229, 230
Gutiérrez, Mike, 130

H
Habermas, Jürgen, 55–56
Hadden, Jeffrey, 2
hate preaching, 235
Heaven's Gate, 201, 209
healing, 8, 213–215, 220, 223
Heitmeyer, Wilhelm, 231
Heresy, 1, 198, 199
Hernandez, Juan, 131
Hikari No Wa, 175
HIV/AIDS, 4, 6, 15–28, 90, 91, 95, 142–153
homosexuality, 218, 219
Hongzhi, Li, 198
honor killing, 229, 233–234, 238, 241
House of Representatives (USA), 128
Hubbard, Ron L., 198

Human Immunodeficiency Virus. *See* HIV/AIDS.
human rights, 54, 55, 58, 133, 138, 154
Huntington, Samuel P., 123

I
Igreja Universal do Reino de Deus. *See* Universal Church of the Kingdom of God
illegal aliens, 6, 122, 130,
immigration, 3, 32, 33, 37, 38, 42, 46, 122–139, 214,
Immigrant Council (Denmark), 33
immigrants, 4, 6, 9, 32–47, 71, 72, 73, 76, 122–139, 230, 238
injustice, 9, 73, 82, 83, 113, 146, 240
Institute for Social and Religious Research, 54
integration, 32–47, 71, 76, 115, 138, 229–242
Interdepartmental Group on Faith (UK), 59
International Society for Krishna Consciousness, 199
intolerance, 239
ISKCON. *See* International Society for Krishna Consciousness
Islam, 4, 7, 8, 15–28, 32–47, 58, 95, 159–171, 198, 229–242

J
Jackson, Jesse, 137
Jehovah's Witnesses, 202
Jesus, 126, 127, 130, 150, 198, 203
John Paul II, pope, 130

K
Kardecist Spiritualism, 215
Kela (The Social Insurance Institution of Finland), 76
Kennedy, Edward (Ted), 129, 130, 131, 132, 134, 138
Kickans, Gerald, 129
Kim, Joon, 131
King, Martin Luther Jr., 126, 127
Kitsuse, John I., 3, 123, 217, 218, 222, 232
Koizumi, Jun'ichiro, 7, 179, 180–182
Koran. *See* Quran
Kuo, David, 188

L
labeling theory. *See* social problems theory

labor policy, 68, 69, 75, 79
Latinos/Latinas, 6, 122–139
law, 28, 33, 58, 122, 124, 125, 126,
  128, 129, 130–139, 151, 188,
  192, 194, 201, 204, 205, 216,
  229, 235, 237; Islamic, 18
Leviticus, 133, 138
Lincoln, Abraham, 137
Logan, Lewis, 130
Luckmann, Thomas, 8
Lutheranism, 5, 47, 67, 68, 78, 79, 90,
  189, 214

M
Macedo, Edir, 219, 220
macumba, 220
Mahony, Roger, 6, 126, 127–131, 133,
  134, 135, 136, 137, 138
Marginalization, 37, 67, 70, 71, 77,
  124, 125
Manson Family, the, 201
marriage, 8, 18, 19, 61, 151, 152, 233,
  234, 237
Mauss, Armand L., 123
McCain, John, 127, 129, 131, 132, 134
McCarrick, Theodore, 129
media, 1, 6, 7, 8, 9, 16, 33, 37, 39, 58,
  60, 62, 85, 132, 133, 159, 160,
  166, 170, 200, 206–207, 214,
  229, 232, 233, 237, 239, 240,
  242
merchant ethos, 36
metaphysical traditions, 122
Methodists, 191, 198
Mexican Americans, 125, 126, 127,
  136
mind control. *See* brainwashing
Ministry for Social Affairs and Health
  (Finland), 76
Minute Men, the, 125, 129
Miranda, Jesse, 131
Mohammed, prophet, 37, 198
Moonies. *See* Unification Church.
moral communities hypothesis, 16
moral panics, 159
mosques, 127, 230, 233, 235–236, 238
Muhammad, Abdullah, 130
Muhammad, prophet. *See* Mohammed,
  prophet.
Müller, Joachim, 231
multiculturalism, 62, 160, 161, 162,
  170, 239, 240
Murguia, Janet, 136

Muslims, 7, 8, 9, 16, 15–28, 159–171,
  198, 216, 229–242
Muslim countries, 4, 15, 16
Myers, Richard, 123, 219

N
Nakanishi, Hiroko, 178
Napolitano, Janet, 135
National Hispanic Prayer Breakfast
  (USA), 134
Nation of Islam, 198
National Research Foundation (South
  Africa), 98
Neo-Pentecostalism, 213–216, 218,
  220
New Labour, 59
new religious movements, 2, 8, 56, 58,
  176, 199
new social movements, 55
NGOs. *See* non-governmental organizations
Nishiyama, Toshihiko, 180
non-governmental organizations, 5,
  68, 70, 71, 82, 84, 85, 86, 87,
  88–96, 98, 103, 113, 114, 115,
  143, 154. *See also* religious non-
  governmental organizations
norms, 4, 15–28, 100, 123, 145, 149,
  161, 205, 213, 214, 216, 217,
  221, 223, 234, 237, 238
NRF. *See* National Research Foundation
NRMs. *See* new religious movements

O
Obama, Barack, 8, 122, 127, 135, 137,
  139, 186, 194, 195
Office of Faith-Based and Community
  Initiatives (USA), 187, 188, 194
oppression of women, 233–235, 237
Orthodox Christianity, 5, 15, 82–96
Orthodox social theology, 5, 82, 86

P
palmistry, 178
parallel societies, 9, 233, 236–239, 240,
  241
parishes, 67–79
Pearce, Russell, 136
peer education, 143, 148
Pelosi, Nancy, 132, 134
Pentecostalism, 122, 131, 136, 143,
  144, 150, 151, 152, 155, 194,

213, 214, 215, 220, 222, 223; *See also* Neo-Pentecostalism
Peoples Temple, 201
police, 58, 135, 137, 238,
polygamy, 21, 26, 27
polygyny, 15, 18, 19, 21, 22, 26, 27
poverty, 1, 5, 36, 54, 62, 82, 83, 90, 91, 95, 96, 98, 101, 110, 112, 115, 116, 117, 118, 124, 145, 155, 186, 194, 202, 219, 221
Poole, Paulette, 123
Praxeology, 145–146
prejudice, 36, 102, 125, 161, 169, 170, 239
prisons, 57, 58, 60, 71, 72, 73, 128, 175, 179, 202
prisoners, 57, 60, 72, 74, 76
private sector, 68
privatization, 67, 224
problematization, 147, 148, 150, 155
proselytization, 150, 173, 176, 178, 189, 190, 191, 195, 196
Prostitution, 18, 21
Protestantism, 4, 42, 82, 84, 126, 139, 214, 218
public sector, 5, 68, 72, 73, 75, 76, 100
Putnam, Robert, 6

Quakers, 204
Quran, 36, 159, 235, 238; Quran schools, 233, 235–236, 241

R
race, 3, 62, 114, 125, 127, 131, 134, 135, 136, 138, 139, 160, 170, 230
Reagan, Ronald, 137
Reid, Henry, 131, 132, 134
reikan/reishi shoho, 176
re-Islamization, 231
religiosity, 37, 39, 42, 43, 44, 46, 47, 231, 238; popular religiosity, 215
religious diversity, 5, 53, 56–58, 159
religious non-governmental organizations, 82, 85, 91, 96
religious sector, 99, 101, 102,110, 112, 113, 114
Ritual, 6, 115–117, 118, 146, 213, 215, 220, 224
Rivera, Miguel, 131
Rivera, Raymond, 131

RNGOs. See religious non-governmental organizations
Robertson, Pat, 188
Robertson, Roland, 55
Rodriguez, Samuel, 6, 126, 131–135, 136, 137
Romans, Paul's letter to, 138
Ryan, Leo, 201

S
Sakurai, Yoshihide, 178
Salazar, Ken, 134
salvation, 35, 85, 138, 150, 152, 213, 215, 219
Salvation Army, 1
Satanism, 2
Schally, Phyllis, 134
Schetsche, Michael, 232, 241
schools, 7, 22, 42, 45, 58, 60, 124, 128, 143,149, 153, 159–170, 193, 236, 238, 239, 241; *See also* Quran schools
school vouchers, 193
Schröder, Helmut, 231
Scientology, 188, 198, 199, 203
secularism, 1, 61
secularization, 9, 41, 47, 55, 190, 224
separation of church/religion and state, 8, 79, 179, 187, 190
September 11, 2001, 1, 7, 8, 59, 126, 159, 229, 233, 240
sex: extramarital, 17, 19, 154, 219; heterosexual, 17, 18, 27, 28, 142; homosexual, 27, 28; premarital, 16, 149
sex workers, 21, 24
sexuality, 142–155; abstinence, 149, 150, 152; perversion, 198
sexually transmitted diseases, 17, 18, 149, 150
Shinto, 176, 177; sect Shinto, 177
Siddiqui, Ali, 130
Slavery, 137, 139, 234
social capital, 2, 6, 98–118, 222
Social Compass, 54
social control, 235
social constructionism. *See* social problems theory
social movements, 55, 56, 58
social policy, 61, 67, 68, 78, 79, 82, 85
social problems theory, 2–3, 8, 9, 124, 143, 144, 213, 215–219, 221; labeling theory, 3, 123, 217;

social constructionist, 2, 3, 6,
8, 54, 58, 123, 124, 125, 143,
145–148, 154, 155, 198, 199,
200–201, 205–206, 208, 210,
213, 214, 217–219, 221, 222,
223, 224, 232–233
social services, 61, 72, 76, 82, 83,
85–91, 95, 96, 110, 113,
186–196
social work, 5, 68, 69, 72, 73, 77, 78,
90, 93, 95, 153
Society of Friends. *See* Quakers
sociology: cultural sociology, 143, 145,
147, 155; of religion, 2, 5, 6,
9, 16, 54, 178, 182; of social
problems, 2, 3, 5, 9, 145
Soka Gakkai, 206–207
Solar Temple, 201
Sò-mûi, Ko Kim, 181
Soto, Jaime, 129
Sotomayor, Sonja, 136
Spiegel, Der, 8, 9, 229, 235, 237, 238,
240
spirits, 174, 176, 177, 178, 215, 216,
219, 220, 221
spirit possession, 213, 216, 218,
219–223
STDs. *See* sexually transmitted diseases
stereotypes, 125, 139, 159, 160
stereotyping, 7, 160, 162, 163
stigma, 125, 142, 143, 148, 152
suicide, 4, 145, 201, 206, 209
Supreme Court (United States), 7, 136,
175, 178, 180, 181, 187, 191,
192, 193, 194
Sürücü, Hatun, 234

H

Tanaka, Nobumasa, 180, 181
Tancredo, Tom, 134
terrorism, 1, 126, 159, 165, 166, 175,
229, 233, 235, 236–239, 240
theology, 5, 82, 83, 86, 143, 144, 153,
213, 215, 216, 223
third sector, 5, 68, 69, 71, 75, 76, 78,
Thomä-Venske, Hanns, 231
Tithing, 214, 215, 221, 223

tolerance, 162, 170, 239, 241; *see*
intolerance
Treaty on the Functioning of the EU,
the, 67
Treviño-Cummins, Lisa, 131
trust, 6, 98, 100, 101, 102, 103, 110,
114, 116, 118, 173

U

UC. *See* Universal Church of the King-
dom of God
UK Inter Faith Network, 60, 61
Umbanda, 213, 215, 220
Unemployment, 4, 32–47, 54, 62,
67–79, 95, 115, 124, 216, 230
Unification Church, the, 176
Unit for Religion and Development
Research (South Africa), 98, 118
Universal Church of the Kingdom of
God, 8, 213, 216, 219
University of Chicago, 3

V

Van Gogh, Theo, 229, 237
veiling, 8, 233–235, 236, 239

W

war criminals, 7, 179, 182
welfare, 5, 34, 67, 68, 72, 79, 83, 84,
91, 96, 99, 170, 195
welfare state, 1, 4, 5, 32, 68, 73, 75,
78, 79, 154
Welfare Reform Act (United States),
191
Wesley, John, 198
West, Cornell, 137
Wicca, 188
World Bank, 94
work ethic; 4, 34, 35, 44; Islamic, 4,
35, 36, 42, 47

Y

Yamaguchi, Hiroshi, 176
Yasukuni Shrine, 173, 178–182

Z

Zapata, Emilio, 127